I0820557

Spring 2026—Spring 2027

CONTAINING pictorial and explicit delineations of the magical phases of the Moon together with information about astrological portents of the year to come and various aspects of occult knowledge enabling all who read to improve their lives in the old manner.

The Witches' Almanac, Ltd.

Publishers Providence, Rhode Island

www.TheWitchesAlmanac.com

Address all inquiries and information to
THE WITCHES' ALMANAC, LTD.
P.O. Box 25239
Providence, RI 02905-7700

© 2025 BY THE WITCHES' ALMANAC, LTD.
All rights reserved

13-ISBN: 978-1-938918-00-1 The Witches' Almanac—Classic Edition
13-ISBN: 978-1-938918-01-8 The Witches' Almanac—Standard Edition
eBook 13-ISBN: 978-1-938918-02-5 The Witches' Almanac—Standard Edition
Español 13-ISBN: 978-1-938918-03-2 The Witches' Almanac—Standard Edition
eBook Español 13-ISBN: 978-1-938918-00-1 The Witches' Almanac—Standard Edition

ISSN: 1522-3184

First Printing July 2025

Printed in USA

Established 1971 by Elizabeth Pepper

Power doesn't always come with noise or force. Sometimes, it's quiet, subtle and transformative. Pluto has moved from Capricorn into Aquarius, and we now find ourselves at a crossroads—a shift from tradition to innovation, from rigid structures to collective change. It's a time when past and future meet, challenging us to rethink what we know and how we live. The choices we make now will forever shape the future.

For years, Pluto in Capricorn exposed cracks in our institutions—government, finance and tradition. It didn't just tear down outdated systems; it revealed flaws that had been hidden. We saw power struggles, financial upheavals and debates over authority. This was Pluto's work—forcing us to face reality rather than cling to illusion. Now, as Pluto enters Aquarius, it's about transformation, not destruction. Aquarius brings innovation, community and rebellion. It's about new ways of thinking, connecting and building a future for the many. This change challenges us to be open-minded and envision new possibilities.

This shift won't always be comfortable. Change rarely is. But it's a chance to move past old patterns and work toward something more forward-thinking. We may see advances in technology, shifts in social structures and challenges to long-held beliefs. It's not just about progress—it's about progress with purpose. We must embrace new ideas while honoring lessons from the past, both in the physical and spiritual realms.

As Witches, we know that power is not just in dramatic moments, but in the quiet, deliberate choices we make. It's about being aware, staying true to our values and working toward a future that balances old with new. Pluto in Aquarius reminds us that real change comes from within—from our willingness to adapt and embrace the unknown. Our magic lies in our ability to grow while staying rooted in who we are.

So, as the world shifts, keep your focus steady but stay curious. Light a candle not just for what was but for what can be. Listen to the whispers of transformation and be ready to move with the tide, shaping the future, not fearing it. The power to change is in our hands—it always has been.

Holidays

Spring 2026 to Spring 2027

Date	Holiday
March 20, 2026	Vernal Equinox
April 1	All Fools' Day
April 30	Walpurgis Night
May 1	Beltane
May 1	Vesak Day
May 8	White Lotus Day
May 29	Oak Apple Day
June 5	Night of the Watchers
June 20	Summer Solstice
June 24	Midsummer
July 23	Ancient Egyptian New Year
July 31	Lughnassad Eve
August 1	Lammas
August 13	Diana's Day
August 17	Black Cat Appreciation Day
September 14	Ganesh Chaturthi
September 22	Autumnal Equinox
October 31	Samhain Eve
November 1	Hallowmas
November 16	Hecate Night
December 16	Fairy Queen Eve
December 17	Saturnalia
December 21	Winter Solstice
January 9, 2026	Feast of Janus
February 1	Oimelc Eve
February 2	Candlemas
February 15	Lupercalia
February 17	Chinese New Year
March 1	Matronalia
March 19	Minerva's Day

Astrologer . . . . Dikki-Jo Mullen
Climatologist . . . . Tom C. Lang
Cover Art and Design. . . . Kathryn Sky-Peck
Sales. . . . . Roy Singleton
Bookkeeping . . . . D. Lamoureux

ANDREW THEITIC
Executive Editor

GWION VRAN
Art Director

MAB BORDEN
Copy Editor

Contents

Contents

Witches' Coven

How silently the purple duck
Had yielded to the night!
The oaks, the pines, my neighbor's house
Had vanished from my sight!
A murky gloom had mantled them,
Somber, deep, and still
And held the quiet, rustic vale
In a kind of runic spell!
Through the darkened sky came the lonely cry
Of a loon o'er the misty pond
While an aura of deep mystery
Encompassed me around!
I stood alone in the darkness,
No moonbeam glimmered there
As the eerie call of the great homed owl
Boomed out on the autumn air.
The haunting beauty of the dusk
Had brought me to this spot,
The oaks, the pines were friendly then
And close, my neighbor's cot.
Oh, deceptive witchery that lured me to this dell
And held me in the circle of this magic spell!
Oh, bewitching magic! Enchanted I had been
To tarry in its circle
Till darkness closed me in!

–GLADYS BIRONG

Yesterday, Today and Tomorrow

by Timi Chasen

ON THE SURFACE The stone sentinels of Rapa Nui—commonly known as the Easter Island heads—have long gazed inland from their windswept perches. But in recent years, excavations have revealed what whispers of old may have always known: these heads are merely the visible crowns of fully-formed statues, their bodies buried deep in volcanic soil. Giants asleep in the earth.

How they came to be sunken remains an enigma. The scale suggests a people of extraordinary ingenuity, though the island itself could never boast the resources or population of an empire. Much like the basalt marvels of Nan Madol or the buried enclosures of Göbekli Tepe, these immense constructions defy easy explanation. They point toward ancient hands with knowledge now forgotten—perhaps shaped by a world before catastrophe.

Some esoteric thinkers suggest these sites are not merely monuments, but geocentric memory nodes—ritual loci marking intersections between terrestrial power and celestial rhythm. Their burial, intentional or otherwise, may have been a sealing away of ancient knowledge, preserved not just in stone, but in silence.

Some propose a prehistoric cataclysm, a celestial bombardment that forever altered the planet's face. If so, what we call myth may be memory: a long-lost age of builders and watchers, cast beneath the veil of time. The buried giants of stone may yet stir the minds of those who remember how to listen.

THIS WAY DOWN Long before the rise of papal Rome, the hill we now call the Vatican bore the name of an ancient Etruscan Goddess: Vatika. Guardian of the liminal space between life and death, Vatika presided over burial grounds and the hidden mysteries of the underworld. The hill itself was once a necropolis—a city of the dead—named in her honor. From Vatika came Vaticanus and eventually, the name of the global center of Catholicism.

She was a Goddess of thresholds: birth, death and all that lies between. Her name is also linked to the Latin vagina, not in vulgarity, but as a sacred gateway—life's passage into and out of the world. In some depictions, a symbol associated with her—often interpreted as the vesica piscis—adorns her brow, representing the sacred feminine, fertility and the generative power of the unseen. Her presence was not merely symbolic; she was invoked in rites of transition, especially in guiding souls between the worlds and as a protectress of pregnant women, ensuring safe passage for lifc both entering and departing.

When Emperor Constantine built the basilica atop Vatican Hill, he did so over the bones of the forgotten dead and beneath the shadow of Vatika. What was once the domain of a Goddess became the seat of an empire's new God. Yet her legacy lingers, hidden in plain sight—in the name, the hill and the whisper of the earth beneath stone. Even now, beneath the grandeur and marble, the spirit of the threshold endures.

SOUNDS GOOD In the shifting landscape of modern Witchcraft, the ancient art of sound healing has found new life through the immersive practice of location-specific sound baths. These contemporary rituals blend traditional meditation techniques with the unique acoustic signatures of natural and urban environments, creating profound auditory experiences that resonate deeply with practitioners.

Imagine a gathering at the edge of a dense forest, where participants recline on the Earth as the sounds of rustling leaves and distant bird calls intertwine with the harmonic vibrations of singing bowls and chimes. Each note is carefully selected to harmonize with the surroundings, fostering a deep connection between the individual and the living landscape. This fusion of natural ambiance and intentional soundscapes serves to ground participants, aligning their personal energies with the rhythms of the environment.

In urban spaces, Witches have adapted this practice to rooftops, abandoned buildings and even subway tunnels—anywhere the acoustics speak. Many now incorporate field recordings, portable synths and looping devices to layer sacred chants with ambient noise, creating a liminal sonic space between worlds. Technology, in this context, becomes an ally of the Craft, extending the reach of traditional tools and opening new channels for experiential magic.

The resurgence of such practices reflects a broader movement within the magical community toward integrating sensory experiences with spiritual work. By attuning to the specific resonances of a place, Witches and Pagans are rediscovering the power of sound as a conduit for transformation and healing. These sonic journeys not

only facilitate personal introspection but also generate a collective field of energy, echoing the timeless understanding that vibration and intention are at the heart of magical practice.

As the boundaries between the ancient and the modern continue to blur, the incorporation of site-specific sound baths into contemporary Witchcraft exemplifies the enduring adaptability of the Craft. It is a reminder that magic is not static but a living, breathing practice that evolves in harmony with the world around it.

NEW DIRECTIONS Our understanding of direction is shaped by Earth—its horizon, its poles, its Sun and Moon. But should Pagans one day find themselves among the stars, in places without true East or West, those deeply held assumptions must shift. The cardinal points, so integral to ritual and worldview, would no longer be tied to sunrise or magnetic field. Direction would become relational—East might simply be the right-hand side from where one begins.

Up and down would still matter, but only relative to body or vessel. The sacred center would hold greater significance, anchoring ritual in personal orientation rather than planetary position. Without the visible Sun or Moon, symbols of the God and Goddess might evolve—taking on the aspect of distant stars, pulsars or even abstract forces of light and dark. In time, whole pantheons could be imagined from stellar phenomena—deities of nebulae, of rotation, of gravitational breath.

In this new paradigm, Pagan cosmology could become more stellar, even mathematical, built on vectors and movement rather than fixed ground. It's not a loss, but a profound reimagining—a way to root magic even in the rootless. And in that motion, a deeper mystery emerges: direction not as geography, but as choice—an inner compass tuned to the vastness of becoming.

www.TheWitchesAlmanac.com

Come visit us at the
Witches' Almanac website

News from The Witches' Almanac

Glad tidings from the staff

In a world adrift with turmoil and uncertainty, we at The Witches' Almanac pressed forward, steadied by purpose and fueled by hope. Across the globe, a restless energy thrummed—a mixture of fear, resilience and fierce will. Against this shifting backdrop, we embraced the challenge of weaving a volume where kindness shines and the enduring power of magic prevails. We rolled up our sleeves and turned to the deeper currents of enchantment, invoking the wisdom of Thoth, the inspiration of Saraswati and the creative fire of Brigid. Their blessings helped us gather the diverse thoughts of many into a tome of light and spirit. In such times, creation itself becomes a sacred act—and by the Gods, we have conjured it once again!

This year, The Witches' Almanac focused on moving to a more efficient, centralized fulfillment center—a seemingly mundane task vital to the magic behind the Almanac. Our large cache of publications, once spread across multiple locations, had to be reinventoried and consolidated. New staff were trained and those in the office navigated the steep learning curve of an entirely new system. True to form, gremlins made mischief, but we turned our wands toward them and prevailed. The result, a fulfillment process faster, more reliable and enchanted—delivering our titles swifter than ever, as if carried by sylphs.

The *Witches' Almanac Issue* 45 welcomes exciting new voices alongside familiar ones. We are delighted to introduce Castor, Loren Crawford and Rebecca Hallaway, each bringing unique insight and magickal wisdom. Returning to enrich this year's volume are beloved contributors Barbara Stacy, Ifadoyin Sangomuyiwa, Dikki-Jo Mullen, Mab Borden and Devon Strong. Don't miss the *2026 Witches' Almanac Wall Calendar,* featuring the mythological magic of the planets, filled with evocative imagery and thoughtful explanations.

This year, we also bid farewell to Casey M. Casey was integral to the magic behind the scenes, coordinating fulfillment across warehouses and maintaining our online presence with great care. In his final months, he chaperoned the complex transition to our new system. His gentle soul, keen mind and steady presence will be deeply missed. As we say goodbye, we warmly welcome Michelle MaBelle, a true tour de force. With decades of Craft experience and as a former shop owner, Michelle brings wisdom, passion and a deft touch to sales.

As always, The Witches' Almanac hums with excitement for the year ahead. David Conway has revisited *Magic: An Occult Primer,* expanding theory and practices for a new generation. Meanwhile, the beloved *Celtic Tree Magic* has been thoughtfully reviewed and expanded, ready to find a home on many new bookshelves.

The Demonization of the Other

From Devils to Dissidence

Dichotomy and Otherness

HUMANS HAVE, by instinct for survival and competitive inclinations, sought to simplify and polarize the world into that which is recognizable, known or otherwise acceptable, in contrast to that which poses a potential or established threat to his persons or personal belief systems.

Organizing various complexities and complicated phenomena in a diverse and largely unknown world becomes a means to categorize acceptability by identifying those elements that establish a sense of common identity, inclusion and safety.

In contrast, that which is unknown or portends changes or threats is imbued with a sense of *monstrum*—the quintessential *other* that exists both on the physical plane and in a liminal sense by eluding comfortable categorization through its defiance of a dichotomous or systematic worldview.

But who—or what—is definably or undeniably other?

It is the distinctive processes within the human mind that allowed for millions of years of survival and which still regulate patterns of recognition of threat versus safety. Those who lived remotely—outside the protection and uniformity of cities and towns—or who maintained views which were juxtaposed to mainstream ideas or conduct of the times were viewed with suspicion or derision—and were often considered a threat or even unnatural.

As humans increasingly ventured beyond the limits of the immediately recognizable world, the unknown became not only that which was different or which ran contrary to accepted thought, but became increasingly imbued with a measure of perversity or monstrosity in terms of what was considered the natural order of the world. Encounters with previously unknown peoples and fantastic creatures or the observation of seeming cataclysmic celestial events served to ignite early imaginations and reinforce the concept of otherness as a manifestation of the supernatural.

Human experience and perspective gave rise to a dichotomous worldview even as polarity inevitably leads to cultural bias, alienation and censorship. Often, as historical records inconsistently or unreliably portray, this resulted in displacement or erasure of marginalized groups or longstanding traditions and ideologies.

In such instances, the experience of time-honored knowledge handed down through generations as a healing art to one person is, to another's perspective, an act of extraordinary ability and suspected malediction. Communing with and venerating ancestors might be perceived as a misguided or possessed individual seeking to enter a pact with the Devil. In both cases, the contrasting interpretations are based on the specific, normative behaviors inherent to the two individuals.

The unknown or the nonconforming—in the guise of other or outsider—is undeniably subjective. The other is therefore mutable and controversial—it constantly challenges and often transcends human perceptions and perspectives not only across geographic boundaries but as a temporal phenomenon. As artistic expression, otherness is evoked through the fusion of experience and imagination and represented in literature and art as both the unique individual expression of the writer or artist and as a mirror of the prevalent social perspectives of the times.

From devils to dissidence—otherness in art

Art is revealing and evocative, not simply as an aesthetic but as a potential window into the prevailing ideas and mores at a given historical point in time. Through examination of artistic works, you can trace the development of social values and norms and gain better understanding of how these arise, become dominant themes and continue to evolve. Much like language, they often contrast with their original interpretations. Unlike the process of unearthing relics from the past with an often-ambiguous timeline and provenance and then having to extrapolate meaning from incomplete fragments, you are provided with a more comprehensive view into the universal thought processes that are inherent in a work of art.

The following artworks range across a broad timeline and, taken purely as examples, may be considered suggestive of the concept of otherness that emerges at pivotal points in European history. This timeline takes the view of the Pagan as the social and religious outsider to depict the evolution of the monstrous other, the contemplation of dissent and objection and the consideration of queerness as a deviation from normalcy and socially imposed and regulated behavioral confines. Contained within all is the discovery that otherness is an embrace of that which defies mainstream conventions—it is that state of mind and of being which permits you to seek out and embrace new paradigms and invites you to explore possibilities that exist outside stale or dated conventions that would no longer serve you.

Paganus

The term Pagan evokes images of heathen sacrifices or of barbarians from the less civilized corners of the world. While considerable debate has been devoted to establishing a contextualized meaning, there is the assertion that Pagan simply applies to one who is an outsider or who does not belong. But who exactly doesn't belong and is this indicative of a sense of contempt for those who fall in this category?

Two theories tend to drive the discussion about the origin and meaning of the word. The first suggests the use of the term to differentiate between a civilian and a soldier, the latter being deemed *milites Christi* (Soldiers of Christ). A second theory promotes the

A Pagan Sacrifice. c.1645-50.
Giovanni Benedetto Castiglione.

use of *paganus* to identify an individual from a rural area as opposed to more populous areas. Alan Cameron, in *The Last Pagans of Rome*, posits that paganus was increasingly used to identify an outsider—one who doesn't belong to a specific group or who is different in some way from the majority.

Castiglione's baroque painting *A Pagan Sacrifice* offers a perspective of otherness. With its original audience being the upper classes of Rome in the 17th century, the Pagan subject matter implies selective differentiation between social groups and ostensibly between religious ideologies, where the outsider maintains tradition in the face of more accomplished and civilized members of Roman society. As the work is based on historic interpretation centuries after the imagined event, the depicted other may be a designation with no specific nor finite duration, dependent upon closely held ideas of who or what belongs.

Sparagmos

Influenced by Euripides' *Bacchae*, this image of the mural at Pompeii depicts the dismemberment of the Greek King Pentheus by the Bacchae when he is discovered hiding after venturing forth to confront and abate the activities of the God Dionysus. The narrative suggests a dichotomy between both characters in terms of their physical presence as well as their characters while the setting and circumstances of their encounter and Pentheus' final plight are played out.

The central theme of dichotomy is realized in the social struggle between the king and his subjects as compared to the cult of Dionysus where the ruled class and those without specific rights or privileges honor the God who provides them unconventional freedoms through his rites.

Pentheus and the Bacchae.
Pompeii Mural.

The Taking of Arkona, the last stronghold of the Pagan Slavs. c.1890. Laurits Tuxen.

Contrasts also exist in the characterization of Dionysus in which the God—a stranger who is dually connected to obscure, foreign daytime (light) and nighttime (dark) rites—is initially deemed untrustworthy since he is not easily confined to one aspect or the other. The God's motivations are thereby deemed unclear. As premeditated other he defies clear categorization and that leads Pentheus to condemn him even before they meet.

As the encounter between Pentheus and Dionysus and his attendants unfolds, there is a notable reversal of circumstance and providence, whereby that which is normative becomes other and the other evolves as the protagonist in restoring order. Pentheus considers himself to be pure and rational but is seen to be corrupted by his own emotions and circumstances by the end of the account, while Dionysus is accused of being corrupt but inevitably proves himself to be a powerful deity. By ordering the *sparagmos* (the tearing apart,) the deity achieves a point of equilibrium: balance is achieved through the reconciliation that the community has achieved through the death of the tyrant king.

Dissident

The Middle Ages saw the expansion of Christianity and forced conversion to the Roman Catholic faith into every corner of Europe. The Slavic Rani Tribe inhabited the Island of Rügen in the southwestern Baltic Sea as well as nearby areas in northeastern Germany. Fiercely defiant of Christian conversion, they maintained a stronghold and thriving Pagan center at Cape Arkona on Rügen even as other Pagan centers across Europe fell to Christian forces and were forcibly converted.

Following an initial invasion and defeat by the Danes in 1136, the Rani agreed to adopt the Christian faith—but returned to their Pagan practices shortly after the Danes departed. In 1169, Arkona was the last stronghold of Pagan (Slavic) faith to be forcefully converted to Roman Catholicism in a prolonged attack by Christian Danes under King Valdemar I. The Rani subsequently became vassals of Denmark and what was left of Slavic Paganism, mythology and folklore was lost to history.

Laurits Tuxen's Victorian-era work *The Taking of Cape Arkona* depicts that pivotal point in Pagan history in 1169 as the army of Danish King Valdemar I and Bishop Absolon topple the idol of the Slavic God Svantevit at the temple at Arkona as the defeated Rani look on.

The Rani and the history of Arkona reveal much about the concept of the other. Persevering in times of turmoil and often against overwhelming odds and a majority position, the other defies convention, uses cunning and resists conversion. Otherness also says much about belonging and resilience nearly one thousand years later as those with Slavic heritage attempt to reclaim and memorialize aspects of their Pagan faith and history as Rodnovery—the new Slavic Native Faith.

Monstrum

> *A monster is born only at [a] metaphoric crossroads, as an embodiment of a certain cultural moment—of a time, a feeling, and place—the monstrous body is pure culture.*
>
> *–Jeffrey Jerome Cohen*

The word *monstrum* is Latin, meaning an evil omen or something that evokes fear but is also wondrous—it is that which reveals and warns. The other as

Circle Dance of the Imps.1651. David Ryckaert III.

monster is that which defies definition or explanation—it lies outside normal or anticipatory human experience and is therefore deemed to be that which cannot or should not exist.

Monstrum is that which is not merely grotesque or supernatural but, when taken in a cultural context, is what invites you to bridge the divide between the mundane or tangible and the psychological or supernatural in order to understand not only the definition of what is purely monstrous but also why it should be considered so.

David Ryckaert's 17th century painting entitled *Circle Dance of the Imps* reflects a fascination with the supernatural that was common in the Early Modern Period—a time of significant political, religious and social upheaval in Europe. Art during this period often explored the dark, weird and whimsical while incorporating depictions of Witchcraft and otherworldly creatures. Ryckaert's timeless painting illustrates how art can embody humanity's universal fear and fascination with the unknown, blending seemingly disparate attributes of both humor and horror.

Here the other takes on monstrous proportions—it defies standard nomenclature and arouses human curiosity by maintaining the illusion of otherworldliness while transgressing the mundane. It asks the viewer, "to what does this belong?" As others, these fantastic creatures portrayed as imps or devils are engaged in a human-like dance macabre. By their very nature they are neither fully of one world nor the other. In belonging to neither, they move in and between both with apparent unconcern for—or apparent defiance of—the mundane world of humanity.

Queer as... "Queer"

> *By [contemporary] definition,* queer *is everything that is at odds with what is normal, what is legitimate, what is dominant.*
>
> –*David Halperin*

The term "queer" is thought to have entered English usage in the early 16th century as implying that which is strange, odd, peculiar and eccentric. Even as the peculiar or strange may invoke a sense of separation of identity or departure from the mundane, the abstraction of what is familiar and recognizable can similarly alter perception. The appearance or combination of otherwise identifiable elements in an unexpected or peculiar way recasts that which is known into the role of other by showing the commonplace manifesting as surreal, or as an unanticipated change or alteration in shape or form.

Rudolph II, the 16th century ruler of the Holy Roman Empire, brought together in his court at Prague a select group of artists, scientists, alchemists and philosophers who promoted his interests in the occult sciences. Among these notables was the Milanese Mannerist painter Giuseppe Arcimboldo, who was commissioned the portraiture of the king as Vertumnus, after the Roman God of the changing seasons and verdant plant growth. In this painting, Rudolph II is envisioned as a cornuco-

Vertumnus. c.1590.
Guiseppe Arcimboldo

pia with his features displayed as an abundance of plants, fruits, and flowers from all seasons.

The interpretations of Arcimboldo's work are multifold and are suggestive of political ambitions where Rudolph II's power as the Holy Roman Emperor extends to Nature itself in his depiction as Vertumnus. The God of the seasons could change form at will and this attribute aligned with the idea of an underlying permanence to the Holy Roman Emperor's rule—a "metamorphosis of power over the world for a ruler," as art historian Thomas DaCosta Kaufmann put it. The work also imbues a sense of the occult—the interplay of humanity emerging from Nature to return to Nature again—where the emperor is not considered separate nor independent from what is above nor below.

The peculiarity and strangeness of Arcimboldo's art—and especially the initial impressions of Vertumnus as *scherzo* (humorous)—exemplified the Renaissance period's fascination with the bizarre, the unexpected—the queer. This otherness was an invitation to fascinate, to engage, to challenge the mind as well as social conventions. The Holy Roman Emperor, costumed in decadent fruits and vegetables as Vertumnus, presents a queer characterization by defying traditional ideas of portraiture and using that discernment to establish a unique interpretation to his imperial role.

In conclusion: "as above, so below"

From a magickal perspective, how does an understanding of history and artistic expression enable a person to embrace a sense of otherness? Identifying as other is not to proclaim deviation from the norm and the mundane but to impart acceptance of the principles of diversity, change and evolution as they exist within the natural world. Otherness recognizes and enables a relationship with magickal intention and practice as well as communion with the Gods—for those who seek that—as agents of these creative forces.

What you imbue in your sense of self, in the practice of the Magickal Arts or as Pagans is an affirmation not of your separateness nor acknowledgement of a dichotomy but of participation in a timeless, cyclical sacred dance and union with the Great Mystery.

–LOREN CRAWFORD

THE MYSTICAL POWER OF A WATER DROPLET

A Journey Through Magic, Witchcraft, and Paganism

IN THE REALMS of Magic, Witchcraft and Pagan traditions, a water droplet transcends its physical form to become a vessel of transformation, a symbol of life and a potent magical tool. Though seemingly ordinary, a single droplet carries profound spiritual, elemental and metaphysical significance, making it a vital Element in many sacred practices.

Water Droplets and the Element of Water

Within the framework of Witchcraft and Paganism, Water is one of the four foundational Elements, alongside Earth, Air and Fire. It embodies emotions, intuition, healing and purification. A single droplet serves as a concentrated embodiment of these qualities, acting as a reminder of water's duality: gentle enough to nurture life, yet powerful enough to carve valleys and shape landscapes.

In rituals, a water droplet often symbolizes the unity of the vast ocean with the individual soul. Practitioners use droplets to cleanse spaces, objects or themselves, invoking Water's purifying energy. This makes each droplet a focal point for transformation and emotional healing.

Scrying with Water Droplets

Scrying, the ancient art of divination utilizing visions in a medium, finds a unique application in the use of water droplets. While bowls of water are traditional tools, a single droplet can act as a microcosmic mirror, reflecting hidden truths. Gazing into a droplet can allow the practitioner to enter a meditative state, seeking visions or guidance from the Spirit World.

Amplifiers of Intention

Water is known for its ability to hold memory and energy, which makes droplets powerful amplifiers of intention in magical practices. Charged with specific energies, prayers or affirmations, a droplet becomes a vessel of transformation. For instance, a droplet imbued with healing energy might be used to anoint the body or mixed into a potion to restore physical or emotional balance. Similarly, droplets charged with protective blessings can create a shield of energy around a person or space. When infused with wishes or desires, a single droplet released into a natural body of water carries those intentions into the wider world, aligning personal goals with the flow of nature. If you cannot reach the body of water, you can sit in quiet contemplation, holding the droplet in your hands and visualizing yourself placing it into the body of water. A photo or a map of the body of water can also be helpful.

Dew Drops and Moon Magic

Dew, often referred to as the "morning tears of the Goddess," is highly revered in Witchcraft for its magical potency. Collected at dawn, dew symbolizes renewal, purity and divine blessings. When harvested during specific lunar phases—especially the waxing or Full Moon—it is believed to carry lunar energy, making it ideal for spells focused on intuition, fertility, transformation and emotional clarity.

Dew is often used to craft enchanted elixirs, anoint sacred tools or perform beauty spells. Many practitioners believe its mystical properties enhance both inner and outer radiance, providing a tangible connection to the gentle power of the Moon and the divine feminine.

Rain Drops: Gifts from the Divine

Rain droplets are seen in Pagan traditions as sacred gifts from the heavens, often interpreted as blessings from water deities like Poseidon, Yemaya, Aphrodite or Tethys. The energy of rain varies with the nature of the storm, and rainwater collected during specific weather events carries unique properties.

Gentle rain facilitates emotional and spiritual renewal, washing away negativity and burdens. Thunderstorm rain, imbued with the ferocity of the storm, holds raw power ideal for spells requiring strength, courage or rapid transformation. Each droplet collected becomes

> The ephemeral nature of a water droplet reflects the cycles of birth, death and rebirth celebrated in Paganism.

Gentle rain facilitates emotional and spiritual renewal, washing away negativity and burdens.

a magical tool, ready to channel the energy of the storm into ritual practices.

Symbol of Impermanence and Sacred Cycles

The ephemeral nature of a water droplet reflects the cycles of birth, death and rebirth celebrated in Paganism. Clinging to a leaf or evaporating into the air, a droplet reminds us of life's fleeting beauty and interconnectedness.

Using Water Droplets in Ritual Practice

Incorporating water droplets into rituals allows for both simplicity and depth. A single droplet can cleanse, charge or connect. For cleansing, practitioners might dip their fingers into a droplet and trace protective symbols on their skin or on ritual tools. Droplets can also be placed on crystals or talismans to charge them with specific energies. In offerings to water deities, a droplet combined with appropriate herbs or flowers becomes a sacred gift, strengthening the bond between the practitioner and the divine.

The Hidden Magic in Nature's Microcosm

When viewed under a microscope, a water droplet reveals a world teeming with microscopic life and intricate structures. This hidden complexity resonates with the magical principle of "as above, so below," emphasizing that infinite worlds exist within even the smallest elements of nature. Recognizing this, practitioners may view a water droplet as a bridge between the visible and invisible realms, deepening their connection to its sacred power.

Conclusion: A Sacred Gift

A single water droplet holds immense spiritual and magical potential, reminding us that even the smallest aspects of nature are vessels of profound energy. Whether used in rituals, spellwork or meditation, the droplet's properties evoke wonder, inspire transformation and foster spiritual growth. For Witches, Pagans and magical practitioners, this humble bead of moisture is a treasure, offering infinite possibilities to align with nature, the divine and the mysteries of existence.

From the Diary of a Dubious Witch

I Just Did What?

HERE I SIT on the porch with my phone in my hand. I just typed in a google search for covens. WHAT am I thinking? Look at all the information! Who knew? Quick, there's still time, back out. Are coven, Witch and magic target words for the police, government or, worse, "the" church? Stop it, that's silly, I'm not a threat—words said by every free thinker since the beginning of time. I'm not dangerous, maybe a little eccentric, but definitely not dangerous. I may be watching too many horror movies. Be brave, get back online. You know you've wanted to do this for a very long time.

Wow, look at all these resources, covens, Witches, esoteric groups, trainings and stores. Where to begin? I'll just start clicking, I won't contact anyone. No one is going to know. No one would believe that I was thinking of becoming a Witch. My somewhat conservative, professional, quiet, white toast life (actually more like boring) is a great cover. Ok, go ahead, click on something. Wait, if I click on something will "they" know I looked? Who is "they" anyway? Then, they will send me something or possibly contact me. Really? That's silly, isn't that what you want? Crazy self talk, who asked you your opinion anyway?

I've been reading and studying this topic since I was in elementary school. Seems I've been putting my soul on the line for a long time. How much more trouble could I be in moving to the next step? It wouldn't hurt to look. Which coven do I look at first? What do I ask? What am I looking for? Simple but somewhat vital

questions. What do I tell them I am looking for? **Wanted**: *a nice group of people to meet with that will teach me magic, tell me I am a natural and make a fuss over my really cute dog.* It's important to know your priorities. Look at all the different groups. How will I ever know which one is right for me? What if you join one and then…it's too late? Hmm, I definitely need to research a little further.

There are some other really import factors for me to think about. I know I have some hard **NOs** .

1. No naked in the woods—wait, actually no naked at all. There are parts of this body that have never seen the light of day much less moonlight in a haunted forest.
2. Nothing Satanic, painful, excessively embarrassing or scary (well maybe a little scary —I do love a good ghost.)
3. No dangerous initiations, drinking weird concoctions, calling someone Your Majesty, moving to a remote part of the Earth or making live sacrifices. Well on that last one, there are a couple of old relationships… **ABSOLUTELY NOT**! (yet)
4. Lastly, nothing that gets me on the wrong side of anyone's Gods. Best to stay neutral until well researched.

This is turning out to be way more research and thought than I was expecting. I think I just need to send out some GENERAL emails for some information while I'm doing my research. (Big gasp with chills running down my spine!) I really feel I need to express the fear I am experiencing right now. Huh, here's one that sounds promising. I like the word traditional. I'm traditional. I'm the one that saves everything because it

either has a story behind it or it might. I love old things and studying history. I'm very sentimental and always celebrating everyone's holidays. Finally, I'm not fully convinced that computers and technology are a good thing.

Oh my God(s)! (being cautious) I just clicked **send**. What if they actually answer me? What if they want to ask me some questions? What if I don't know the answers? S#%t, I gave them my real name. Did I say too much or not enough? I know… I can send another email saying OOPS! I didn't mean to send that email. Seriously? Like that's going to fly. Wait, maybe they will never answer my email. Yah, nobody answers their email anymore. Oh now I've jinxed it. Maybe I try to delete the email before it really is sent? Who am I kidding? I can barely SEND an email. What a time to be technologically disabled. I guess I just have to wait and see.

Wait! What's that?

THEY ANSWERED…

LÎCWÎGELUNG

10th Century Rites of Exorcism in Anglo-Saxon Leechbooks

VENERATION of the dead is common to all cultures. Its significance to our understanding of otherworldly perceptions should not be underestimated. There is much to support the view held by many scholars that in antiquity a home-based ancestral cult formed basis of religious experience, especially amongst Germanic and Norse peoples. The presence and influence of the dead was such that both fortune and misfortune were attributed to their contentment or spite, respectively—the latter occurred from simple neglect. Former cultic activity focused on the sepulchres of the dead and incorporating *Lîcwîgelung* (necromancy or black magic) suggest the continued reverence of ancestral spirits and heroes. As tribal guardians, these denizens of the Otherworld were called upon to intercede, to mediate on the behalf of their living descendants and to remove or banish illness and disease.

Despite various Penitentials and Confessionals that strictly forbade all acts of bewitchment by means of the dead, the accumulation of charms recorded in the Leechbooks attests to the persistence of belief in such remedial practices. Lîcwîgelung features largely amongst them despite its condemnation. According to popular Anglo-Saxon lore and custom, advice sought from the dead was deemed essential for all aspects of life. Moreover, the ability of the dead to manipulate *Wyrd* (destiny) was an invaluable asset to prosper, gain advantage and to exact revenge. Prayers and incantations made to the dead often involved outsitting—a lengthy vigil lasting several hours on or within the mound or grave of the corpse being consulted. This practise continued post conversion. *Valgaldr* charms and incantations are thought to mimic the mighty spells used by Oðinn to command the Volur to reveal to him the

machinations of fate. Saxo Gramaticus refers to a case where a man Hadingus called upon the knowledge of a barrow spirit to provide information regarding his own fate. Because it was believed that the dead influenced the destinies of the living, the most powerful amulets of protection were formed from the bones and pieces of mummified or desiccated corpses.

The dead played a vital role in the health of the living. Touching a dead person's hand or garment allowed disease to be transferred to that corpse. The same could be achieved by merely stepping over a recently buried corpse. Pregnant women who consistently failed to carry their babies to full term would step over the grave of a recently buried person with the intention of discarding the unwanted demon possessing her that was causing her miscarriages, effectively "earthing" it. Numerous Anglo-Saxon charms are dedicated to exorcisms of disease spirits. Charms involving the transference of disease from the afflicted person to the animistic spirits of the Earth, cleft trees or holed stones were sometimes set up as translocation charms. This meant the illness or bad luck was then contracted by the next person to touch the object, despite official injunctions against translocation activity as a commitment to the Devil, as evidenced by Egbert's Penitential. The oldest charms of transference involve running water. Saxon herbals reveal the popular belief amongst Germanic peoples relating to the virtues and sanctity of running water. Holy water is drawn from a running stream in a holy season, before sunrise and in solemn silence.

Bad luck, illness, death and many other calamities were caused by unseen spirits that attacked the weak and the unwary. The invasion of malefica that inflicted disease was known as elf-shot, a condition that manifested in every malediction from a simple headache to infection and from epilepsy to miscarriage. All contagion and possession were seen as the result of elf-shot. Skin eruptions, swellings, joint pain, hysteria and even melancholia were all deemed to be the result of

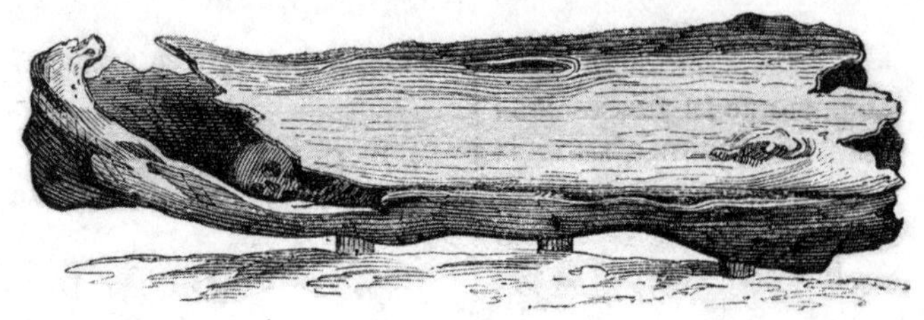

possession by various malignant spirits. Imperceptible to normal human senses, elf-shot attacked at will. Magic was the only recourse. Lîcwîgelung was often practised in graveyards and power was to be gained from contact with the dead. Elf-shot could only be banished from the body by conjuration or transference, achieved through the application of worts (herbs) and words of power—exorcism. Finnish sorcerers banished malevolent spirits into hostile elemental environments. Anglo-Saxon conjurers dispatched Witches and demons to distant mountains.

Skin afflictions such as boils and infected sores or wounds were wiped onto a cloth which was placed into coffins or graves. The corpse was petitioned to take the affliction from the living in the name of God. To invoke a name within a charm or spell is to literally imbue it with magic: no name—no power. It is assuredly apparent how those beliefs—and fears of malefic possession and attack from shades and denizens of the Otherworld—extended into notions of cursing, possession and thence to rites of exorcism. Exorcism is the act of driving out or warding of demons or evil spirits from people, places or inanimate things believed to be possessed by them. This belief demonstrates the requisite rites of expulsion—exorcism, whether that be through Christ by Christians or ancestral spirits by Heathens. Rooted in superstition, the process of exorcism evolved as a strictly religious act or rite, though it is sometimes considered Witchcraft. The means employed for this purpose observe the solemn and authoritative adjuration of the demon in the name of a God or higher power to which that demon is subject.

As a license to depart, many spells sourced in Bald's 10th century Leechbook were adopted into rites of exorcism—one spell even prescribes a salve to prevent the nocturnal wanderings of spirits. The notion that disease is caused by invisible, evil-working demons finds concise expression in the opening words of the following charm: "For a fiend-sick man, when a devil possesses a man, or ravages him internally with disease." Unlike the named spirits of evil we encounter in Classical and Oriental magic, the disease demons found in Anglo-Saxon charms remain largely unnamed. Instead they are simply referred to as elves, dwarves, night visitors, loathsome fiends, mighty Witches, devils and succubae. Exceptions occur in a few Christian spells in which the disease demon or devil is called a diabolus. Several charms exist against the night mare. Exorcisms were dealt with in uncompromising procedures that initially involved flattery and cajolement, which soon escalated to threats, commands, acts of purging and even physical violence in the form of beatings, pricking, bleeding and scourging.

Leechbooks are filled with charms that work against invasion or contagion. Some involve blood-letting, hence the name 'leech' for the doctor. The remedy required the Leech to draw out some of the blood and thus drawing out the disease-spirit with it. The blood was then rubbed over a hazel, oak or elder rod inscribed with the patient's name. Blood drawn in such a manner was often thrown over running water to neutralise the evil demon possessing the blood. Rituals relating to the collection and processing of healing herbs and of holy water were developed according to the superstitions that dictated their use.

Both mandrake and periwinkle were held in high regard; it was believed they were endowed with a mysterious power that could combat insomnia, dementia and insanity—all sure signs of demoniacal possession. Eleanour Sinclair Rohde states in The Old English Herbals that at the end of the description of the mandrake in the *Herbarium* of Apuleius there is this prescription: "For witlessness, that is devil sickness or demoniacal possession, take from the body of this same wort mandrake by the weight of three pennies, administer to drink in warm water as he may find most convenient; soon he will be healed." Of periwinkle, it similarly reads`: "This wort is of good advantage for many purposes, that is to say first against devil sickness and demoniacal possessions."

Artemisia is a potent herb that staves illness and averts the Evil Eye. Herbs that grew in graveyards and burial grounds were deemed to be particularly efficacious against infection and invasion. Many were used in exorcism rites. Claiming to have the power to dispel the demons of possession, various tinctures and decoctions composed of various potent herbs appear in the Leechbooks as 'spew drinks' (emetics.) In one example, lupin, bishopwort and henbane were pounded together and steeped in ale and holy water. Another remedy called "A drink for a fiend" declared the curative potion must be consumed from a church bell. Masses and psalms and benedictions were often sung over the potion before it was administered.

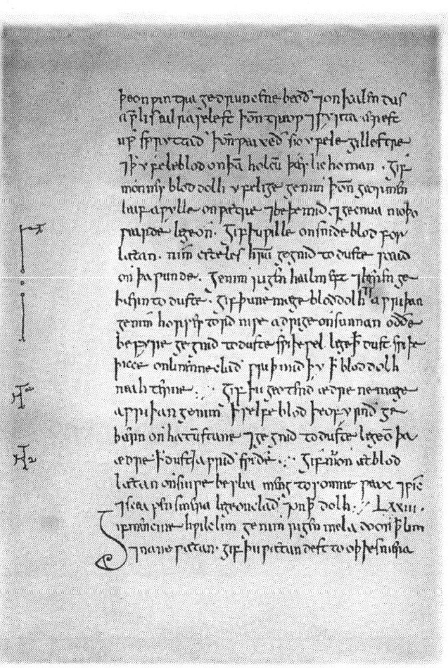

Betony is also cited for use against the nocturnal visions and dreams inflicted by the nightmare. Attacks of elf-shot were not confined to human beings but extended to cattle and draft animals. Cures were similar to those applied to humans. Some involved brass nails and other amuletic warding.

Leechbooks consulted during the early medieval period include *Lacnunga*, the *Herbarium of Apuleius*, *Bald's Leechbook* and *Peri Didaxeon*. The Old English *lœce* (leech or doctor) was a charmer—a healer somewhat akin to a tribal medicine man. The Anglo-Saxons borrowed from diverse sources: Greek, Irish, Hebrew and especially Latin. As such, a number of charm formulas evidently owe their effect to the mystification of a foreign tongue. Doggeral Latin prayers against demoniacal possession were commonplace. The magical character of the text is based on the fact that the words have become unintelligible. Magic operates in accordance with the law of similarity, a metaphysical association unperturbed by modus of belief. Whether Heathen or Christian, the premise relied upon faith in the curative powers ascribed to the objects used in the charms and to the words of power. Charms consisting of unintelligible words follow various instructions involving repetitions in multiples of three. Charms were held secret by the shaman, sorcerer or priest who composed them. Their potency was increased exponentially if sung—hence incantation and *galdr* (magical songs.) Ironically, it was only after conversion to Christianity that Germanic peoples believed all charms and runes, both inscribed and sung, originated from Woden, *Galdrs Fadir*—the father of charms. A significant number of Anglo-Saxon charms are either Christian or have Christian overlays. Very few are outrightly Heathen, as appeals are rarely made to named or specific God forms. Sometimes the Sun or Moon is mentioned. Christianity also transformed elves and dwarves especially into devils.

Bald's Leechbook offers several remedies that demonstrate curative methods. Imbibing herbs in holy water was a technique of exorcism: "Against one possessed by a devil: Put in holy water and in ale bishopwort, water-agrimony, agrimony, alexander,

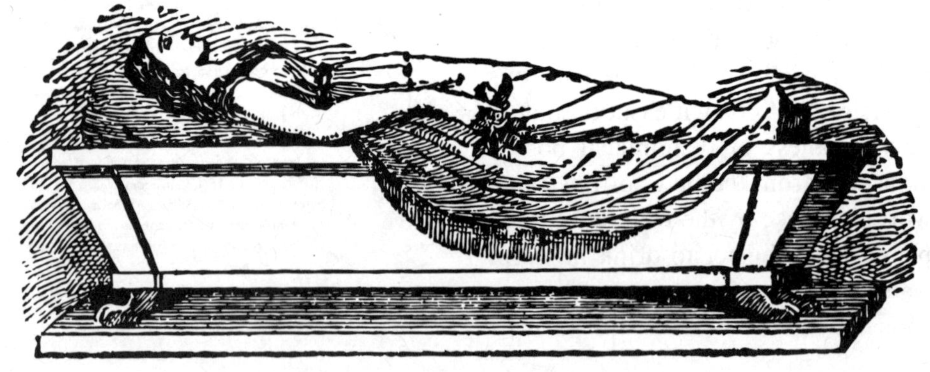

cockle; give him to drink." Methods of cure were sometimes quite brutal and driving out the spirits of possession sometimes involved a beating: "If a man is insane [possessed by a malignant spirit], take the skin of a tortoise, make a whip of it, and beat the man with it. He will soon be well." Emetics were considered less brutal. "Against an elf and against an unknown possession, rub myrrh into wine and an equal quantity of white incense, and shave a little of the agate stone into the wine. Drink it after a night's fasting on three mornings or nine or twelve." This may have induced vomiting.

The belief that illness is caused by demonic possession reaches back into the antique world—it was certainly not new. Exorcism rids the body of possession by obnoxious or demonic intruders. Remedies were varied and included invocations, herbs, salves, smoking and breathing—called *insufflatio*. Laying of hands on the subject or making the sign of the cross were typical elements of a charm. Salves are herb infused butters that were used to ward off Witches and harm from bad spirits, so perhaps this adds another dimension to the purpose of flying ointments? Crosses were accordingly made on various parts of the body—on the forehead, the limbs, the tongue, the breast and the arm—to drive the demons out. It is important to assert the universality of the cross symbolism within these charms. The cross had long existed as a sign of good omen, propitiation, benediction, prosperity and protection. In Germanic tradition, the cross appeared in stylised form with four equilateral arms, either as fylfot or the swastika. Smoke was also employed to drive out evil spirits where possession was suspected. This may demonstrate an influence attributed to the Christian liturgical use of incense—particularly when accompanied by genuflections of the cross—however, smoking out spirits of possession is not unknown outside the Christian world.

By the 12th century, Latin charms referring to the apostles, the trinity or saints became very popular in exorcisms. These ecclesiastical authorities replaced all Heathen appellations. Substitutes included all variations of God or Christ such as Deus, Emanuel or Adonai, the names of saints, the apostles, the evangelists, Mary and sometimes even the biblical patriarchs. An Anglo-Saxon expedient from *Bald's Leechbook* to ward off the evil consequences of flying venom, i.e. infectious diseases, directs the healer or charmer to procure a stick of oak or elder and proceed as follows: "Against flying venom. Cut four incisions in four parts of the body with an oaken stick. Dip the stick into the blood, throw it away and sing this three times: ✠ Matheus me ducat ✠ Marcus me conservet ✠ Lucas me liberei ✠ Iohannes me adiuvet semper. Amen." Note the similarity to the former charm involving bloodletting and a hazel stick—the demon is here drawn out and diffused by the efficacy of the abjurement in the name of the apostles rather than the original Heathen spirits of the springs and watercourses.

–SHANI OATES

THE NOBLE'S CROWN, with its regal form and storied history, holds profound symbolic, magical and occult significance across cultures and through the centuries. Beyond its visible function as a marker of rank and authority, the crown represents divine power, spiritual alignment, sovereign authority and esoteric wisdom. Its materials, design and ritual uses imbue it with layers of meaning, symbolizing sovereignty, cosmic harmony and a duly noted connection to higher planes of existence.

Materials and Their Symbolic Power

The materials used in crafting crowns are chosen not only for their rarity and beauty, but also for their metaphysical properties, each contributing to the crown's power and symbolism.

Gold, often the primary metal, is revered in alchemy and magic as the metal of the Sun. It signifies illumination, divine energy, perfection and incorruptibility. In magical practice, gold aligns with solar energies, granting vitality and enlightenment to the wearer. Crowns made for High Priests ideally use gold, though brass or bronze may serve as substitutes for practicality.

Silver, the metal of the Moon, often complements gold. Its association with intuition, purity and reflection makes it a favorite for High Priestesses' Moon crowns. Silver balances gold's fiery nature with a cool, receptive energy, linking the crown to the mystical realms of transformation and the unconscious.

Precious stones embedded in crowns further amplify their magical significance. Diamonds represent clarity, invincibility and spiritual ascension; sapphires signify truth, wisdom and divine favor; emeralds embody fertility, balance and eternal life, reflecting the prosperity of a ruler's domain; rubies evoke passion, power and protection, warding off negative forces; and amethysts, known for their spiritual insight, offer protection against physical and spiritual intoxication while bringing clarity of thought, an essential quality for leadership.

Pearls, with their oceanic origins, signify purity and hidden knowledge gained through introspection. Their connection to the divine feminine underscores emotional wisdom. Meanwhile, the velvet and silk lining of crowns symbolizes refinement and transformation, often derived from animals or plants within the ruler's territory, enhancing the land's spiritual resonance. Also, the wearer should include a material object which is special to only them—making the crown an extension of the wearer's being.

The Occult and Magical Meaning of the Crown

The crown transcends political symbolism, acting as a conduit for cosmic and spiritual authority. In esoteric traditions, the head represents the mind, spirit and connection to the divine. Placing a crown upon it is a sacred act, aligning the wearer with celestial forces and activating higher consciousness. Of course, take note to first place the crown on the head of its wearer at an auspicious time for beginnings.

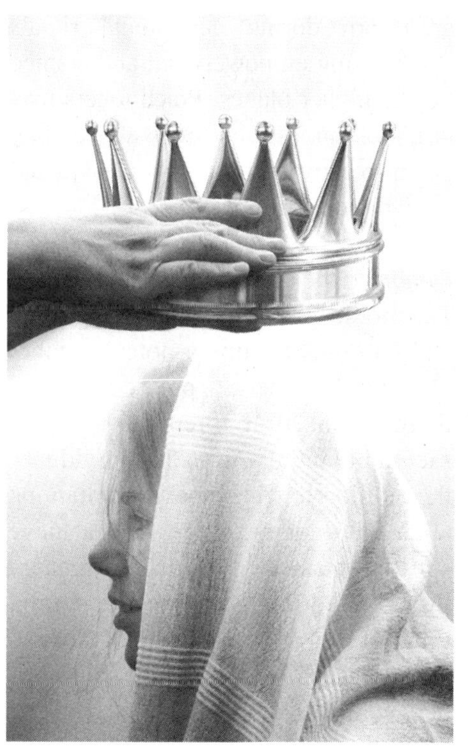

Historically, crowns have been seen as marks of divine favor. In ancient societies, rulers were often regarded as intermediaries between Gods and humanity. The crown, akin to a halo, reinforces this connection, serving as a channel for spiritual energy. Rituals such as placing a crown on the wearer during a Solar return or the Sun's transition into Aries amplify this alignment.

Esoterically, the crown resonates with the Sahasrara Chakra, located at the top of the head. This chakra symbolizes spiritual enlightenment and cosmic unity. Wearing a crown activates this energy center, heightening awareness, wisdom and alignment with universal truths. Mystically, the crown also signifies mastery of the lower self and alignment with the higher self, representing the integration of spirit, mind and body.

The circular design of crowns symbolizes eternity, wholeness and the cyclical nature of life. Often adorned with motifs reminiscent of solar rays or stellar configurations, crowns associate the wearer with celestial power, bridging earthly and cosmic realms.

Historical Uses of the Crown in Ritual and Power

Throughout history, crowns have played significant roles in rituals and as symbols of divine authority. In ancient Egypt, the pharaoh's crown—the pschent—symbolized the unity of Upper and Lower Egypt and conferred God-like status upon the ruler. Materials like lapis lazuli were included in Egyptian crowns, connecting wearers to the heavens.

In medieval Europe, crowns were sanctified during coronations, becoming sacred objects that symbolized divine anointment. Placing the crown on a monarch often signified the transference of divine traits, aligning them with the deity they served. In religious iconography, the halo—a spiritual crown—depicted enlightenment and radiance, mirroring the physical crown's role in manifesting celestial energy.

In mystical orders and secret societies, crowns were ritual objects signifying spiritual initiation and mastery over elemental forces. They often marked a journey into higher states of consciousness and authority within the esoteric hierarchy.

Power Attributed to Crowns

The crown's mystical properties extend beyond symbolism, granting tangible and spiritual powers. It acts as a protective shield, warding off negative forces and curses. Its connection to divine favor makes it a potent barrier against spiritual adversaries. As a manifestation of authority, the crown represents dominion over chaos and mastery over fear and doubt. Esoteric traditions assert that crowns enhance psychic awareness, aiding in connection with higher planes or celestial beings.

In rituals, the act of crowning symbolizes transformation, a moment of

symbolic death and rebirth. The crown marks the culmination of the wearer's spiritual, mental and emotional evolution.

Modern Magical and Occult Use of Crowns

In modern magical practices, crowns retain their mystical significance. They are worn during ceremonial rituals, symbolizing empowerment and connection to higher planes. Practitioners may visualize an astral crown above their heads to activate the Crown Chakra and draw divine wisdom.

Honoring the Crown as a Mystical Tool

The noble crown, transcending time and culture, remains a potent symbol of enlightenment, protection and divine connection. It reminds us of the sacred potential within all individuals: the ability to rise above limitations, align with cosmic forces and achieve spiritual mastery. For modern seekers, the crown offers a path to transformation, serving as both a magical tool and an aspirational symbol of the harmony between self and the universe.

Dionysius and Pan

Kindred Spirits of Wild Nature and Ecstasy

Sing to me, Muse, of Pan, the lord of the wild,
Goat-footed God of the shepherd's fold,
Who roams the hills with echoing cry,
Lover of nymphs and the mountain cold.

He delights in the cliffs and shady glens,
With leaping limbs and a beard so thick,
He dances with joy on the wooded slopes,
And plays the reed pipes swift and quick.

Hail, great Pan, spirit of field and stream!
I sing your name with a rustic dream.

IN THE LUSH tapestry of Greek mythology, Dionysius and Pan stand out as two enigmatic deities whose spheres of influence intertwine in fascinating and deeply resonant ways. Dionysius, the God of wine, revelry, and divine ecstasy, and Pan, the goat-footed deity of wild nature, music, and untamed passion, represent two faces of liberation and connection to the primal forces of life. To view them together through a Pagan lens is to understand the sacred dynamics of wilderness, joy and spiritual transcendence.

Dionysius: The Liberator and God of Ecstasy

Dionysius, often called Bacchus in Roman tradition, embodies the spirit

of ecstatic release. He is a God who bridges the mortal and the divine through the intoxicating powers of wine, theater, and ritual celebration. His rites, known as the Dionysian Mysteries, were said to strip away the constraints of societal norms, allowing initiates to experience a deeper, unifying truth. The vineyards and ivy that are sacred to him speak to a duality of cultivation and wild growth—a balance between order and chaos.

As a God, Dionysius is paradoxical. He is a bringer of joy and a master of frenzy. His followers, the Maenads, danced in ecstatic abandon, often depicted wielding thyrsi—staffs wound with ivy and tipped with pinecones—as they communed with the divine. This ecstatic state was not just drunken revelry but a sacred act of breaking free from mundane existence to touch the divine essence within.

Pan: Guardian of the Wild and Spirit of Lusty Freedom

Pan, a rustic deity tied to the Arcadian mountains and forests, represents the raw and untamed spirit of nature. With the legs and horns of a goat, Pan embodies a liminal, primal force that is at once playful and fearsome. As the God of shepherds, flocks and wild music, his flute, the syrinx, calls forth both pleasure and panic (the latter derived from his name.)

Pan's domain is the wild—those untouched, unrestrained spaces where instinct and freedom reign supreme. He is a fertility God, a figure of lust and vitality whose unions with nymphs and dryads symbolize the generative power of the natural world. His presence evokes a connection to the Earth's rhythms and a reminder of humanity's animalistic roots.

Parallels and Intersections: Dionysius and Pan as Twin Liberators

Dionysius and Pan share profound similarities as deities of liberation. Both inspire humans to transcend the ordinary, urging you to break free from the confines of civilization and reconnect with your deeper, instinctual selves. While Dionysius does so through wine and ecstatic ritual, Pan achieves this through the unfiltered experience of nature's raw beauty and terror.

Their shared association with music further underscores their kinship. Pan's syrinx and Dionysius's lyre-driven revelries both transport participants to altered states of being. Music in their myths is not mere entertainment but a sacred tool for communion with the divine forces of life.

Another intersection lies in their connection to liminality. Both Gods exist at the boundaries—Dionysius as a figure who moves between mortal and divine realms, and Pan as a guardian of the wilds, standing between civilization and the uncharted wilderness. In these spaces, their power is most potent, inviting their followers to explore and embrace the unknown.

A Pagan Perspective: Honoring the Duality of Nature and Spirit

From a Pagan point of view, Dionysius and Pan together represent the dance of opposites: cultivated celebration and untamed passion, divine ecstasy and earthy sensuality. In honoring both, practitioners acknowledge the wholeness of existence. Their energies remind us that spiritual growth often requires stepping outside the safe confines of routine, embracing the ecstatic and the wild, and celebrating life in its fullest, most unrestrained forms.

Rituals that invoke both deities may blend elements of Dionysian mystery with the untamed energies of Pan. A grove under the stars can transform into a sacred space where wine flows, drums beat, and the barriers between human and divine dissolve. Through this union, participants can touch the primal heart of life, experiencing the divine not as a distant ideal but as an immediate and visceral reality.

Conclusion: Eternal Echoes of the Wild Divine

Dionysius and Pan stand as eternal symbols of freedom and ecstasy in the Pagan imagination. Their myths remind us that joy, wildness and spiritual transcendence are interconnected facets of the human experience. By celebrating their energies, we open ourselves to the transformative power of the wild divine, finding harmony between the cultivated and the untamed within ourselves and the world around us.

—AMELIA INGRAM

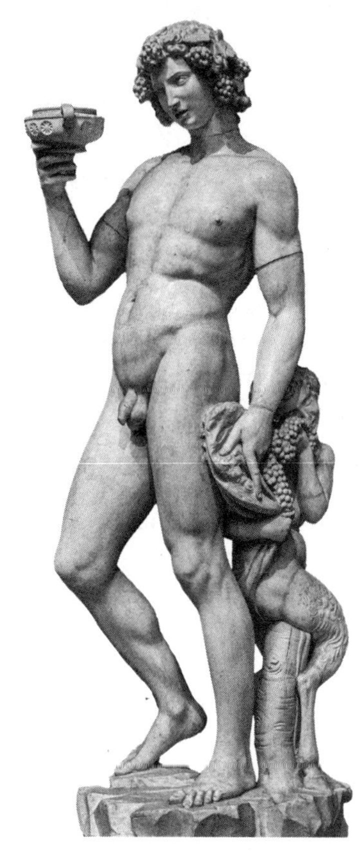

Magical Regalia: Celebrating Graduation Day

GETTING DRESSED for the day: the ritual of creating an image, an identity, by selecting comfortable or at least appropriate garments to greet a new day evokes a unique magic. Dressing for even an ordinary work or school day generates a momentum, an aura. But suppose the day marks a memorable occasion such as a wedding, a recital, public speech, prom or other anticipated event. The occasion of donning a graduation cap and gown often ranks high among these really significant events, the once or twice in a lifetime rites of passage. Years of anticipation, looking forward to receiving a diploma, perhaps shaking the hand of a school principal or dean, walking across a stage and being rewarded with "all of the rights and privileges thereunto appertaining" can be forever etched in memory. Caught up in the drama of the moment, few graduates probably ever wonder why wearing a long robe with an odd hat is a part of the process of completing school. The answer is actually very long, involved and intriguing.

The origins of today's graduation cap and gown are linked with residential life in European universities during the 12th and 13th centuries.

These institutions were founded by the clergy who instituted the wearing of black or brown gowns which were hooded. These gowns signified the students' religious status and were a way to distinguish them from the lay people, the ordinary people in the street. The phrase "town and gown" evolved as quite a literal distinction, separating the educated from the uneducated, the elite from the common. Medieval scholarship was usually connected with taking at least minor religious orders. The voluminous robes also served the practical purpose of protecting the students as they sat studying in cold, unheated and draughty buildings. The early hats resembled hoods and doubled as alms bags to be slung around the neck or over the shoulders. Eventually the hoods morphed into rounded caps with pompons, then into the square, flat, tasseled mortar boards which perch on tops of the heads of today's graduates.

By the late 19th century an Intercollegiate Code of Academic Costume was established. An 1895 version of the code in the United States prescribed that all gowns were to be black. Features on the gowns would be unique to specific degrees of achievement. Pointed sleeves were for recipients of Bachelor's degrees, long, closed sleeves were for Master's degrees, while round, open sleeves belonged with Doctoral degrees. By the late 20th century some institutions selected gowns in school colors. Different features such as stripes added to the sleeves or neck ribbons and badges were sometimes worn to denote academic achievement or affiliations with distinct programs of study. Tiny graduation gowns—usually white and topped by miniature mortar board hats—are sometimes worn today by nursery school graduates who have been preparing to begin kindergarten or elementary school.

Originally the cap and gown tradition wasn't limited to graduation day. Institutions such as New York's Columbia University as recently as the 19th Century established the wearing of a cap and gown as part of everyday uniforms for faculty and students. Those who violated rules could be barred from wearing the cap and gown for a week or more. More serious offenses could result in students being stripped of their academic regalia for longer periods of time.

The deep historical roots of the graduation cap and gown have evolved over centuries. The garments symbolize making powerful statements to denote privilege and intent—to signify the pursuit of knowledge and acquisition of accomplishments.

–ESTHER NEUMEIER

An Excerpt From Gerd Ziegler's

TAROT

Mirror of the Soul

A Handbook For the Thoth Tarot

FORWARD

My relationship with T*arot: Mirror of the Soul* is a rather personal one. My spiritual quest commenced in the early 1990s. I was in my mid-twenties and started to be curious about life, death, love, and the Universe. I turned to the tarot, and *Tarot: Mirror of the Soul* was one of my first forays into the subject.

The book was the perfect companion to—what was then for me—the intimidating Thoth Tarot. The book is extremely accessible to the beginning student in that it provides keywords for each card; a short, digestible description of the card; and ends with Indications, Questions, a Suggestion, and an Affirmation. This simple formula allows one to "enter" the cards and actually live with, experience, and feel each one on a deep soul level. This is one of the original meanings of "Pathworking." It is especially helpful to those familiarizing themselves with the Thoth Tarot by doing daily single card pulls. The cards have an uncanny way of revealing more information and insights as one continues to work with them, and *Tarot: Mirror of the Soul* is the perfect vehicle in which to embark upon this lifelong voyage.

It has been my long-held belief that we stand upon the shoulders of those who have gone before us. The deck has always been referred to as the Crowley-Thoth Tarot, but who was the woman behind the creation of this uniquely influential and enduring masterpiece? Lady Frieda

Harris, as we know her to be called, and the recognition of her role in the creation of the cards is long overdue.

Marguerite Frieda Harris was born on August 13, 1877, in London. She later married Sir Percy Harris, an English Liberal Party Member of Parliament and British baronet, so her actual title is Frieda, Lady Harris; or, more accurately, Lady Harris.

Aleister Crowley and Lady Harris were initially introduced at a dinner party in 1937 by Clifford Bax. In May of 1938, Lady Harris officially joined both the O.T.O. and the A∴A∴, choosing the motto Soror TzBA, translating in Hebrew to "Host" and enumerating to the number 93.

She later became Crowley's student, collaborator, benefactor, artist, executant, and, toward the end of his life, caretaker and one of the executors of his will. By 1947, the year of Crowley's death, there were very few individuals with whom he had not alienated himself.

It was Lady Harris's suggestion that they collaborate on creating a tarot deck similar to the Golden Dawn attributions. In 1938, at the outbreak of the Second World War, Lady Harris was engaged by Crowley to paint the seventy-eight cards. Soon after embarking on this momentous task, they began to realize that the traditional descriptions of the cards were inadequate. Lady Harris suggested that Crowley use his lifetime's worth of study and experience to create the cards. That, coupled with Lady Harris's creative genius, brought the Thoth Tarot to life.

She was approximately sixty years old at the commencement of the project. That alone should be an inspiration to us all! The project was supposed to take six months, but due to both of them being inherent perfectionists and the difficulties brought about by the war, the project ended up taking five years to complete. Part of the delay was that their communication mostly consisted of physical correspondence and that Lady Harris had to paint up to eight different versions of certain cards because of Crowley's painstaking demands. Crowley would later write of the Thoth Tarot: "It is the vindication of my life's work for the last 44 years; and will be the Compass of Power of the good ship Magick for the next 2,000 years."

Lady Harris had been interested in myriad occult subjects prior to the commencement of the Thoth Tarot. She had been drawn to Mary Baker Eddy's Christian Science, anthroposophy, Co-Freemasonry, Indian mysticism, and the teachings of Rudolf Steiner. She had also studied projective synthetic geometry and utilized this technique in the execution of the designs of the Thoth Tarot.

As part of being a Co-Freemason, Lady Harris designed three "tracing boards" based on the original designs. Tracing boards are illustrations illuminating the various emblems and symbols of Freemasonry. The three boards were interpretations of the First, Second, and Third Degree tracing boards. They are distinctively hers in that they are rendered in a modern style and utilize bold and energetic symmetry in the creation of the designs.

Lady Harris would contribute artwork for several other of Crowley's projects, including the image of the Tree of Life on the dust jacket for Little Essays Toward Truth, Crowley's portrait on the dust jacket for Olla: An Anthology of Sixty Years of Song, and, after Crowley's death, the cover and frontispiece for Crowley's funeral program: "The Last Ritual." Finally, in 1962, she provided the cover art for Liber Aleph: The Book of Wisdom and Folly. There also exist several heart-rending sketches of how The Great Beast appeared on his deathbed.

The Book of Thoth was published in 1944 in a limited edition of two hundred copies, but neither Crowley nor Lady Harris lived to see their beloved deck in print. The deck was finally produced in full-color by Grady Louis McMurtry in 1969 in collaboration with Samuel Weiser. Ultimately, Lady Harris bequeathed the original paintings of the Thoth Tarot to Gerald Yorke, another stalwart associate and executor of Crowley's will, who in turn placed them in the safe and capable hands of the Warburg Institute in London where they reside to this day.

As previously stated, Crowley fell out with most of his associates throughout his life, so his heartfelt testimonial of Lady Harris in the beginning of The Book of Thoth speaks volumes:

> *She devoted her genius to the Work. With incredible rapidity she picked up the rhythm, and with inexhaustible patience submitted to the corrections of the fanatical slave-driver that she had invoked, often painting the same card as many as eight times until it measured up to his Vanadium Steel yardstick! May the passionate "love under will" which she has stored in this Treasury of Truth and Beauty flow forth from the Splendor and Strength of her work to enlighten the world; may this Tarot serve as a chart for the bold seamen of the New Aeon, to guide them across the great Sea of Understanding to the City of the Pyramids.*

The tarot aids us to access the spiritual and manifest it in our daily lives. The temple we build on the physical plane is a reflection (mirror) of the one we build within ourselves. To seek the Divine, the Cosmic Source, The All, is verily to peer within the Mirror of the Soul. This classic text has stood the test of time and is an invaluable reference source for beginning and seasoned tarot students alike.

DIANE CHAMPIGNY

PriestessThea-Soror Shahin

PREFACE

Just as we use a mirror to observe our exterior, we can use the images of the Tarot to approach our inner reality. An adventurous expedition! The images of the Tarot are a mirror of the images in our souls. The longer we look inward, the more we discover about ourselves and our lives.

A mirror reflects visible reality without judging it. It shows the beautiful and the ugly, the pleasant and the unpleasant. It cannot do anything else. We can put it aside or shatter it if we don't like our reflection, but doing so won't change our appearance.

The images of the Tarot describe spiritual conditions. In using the cards we see our inner reality from new perspectives. The images are neither "positive" nor "negative," neither "for" nor "against" us. They simply offer hints and clues. We can examine them, choosing either to discard or consider, ignore or use them.

Many people are afraid to confront their inner reality; they may find ugly or unpleasant aspects of themselves. They pretend to know themselves, often believing they really do. They expend enormous amounts of energy in maintaining an illusory facade; the more illusory, the more desperately they defend it and the greater their underlying fear. Yet each defensive action, each denial, reveals, rather than hides, the underlying insecurity. Fear, narrow-mindedness, repression, constriction and a sense of isolation result, and the true inner reality remains unknown.

Surprisingly, we learn to accept and love ourselves only when we stop trying to hide, and hide from, our inner reality. We can only share with others those parts of ourselves which we had discovered and accepted, and can only change those unpleasant aspects in ourselves which we have thoroughly examined, and recognized as needing change.

Self-exploration can be risky at times. Newly won perspectives can upset old habits and attitudes, and shake the very foundation of our belief systems (see The Tower). Yet this is an essential step in any transformational process.

The "rewards" of such an internal cleansing process are great. Each time we reveal and let go of one of our illusions, we come one step closer to our own true, boundless and enduring selves. What we let go and lose in this process never has been really ours; what is destroyed never has been rooted in our true being.

In letting go you arrive at the still place in yourself where you and the stillness are one; you arrive home and you and your home are one.

This book offers suggestions for playing with and increasing your understanding of the Crowley-Thoth Tarot. It will help you in your work with the cards, sometimes guiding your inner exploration, sometimes pointing the way in daily situations and difficult decision-making processes.

Tarot means, above all, subjectivity, and maintaining a vital readiness to being touched. The Tarot's images, as mirrors of our own unconscious impulses, unlock and make these impulses available to our conscious mind. And we learn to interpret the messages of the cards, as we might interpret a muddled dream, we can discover new inner realms, and gain a glimpse into the mysteries of the Universe in its all-encompassing cosmic order.

GERD ZIEGLER

Waakirchen, Germany, August 1984

Zolling, Germany, July 1985

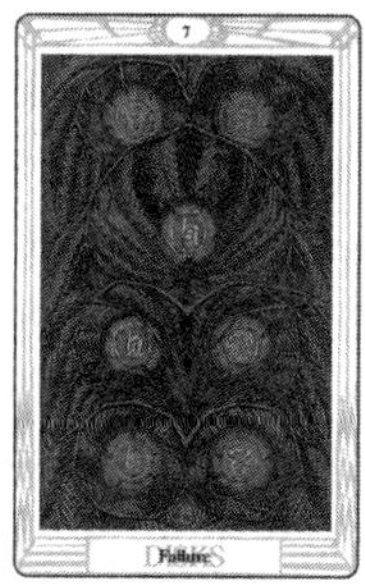

THE FOOL

***Key Words:** openness, trust; ready to take a risk; courage to stand your ground; freedom, independence; creativity; great potential; possibility to take a quantum leap; listening to the heart's voice.*

The Fool is represented by the god of Spring, Dionysus. The green color reminds us of the powerful creative force of Spring. The crocodile (the ancient Egyptian god of creativity) is also the bearer of the greatest creative powers.

The long umbilical cord, connection to cosmic oneness, wraps the Fool in four spirals. The possibility of rebirth is given on all four planes of human existence: spiritual, intellectual, emotional, and physical. The prerequisite is your readiness to change in all areas; your responsibility to self-development.

The four spirals are described as follows:

The first spiral surrounds the heart in heart-shape. It stands for emotional rebirth; the recognition, perception, and acceptance of true emotional needs.

The second spiral bears three symbols. The dove represents vulnerability and sensitivity as requirements for love of oneself and others. The ability to set limits and say "No" in unclear relationships is also needed. The butterfly means transformation (the caterpillar becomes the butterfly). The snakes wrapped around each other (Caduceus) are a symbol for engagement in in healing and health.

On the third spiral lie two naked children entwined. Their presence brings the realm of relationship into the picture. The quality of your relationships with family, friends, business associates, and deep emotional bonds must be reexamined and reevaluated. Which people do you really want around you?

The fourth spiral is occupied by the tiger and the crocodile. The crocodile urges for the development of creative abilities in work and career. The rose it wears symbolizes the unfolding of creative powers. The crocodile's powerful jaws testify to its endurance and leadership qualities, as well as to the ability to work independently and self-sufficiently. It is possible to break through old, worn-out conditioning.

The tiger symbolizes fear (see Princess of Wands). Dionysus is repeatedly bitten by this tiger, but his gaze remains directed forward. He gives no attention to fear, so it has lost its power over him. The tiger cannot injure him at all. His unshakable faith in existence allows him to be aware of fearful feelings without being their victim. He is liberated, able to be receptive for mystical peak experiences and interpersonal interaction. Basic, dynamic powers are released which drive forward. The onrushing creative unfolding process cannot be held back.

The Fool holds a cup with a base of crystal in his right hand and a burning torch in his left. These are alchemical symbols (see the card XIV Art). They show the meeting of opposite forces which creates the energy for the transformation, the quantum leap, to take place.

The grapes, symbols of fertility, are ripe for harvest. The white spots on the golden background mean Fall (harvest time); falling leaves, dropping, letting go, surrender. The coins at the right, engraved with astrological symbols, reflect the overflowing wealth on all planes which comes when you give your creative energies full rein to unfold.

The horns Dionysus wears reflect expanded perception. The rainbow surrounding his head means wholeness, Unity, the bridge between heaven and earth, inner and outer. Between his legs is a cluster of flowers which represents the process of transformation. At the bottom, the active aspect (the three flowers to the left symbolize body, mind, and spirit) combines with the passive aspect, receptivity, willingness to learn. The simple blossoms below, when united, give birth to the many-petalled blossom above.

The sun symbolizes the creative and transformatory powers released by the melting of basic sexual energy.

Indications: You are ready for a new beginning, perhaps even a quantum leap. Give in, dare to leap, even if fear attempts to hold you back. Trust the voice from within your heart.

Questions: What is the "tiger of fear" for you? How do you imagine the courageous leap into the new? What does it look like? Where does your heart call you to go?

Suggestion: Draw other cards for the above questions if their answers are not clear for you.

Affirmation: I now follow my heart. I am open, and ready to go wherever it may lead me.

Gerd Ziegler *(born February 8, 1951) is a therapist specializing in humanistic and spiritual therapy. He studied psychology, political science, theater, and religious studies at Freie Universität Berlin, and also worked with encounter groups, gestalt, psychodrama, neo-Reichian bodywork, and meditation. He studied at the Boyesen Institute in London from 1976–1978. In 1979, his path led him to India, where he spent two years studying and living at the Shree Rajneesh Ashram and Rajneesh International University.*

MOON GARDENING

BY PHASE

Sow, transplant, bud and graft			*Plow, cultivate, weed and reap*	
	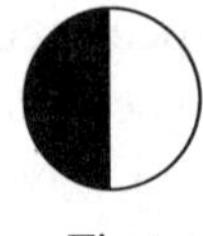	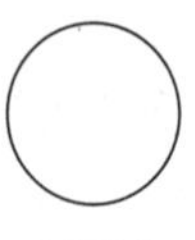	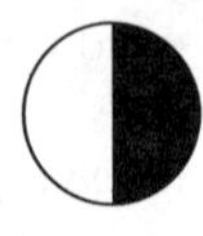	
NEW	First Quarter	FULL	Last Quarter	NEW
Plant above-ground crops with outside seeds, flowering annuals.	Plant above-ground crops with inside seeds.	Plant root crops, bulbs, biennials, perennials.		Do not plant.

BY PLACE IN THE ZODIAC

In general—plant and transplant crops that bear above ground when the Moon is in a watery sign: Cancer, Scorpio or Pisces. Plant and transplant root crops when the Moon is in Taurus or Capricorn; the other earthy sign, Virgo, encourages rot. The airy signs, Gemini, Libra and Aquarius, are good for some crops and not for others. The fiery signs, Aries, Leo and Sagittarius, are barren signs for most crops and best used for weeding, pest control and cultivating the soil.

Aries—*barren, hot and dry.* Favorable for planting and transplanting beets, onions and garlic, but unfavorable for all other crops. Good for weeding and pest control, for canning and preserving, and for all activities involving fire.

♉

Taurus—*fruitful, cold and dry.* Fertile, best for planting root crops and also very favorable for all transplanting as it encourages root growth. Good for planting crops that bear above ground and for canning and preserving. Prune in this sign to encourage root growth.

♊

Gemini—*barren, hot and moist.* The best sign for planting beans, which will bear more heavily. Unfavorable for other crops. Good for harvesting and for gathering herbs.

♋

Cancer—*fruitful, cold and moist.* Best for planting crops that bear above ground and very favorable for root crops. Dig garden beds when the Moon is in this sign, and everything planted in them will flourish. Prune in this sign to encourage growth.

♌

Leo—*barren, hot and dry.* Nothing should be planted or transplanted while the Moon is in the Lion. Favorable for weeding and pest control, for tilling and cultivating the soil, and for canning and preserving.

♍

Virgo—*barren, cold and dry.* Good for planting grasses and grains, but unfavorable for other crops. Unfavorable for canning and preserving, but favorable for weeding, pest control, tilling and cultivating. Make compost when the Moon is in the Virgin and it will ripen faster.

♎

Libra—*fruitful, hot and moist.* The best sign to plant flowers and vines and somewhat favorable for crops that bear above the ground. Prune in this sign to encourage flowering.

♏

Scorpio—*fruitful, cold and moist.* Very favorable to plant and transplant crops that bear above ground, and favorable for planting and transplanting root crops. Set out fruit trees when the Moon is in this sign and prune to encourage growth.

♐

Sagittarius—*barren, hot and dry.* Favorable for planting onions, garlic and cucumbers, but unfavorable for all other crops, and especially unfavorable for transplanting. Favorable for canning and preserving, for tilling and cultivating the soil, and for pruning to discourage growth.

♑

Capricorn—*fruitful, cold and dry.* Very favorable for planting and transplanting root crops, favorable for flowers, vines, and all crops that bear above ground. Plant trees, bushes and vines in this sign. Prune trees and vines to strengthen the branches.

♒

Aquarius—*barren, hot and moist.* Favorable for weeding and pest control, tilling and cultivating the soil, harvesting crops, and gathering herbs. Somewhat favorable for planting crops that bear above ground, but only in dry weather or the seeds will tend to rot.

♓

Pisces—*fruitful, cold and moist.* Very favorable for planting and transplanting crops that bear above ground and favorable for flowers and all root crops except potatoes. Prune when the Moon is in the Fishes to encourage growth. Plant trees, bushes and vines in this sign.

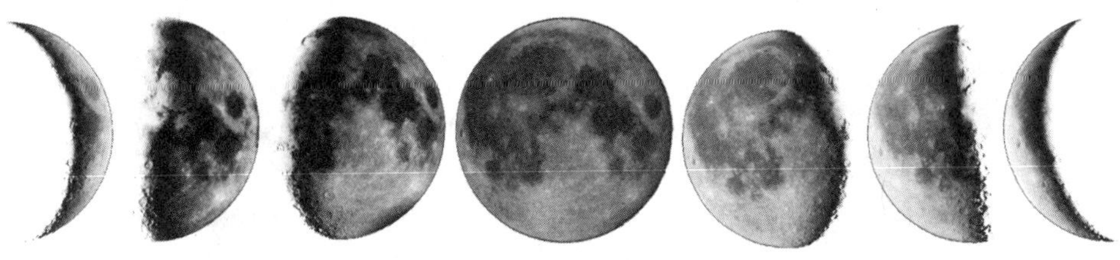

Consult our Moon Calendar pages for phase and place in the zodiac circle. The Moon remains in a sign for about two and a half days. Match your gardening activity to the day that follows the Moon's entry into that zodiacal sign. For best results, choose days when the phase and sign are both favorable. For example, plant seeds when the Moon is waxing in a suitable fruitful sign, and uproot stubborn weeds when the Moon is in the fourth quarter in a barren sign.

The MOON *Calendar*

is divided into zodiac signs rather than the more familiar Gregorian calendar.

2026 2027

Bear in mind that new projects should be initiated when the Moon is waxing (from dark to full). When the Moon is on the wane (from full to dark), it is a time for storing energy and the wise person waits.

Please note that Moons are listed by day of entry into each sign. Quarters are marked, but as rising and setting times vary from one region to another, it is advisable to check your local newspaper, library or planetarium.

The Moon's Place is computed for Eastern Time.

aries

March 20 – April 19, 2026

Cardinal Sign of Fire △ Ruled by Mars ♂

S	M	T	W	T	F	S
	Mars ***Drive, courage, initiation*** Raw will and decisive action shape the domain of the ancient God Mars, patron of warriors. In myth, he is not only the bringer of battle but the protector of boundaries, the embodiment of passion and the spark that drives creation forward. His presence ignites courage and the instinct to move, to begin, to break inertia. Associated with ↓				Mar **20** Vernal Equinox 5:01 AM Aries	**21** *Wake up early* Taurus
22	**23** Gemini	**24** *Set bold intentions*	**25** ◐ Cancer	**26** *Take the lead*	**27**	**28** Leo
29 *Elevate your confidence*	**30** Virgo	**31**	April **1** Seed Moon Libra	**2** WANING All Fool's Day ⇦	**3** Scorpio	**4** *Relax fear*
5	**6** *Recognize yourself* Sagittarius	**7**	**8** *Share progress* Capricorn	**9**	**10** ◑	**11** *Use black thread* Aquarius
12	**13** *Take a ritual bath* Pisces	**14**	**15** *Burn a letter* Aries	**16**	**17** ● Taurus	**18** WAXING
19 *Sunshine musings* Gemini	blood, iron and the pulsing force of life itself, Mars governs the sacred aggression needed to manifest intention. In magic, he is invoked for strength, protection and the forging of one's path with unflinching clarity. Though often linked with conflict, his deeper essence lies in the empowerment to act. When aligned with Aries, the zodiac's initiator, Mars assumes the mantle of the flame bearer—beckoning us to rise, act and claim our place in the unfolding cosmos. Motion becomes magic and right action kindles transformation in the forge of Mars' relentless fire.					

Hawthorn

Uath

THE HAWTHORN is a small tree seldom exceeding 15 feet in height. Its long thorns protect against storms and grazing animals, sheltering young trees like oak and ash that grow beneath it and eventually supplant it. It also provides thorny refuge for birds and wildlife that feast on its scarlet autumn berries.

Though it thrives in most soils, hawthorn prefers damp, sandy earth for germination and is often bird-sown. Its bark is dark grey-brown, splitting into random square patterns with age. Flowers grow in clusters of white or pale pink and exude a strong, unusual scent.

Hawthorn is strongly tied to the Celtic May Eve festival—"May" being a folk name for it. "Whitethorn" is another name, especially in Brittany, where the tree marks fairy trysting places. In Ireland, sacred hawthorns guard wishing wells, their thorns often hung with scraps of cloth to symbolize wishes. The Roman Goddess Cardea, mistress of Janus, used a hawthorn bough as her emblem of protection—"her power is to open what is shut; to shut what is open."

Thorn trees are considered bewitched in legend, and hawthorn in particular captured the imagination of Western Europe from earliest recorded time. In some traditions, it protected against lightning; in others, it held purifying powers. The Old Irish deemed it a tree of chastity. Greek brides wore crowns of hawthorn blossoms in May, yet Romans considered both the month and the flower ill omens for marriage, especially if brought into the home. To the Turks, hawthorn symbolized erotic desire.

—ELIZABETH PEPPER

taurus

April 20 – May 20, 2026

Fixed Sign of Earth 🜃 Ruled by Venus ♀

S	M	T	W	T	F	S
	April **20**	**21** Cancer	**22** *Beat a drum*	**23** ◐	**24** Leo	**25**
26 *Keep your balance* Virgo	**27**	**28** Libra	**29** *Revel with the devil*	**30** Walpurgis Night	May **1** Hare Moon Scorpio	**2** WANING Beltane ⇦ Vesak Day
3 *Build a needfire* Sagittarius	**4**	**5** *Bind the spell* Capricorn	**6**	**7** *Heed ye flower*	**8** White Lotus Day Aquarius	**9** ◑
10 *Water the seedlings* Pisces	**11**	**12**	**13** *Remain steadfast* Aries	**14**	**15** *Cook for your love* Taurus	**16** ●
17 WAXING Gemini	**18** *Help a toad*	**19** Cancer	**20**			

Ceres ***Fertility, sustenance, seasonal wisdom*** Guardian of Earth's bounty, the ancient grain mother Ceres oversees nourishment, harvest and the sacred pulse of seasonal return. She teaches us to honor what sustains—not only the body, but the soul. Her myth, in which her daughter Persephone is taken to the Underworld, reveals the alchemical link between loss and restoration. In magic, Ceres governs abundance, agricultural rites and food blessings. She is the cultivated Earth herself—provider, healer and bearer of sacred grain. Taurus, grounded and sensual, harmonizes with Ceres' roots in the physical. Together, they remind us that care is a form of power and feeding others is holy. Ceres calls us back to rhythm, simplicity and the gentle reverence found in soil, breath and ritual. To tend, to feed, to rest—these become sacred acts. Within her cycle lies the mystery of return and in her arms, we remember how to belong.

Notable Quotations

WATER

Water is the softest thing, yet it can penetrate mountains and Earth. This shows clearly the principle of softness overcoming hardness.

Laozi

The memory of life arrived on this Earth carried by the soul of water.

Masaru Emoto

The soul is like water: it comes from Heaven, flows to the Earth, rises up again to the sky.

Paracelsus

In one drop of water are found all the secrets of all the oceans.

Kahlil Gibran

A lake carries you into recesses of feeling otherwise impenetrable.

William Wordsworth

Empty your mind, be formless, shapeless—like water.

Bruce Lee

The water in which the mystic swims is the same water a madman drowns in.

Joseph Campbell

The soul of man is like to water: from Heaven it comes, to Heaven it rises, and then returning to Earth, it must go back and forth eternally.

Johann Wolfgang von Goethe

You are like water. You go everywhere and fill everything. But when you face resistance, you do not break—you flow around it, you wear it down.

Thich Nhat Hanh

The sound of water is worth more than all the poets' words.

Octavio Paz

Silence is as deep as eternity, speech as shallow as time. But water belongs to both.

Thomas Carlyle

gemini

May 21 – June 20, 2026

Mutable Sign of Air △ Ruled by Mercury ☿

S	M	T	W	T	F	S
Mercury ***Thought, movement, communication*** The great connector between minds, realms and meanings, Mercury weaves the fabric of thought and speech into potent spells of becoming. As trickster and guide, he governs not only speech and thought, but the magic of transformation through language. In myth, Mercury escorts souls between realms—a liminal deity of ↓				May **21** Leo	**22** *Bird's eye view*	**23** Virgo
24 *Sing golden notes*	**25** Libra	**26**	**27** *Tell the bees*	**28** *Perfect Love Perfect Trust* Scorpio	**29** Oak Apple Day	**30** Sagittarius
31 Dyad Moon	June **1** WANING *Be ready*	**2** Capricorn	**3** *Speak to the stars*	**4** Aquarius	**5** Night of the Watchers	**6**
7 Pisces	**8**	**9** Aries	**10** *Flute with the fae*	**11** Taurus	**12**	**13** *Quiet the mind* Gemini
14	**15** WAXING *Self reflect* Cancer	**16**	**17** Leo	**18** *Pass the grapes*	**19** Virgo	**20** Summer Solstice 10:42 PM

invention, cleverness, sudden insight—he is the spark behind wit, the voice weaving meaning, the feet crossing paths in spirit and flesh. In magic, Mercury supports communication, divination, swiftness, and cunning. He rules commerce and exchange—stories, contracts, intention. Gemini reflects his agile energy—dual, bright, curious. Together, they dance through paradox, teaching humor and perspective. Every word is a spell. Mercury reminds us: think sharply, speak wisely, move like wind.

FULL MOON NAMES

Students of occult literature soon learn the importance of names. From Ra to Rumpelstiltskin, the message is clear—names hold unusual power.

The tradition of naming full Moons was recorded in an English edition of The *Shepherd's Calendar*, published in the first decade of the 16th century.

Aries—Seed. Sowing season and symbol of the start of the new year.

Taurus—Hare. The sacred animal was associated in Roman legends with springtime and fertility.

Gemini—Dyad. The Latin word for a pair refers to the twin stars of the constellation Castor and Pollux.

Cancer—Mead. During late June and most of July the meadows, or meads, were mowed for hay.

Leo—Wort. When the sun was in Leo the worts (from the Anglo-Saxon wyrt-plant) were gathered to be dried and stored.

Virgo — Barley. Persephone, virgin goddess of rebirth, carries a sheaf of barley as symbol of the harvest.

Libra — Blood. Marking the season when domestic animals were sacrificed for winter provisions.

Scorpio — Snow. Scorpio heralds the dark season when the Sun is at its lowest and the first snow flies.

Sagittarius — Oak. The sacred tree of the Druids and the Roman god Jupiter is most noble as it withstands winter's blasts.

Capricorn — Wolf. The fearsome nocturnal animal represents the "night" of the year. Wolves were rarely seen in England after the 12th century.

Aquarius — Storm. A storm is said to rage most fiercely just before it ends, and the year usually follows suit.

Pisces — Chaste. The antiquated word for pure reflects the custom of greeting the new year with a clear soul.

Libra's Full Moon occasionally became the Wine Moon when a grape harvest was expected to produce a superior vintage.

America's early settlers continued to name the full Moons. The influence of the native tribes and their traditions is readily apparent.

AMERICAN	**Colonial**	**Native**
Aries / April	Pink, Grass, Egg	Green Grass
Taurus / May	Flower, Planting	Shed
Gemini / June	Rose, Strawberry	Rose, Make Fat
Cancer / July	Buck, Thunder	Thunder
Leo / August	Sturgeon, Grain	Cherries Ripen
Virgo / September	Harvest, Fruit	Hunting
Libra / October	Hunter's	Falling Leaf
Scorpio / November	Beaver, Frosty	Mad
Sagittarius / December	Cold, Long Night	Long Night
Capricorn / January	Wolf, After Yule	Snow
Aquarius / February	Snow, Hunger	Hunger
Pisces / March	Worm, Sap, Crow	Crow, Sore Eye

– ELIZABETH PEPPER
Moon Lore

cancer

June 21 – July 22, 2026

Cardinal Sign of Water ▽ Ruled by Moon ☽

S	M	T	W	T	F	S
June 21 ◑	22 Libra	23	24 Midsummer Scorpio	25 *Times two*	26	27 *Resist injustice* Sagittarius
28	29 Mead Moon Capricorn	30 WANING	July 1	2 Aquarius	3 *Gaze at the tide*	4 Pisces
5	6 *Lucid dreams reign* Aries	7 ◐	8 *Contemplate the eye*	9 Taurus	10	11 *Scry the foe* Gemini
12	13 *Embody the narwhal* Cancer	14 ●	15 WAXING Leo	16 *Collect water stones*	17 Virgo	18 *Speak in riddles*
19 *Conjure a shield* Libra	20	21 ◑ Scorpio	22 *Smell lemon balm*			

Moon *Emotion, memory, reflection* Luminous and ever-changing, the Moon reflects the hidden rhythms of tides, wombs, dreams and emotion. She governs instinct and the invisible currents that shape our lives. Across cultures, the Moon is honored as Goddess, protector and weaver of cycles—overseeing birth and death, ebb and flow, shadow and light. Her pull governs not only oceans, but the inner tides of intuition, longing and deep knowing. In magic, she's evoked for dreamwork, divination, fertility and psychic growth. Her phases offer a map of becoming and release. Aligned with Cancer, her rulership is nurturing, lunar and sacredly feminine. The Moon teaches that feeling is knowing, softness is strength and the unseen is sacred. She is rhythm in the dark, breath in stillness, the soul's silver mirror.

Lukumi Orisha Shrine

Havanah, Cuba

leo

July 23 – August 22, 2026

Fixed Sign of Fire △ Ruled by Sun ⊙

S	M	T	W	T	F	S
	Sun *Vitality, illumination, divine self* At the center of our celestial stage blazes the Sun, radiating power, joy and unwavering presence. It is the divine spark made visible, the fire at the heart of all becoming. In myth, the Sun is the chariot of Gods, the golden eye of truth, the ➜			July 23 Ancient Egyptian New Year	24 Sagittarius	25 *Create a legacy*
26 Capricorn	27 *Calm the fire*	28	29 Wort Moon Aquarius	30 WANING	31 Lughnassad Eve Pisces	Aug 1 Lammas
2	3 *Evoke confidence within* Aries	4	5 Taurus	6	7 *Ready the lemons* Gemini	8
9 *Swim with friends* Cancer	10	11 Total Solar Eclipse ⇨ Leo	12	13 WAXING Diana's Day Virgo	14	15 *Ground yourself* Libra
16	17 Black Cat Appreciation Day	18 Scorpio	19	20 *Be spontaneous* Sagittarius	21 *Shine your light*	22

sovereign that commands the day. It governs identity, courage, creativity and the will to express the self fully. In magic, the Sun is invoked for vitality, success, strength and the illumination of purpose. Its energy burns away illusion and charges the spirit with warmth and clarity. Aligned with Leo, the Sun becomes a crown of fire—reminding us to lead from the heart and shine without shame. It strengthens the lifeforce, awakens boldness and restores confidence. The Sun teaches that true sovereignty begins within—and that the brightest light is often born from devotion, not dominance. To honor the Sun is to honor the sacred joy of being fully, gloriously alive.

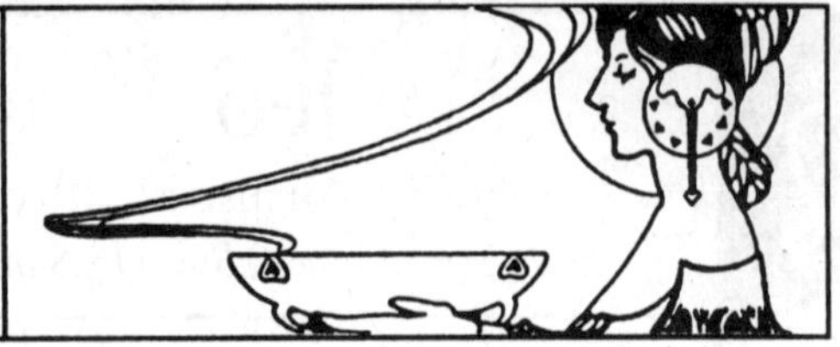

May Blossom Honey Cakes

BELTANE ARRIVES with bright blossoms and the crackle of sacred flame. This Sabbat, steeped in ancient custom, celebrates the turning of the Wheel toward Summer. In the old Celtic calendar, it was the season when livestock were driven to open pasture, blessed as they passed between twin fires. Homes were decorated with hawthorn, and lovers wandered into the woods to welcome fertility, revelry and the promise of new life. On this liminal night, when the veils are thin, spirits and fae walk freely, and offerings of food and drink are often left beneath trees or on thresholds to court their favor.

Among the delights of the Beltane table are herbal sweets and honeyed cakes—simple, fragrant and rich with meaning. These may blossom honey cakes are ideal for sharing at bonfires, tucking into picnic baskets, or leaving as gifts for unseen visitors who may pass your way on a spring night.

Making May Blossom Honey Cakes

1½ cups all-purpose flour
½ tsp baking powder
½ tsp baking soda
½ tsp salt
1 tsp dried edible flowers (such as chamomile, lavender, or rose)
1 tsp chopped fresh thyme or lemon balm
⅓ cup honey
½ cup unsalted butter, softened
¼ cup brown sugar
1 large egg
1 tsp vanilla extract
¼ cup milk

Preheat oven to 350°F. Line a baking sheet with parchment.

In a mixing bowl, combine the flour, baking powder, baking soda and salt. Gently stir in the herbs and blossoms.

In a separate bowl, cream the butter, honey and brown sugar until light and fluffy. Beat in the egg and vanilla until smooth. Add the dry ingredients gradually, alternating with the milk, mixing just until a soft dough forms.

Scoop tablespoon-sized portions of dough onto the prepared baking sheet, spacing them an inch apart. Press each gently to flatten. Bake for 10 to 12 minutes, or until the edges turn golden.

Let cool completely on a wire rack. These delicate cakes carry the sweetness of the season—ideal for Beltane offerings, or simply for savoring in a field of flowers.

–DEVON STRONG

virgo

August 23 – September 22, 2026

Mutable Sign of Earth 🜃 Ruled by Mercury ☿

S	M	T	W	T	F	S
Aug **23** Capricorn	**24**	**25** *Vision with precision* Aquarius	**26**	**27**	**28** Barley Moon Pisces	**29** Partial Lunar Eclipse ⇦
30 WANING Aries	**31** *Follow an astral thread*	Sept **1** Taurus	**2**	**3** *Enjoy the harvest* Gemini	**4**	**5** Cancer
6	**7** Leo	**8** *Open the gate*	**9** Virgo	**10**	**11** WAXING *Give thanks*	**12** *Organize and declutter* Libra
13 Ganesh Chaturthi ⇨	**14** *Drink peppermint tea* Scorpio	**15**	**16** Sagittarius	**17** *Circle back*	**18**	**19** Capricorn
20 *Ready the altar*	**21** *Gather round the rue* Aquarius	**22** Autumnal Equinox 2:19 PM				

Vesta ***Devotion, sacred order, inner flame*** As guardian of Rome's inner fire and temple sanctity, she was revered not through spectacle, but through stillness, purity and unwavering care. Vesta represents focus, clarity and the art of maintaining what is essential. In magic, she governs ritual space, consecration, and the invisible thread binding intention to outcome. She teaches the grace of tending—whether flame, home, or spirit—with patience and precision. Virgo, deeply connected to healing and holistic order, resonates with Vesta's archetype. Together, they express a devotion not only to doing, but to doing well, to embodying service as a spiritual act. Vesta in Virgo is the priestess at the threshold, the healer who sanctifies through action and the keeper of rhythm in a chaotic world. She reminds us that true sanctity is not loud—it is deliberate, intentional and eternal.

The Ant and the Dove

An ant went to a river to quench its thirst, and, being carried away by the rush of the stream, was on the point of drowning. A dove sitting on a tree overhanging the water plucked a leaf and let it fall into the water close to her. The Ant climbed onto it and floated in safety to the bank. Shortly afterwards a bird catcher came and stood under the tree, and laid his lime-twigs for the Dove, which sat in its branches. The Ant, perceiving his design, stung him in the foot. In pain, the bird catcher threw down the twigs, and the noise made the Dove take wing.

Moral: One good turn deserves another.

Illustration by
Percy James Billinghurst

♎

libra

September 23 – October 22, 2026

Cardinal Sign of Air 🜁 *Ruled by Venus* ♀

S	M	T	W	T	F	S
Venus ***Love, beauty, harmony*** From seafoam and starlight rises Venus, Goddess of love whose grace shapes both passion and peace. She governs the arts of union, aesthetics and value. Born of ocean and spirit, she moves with irresistible allure, drawing all toward ↓			Sept **23**	**24** *Cultivate partnerships* Pisces	**25**	**26** Blood Moon Aries
27 WANING *See the beauty*	**28** Taurus	**29** *Challenge yourself*	**30** Gemini	Oct **1**	**2** *Cherish your friends*	**3** Cancer
4 *Live and let live*	**5** Leo	**6**	**7** *Weigh the details* Virgo	**8**	**9** *Confide in a loved one* Libra	**10**
11 WAXING Scorpio	**12** *Look inside*	**13**	**14** Sagittarius	**15** *Have grace*	**16** Capricorn	**17** *Be fair*
18	**19** Aquarius	**20**	**21** *Listen to music* Pisces	**22**		

balance, attraction and beauty. She rules not only romantic love, but principles of charm, sensuality and the harmonics of the universe. In magic, Venus is invoked for enchantment, elegance, seduction and heart healing. She inspires artists, lovers and peacemakers. Her blessings extend to acts of devotion—adorning altars, crafting beauty from intention, nurturing the sacred through refinement. Libra, as her airy mirror, reflects the fairness of her gaze and the subtle justice in her touch. Venus teaches that to love is to recognize divinity in the other—and when beauty is honored, it becomes a portal. What we cherish shapes who we become—tenderness is strength.

The Geomantic Figures: Rubeus

GEOMANCY IS AN ANCIENT SYSTEM of divination that uses sixteen symbols, the geomantic figures. Easy to learn and use, it was one of the most popular divination methods in the Middle Ages and Renaissance. It remained in use among rural cunning folk for many centuries thereafter, and is now undergoing a renaissance of its own as diviners discover its possibilities.

The geomantic figures are made up of single and double dots. Each figure has a name and a divinatory meaning, and the figures are also assigned to the four Elements, the twelve signs of the Zodiac, the seven planets and the nodes of the Moon. The dots that make up the figures signify their inner meanings: the four lines of dots represent Fire, Air, Water and Earth, and show that the Elements are present in either active (one dot) or latent (two dots) form.

The eighth of the geomantic figures is Rubeus, which means Red. Yes, it's also the first name of Hagrid, the character from the Harry Potter novels, and if you think of the character you already know more about the geomantic figure than you think you do! Rubeus belongs to the element of Water, the Zodiacal sign Scorpio and the planet Mars (or in some accounts, the dwarf planet Pluto.) The pattern of dots that forms this figure resembles a goblet that has been emptied and turned upside down.

Read as symbols of the Elements, the dots that form Rubeus reveal much about the nature of this figure. In this figure the elements of Fire, Water, and Earth are latent, while Air alone is active. The restless, turbulent, troubled energy of Air pervades this figure, though that turbulence very often expresses itself in the sphere of the emotions—thus the attribution to Water noted above.

In divination Rubeus represents passion, fierceness and violence. It is favorable in any situation that calls for a headlong plunge into the maelstrom of experience, and unfavorable in any situation that calls for a clear head and calm decisions. It can also be a warning that you are fooling yourself, or that someone else is trying to fool you.

–JOHN MICHAEL GREER

scorpio

October 23 – November 21, 2026

Fixed Sign of Water ▽ Ruled by Pluto♇

S	M	T	W	T	F	S
	Pluto ***Power, transformation, initiation*** Beneath the surface of things lies Pluto's realm—where endings deepen, secrets fester and transformation is forged in fire. As Lord of the Underworld, he reigns in silence and depth—where endings breed beginnings and truth waits beneath illusion. His mythic abduction of Persephone is not merely conquest but catalyst,🡓				Oct **23** *Enchant a balm*	**24** Aries
25	**26** Snow Moon Taurus	**27** WANING	**28** *Guard your secrets* Gemini	**29**	**30** *The bone dust calls* Cancer	**31** Samhain Eve
Nov **1** Leo	**2** Hallowmas ⇦ *Honor the dead*	**3** Virgo	**4**	**5** *Scatter the ashes* Libra	**6**	**7** *Move into silence*
8 *Steer the wind* Scorpio	**9**	**10** WAXING Sagittarius	**11** *Silence*	**12**	**13** *Redeem the shadow* Capricorn	**14**
15 Aquarius	**16** Hecate Night	**17**	**18** *Throw the bones* Pisces	**19**	**20** Aries	**21**

pulling her and the world into a deeper rhythm of becoming. Pluto governs the hidden, the taboo, the regenerative cycles of decay and rebirth. In magic, he is called upon in banishing, ancestral rites, deathwork and deep shadow integration. His is the domain of thresholds, where the soul sheds what cannot pass through fire. Pluto also rules obsession, karmic unraveling and the primal urges that haunt and awaken. Scorpio, with its intensity and intimacy, echoes this alchemical process. Together, they transform pain into power and wounds into wisdom. Pluto reminds us that no transformation is gentle—but that what dies in darkness may rise in power.

YEAR OF THE FIRE HORSE

February 17, 2026–February 5, 2027

This is the oldest of the world's zodiacs. It follows a cycle of twelve years. The lunar (Chinese) calendar is found throughout the Orient and is followed by a greater number of people than any other. It is observed in China, Japan, Korea, Vietnam, Cambodia and neighboring countries. The legend is that Buddha invited all of the animals to his birthday party. The twelve who came were each rewarded with a year with the promise that they would be the animals to hide in the heart of the year itself and also within the hearts of those born during that year. The Horse is the seventh of the twelve animals Buddha rewarded with stewardship of a year. Five Elements (Fire, Water, Metal, Earth and wood) distinguish the animals. Every sixty years the pattern of element-animal pairs repeats.

February 17, 2026–February 5, 2027 is the Red Fire Horse's Year. Strong willed and adventurous, Fire Horse tosses its head with determination. This Horse seeks challenging new experiences and inspirations. Innovative techniques, strategy, courage and using the element of surprise leads to winning situations. Remember the legend of the Trojan Horse. Fire Horse cherishes and nurtures a free spirit. Persistently it trots along its chosen path without compromising. Success awaits at the end of the trail. Remember to allow others ample liberty, though. Be supportive of those who have goals and ideals which might differ from yours in order to make this year a favorable one.

Those born during a Horse Year are passionate in love, enthusiastic, independent, optimistic and quite strong—both physically and intellectually. They do have a tinge of selfishness, though, and can be quick tempered.

More information on the Fire Horse can be found on our website at TheWitchesAlmanac.com/pages/almanac-extras

Years of the Horse

1942, 1954, 1966, 1978, 1990, 2002, 2014, 2026, 2038

Illustration by Ogmios MacMerlin

sagittarius

November 22 – December 20, 2026

Mutable Sign of Fire △ Ruled by Jupiter ♃

S	M	T	W	T	F	S
Nov 22 Taurus	23 *Bathe under the Moon*	24 Oak Moon Gemini	25 WANING	26 Cancer	27 *Dance to release*	28 Leo
29	30 Virgo	Dec 1 ◑	2	3 *Travel afar* Libra	4	5 *Slumber deep* Scorpio
6	7 *Take a midnight walk* Sagittarius	8 ●	9 WAXING *Learn something new*	10 Capricorn	11 *Give a gift*	12 Aquarius
13	14 *Behold cosmic reflection*	15 Pisces	16 Fairy Queen Eve	17 ◐ Aries	18 Saturnalia ⇦	19 *Break the rules*
20 *Light the log* Taurus						

Jupiter *Expansion, wisdom, revelation* Ruler of thunder and sky, Jupiter opens doors to vastness—spiritual, intellectual and physical. In myth, he is benevolent and fierce: king of Gods, guardian of law and bringer of blessing. His domain includes expansion, justice, philosophy and the high road of growth. In magic, Jupiter governs good fortune, sacred timing, elevation and broad perspective. He is invoked for spiritual blessing, abundance, legal favor and journeys of meaning. Sagittarius carries his flame across the unknown, seeking truth not as destination, but as horizon. The archer's arrow is drawn toward ideals, guided by faith and fire. Jupiter teaches that wisdom grows through courage and that belief is a choice made sacred by experience. His presence stirs bold dreams, deeper convictions and an appetite for life's mysteries. To walk with Jupiter is to not only accept greatness as your due—but to earn it by seeking, risking and believing that the universe responds to vision.

We are only one bigot away from persecution.

Maxine Sanders

♑

capricorn

December 21 2026 – January 19, 2027

Cardinal Sign of Earth ♁ Ruled by Saturn ♄

S	M	T	W	T	F	S
	21 Winter Solstice 10:03 AM	**22** *Focus the now* Gemini	**23** Wolf Moon	**24** WANING Cancer	**25**	**26** *Seek ancestral wisdom* Leo
27	**28** *Align your purpose* Virgo	**29**	**30** Libra	**31** *Save money*	Jan **1** *Honor your word* Scorpio	**2**
3	**4** Sagittarius	**5**	**6** *Speak with intention* Capricorn	**7**	**8** WAXING *Step beyond*	**9** Feast of Janus Aquarius
10 *Be strategic*	**11** Pisces	**12** *Refine goals*	**13**	**14** *Embrace the chaos* Aries	**15**	**16** Taurus
17	**18** Gemini	**19**				

Saturn ***Structure, endurance, time*** Through law, limit and sacred labor, Saturn teaches what is lasting, earned and real. As the great taskmaster, he rules over time, responsibility and the architecture of achievement. In myth, Saturn devours his children, yet also governs golden ages—where order, peace and purpose prevail. He is invoked in magic for protection, boundaries, karmic reckoning and the strengthening of resolve. His influence is somber but powerful, demanding clarity of intent and depth of commitment. Capricorn reflects this ambition with steadfastness and high standards, climbing toward a summit not of comfort, but of mastery. Saturn's path is not quick, but it is profound. He guides us to build what lasts, endure what tests and respect the effort sacred work requires. His are the lessons that forge excellence. To work with Saturn is to accept the challenge of real growth—and to shape time itself into a vessel that holds meaning.

Shinto torii gate of the Itsukushima Shrine

Seto Inland Sea of Japan

♒

aquarius

January 20 – February 18, 2027

Fixed Sign of Air 🜁 Ruled by Uranus ♅

AQVARIVM

S	M	T	W	T	F	S
Uranus ***Change, revelation, higher vision*** Electric and unrelenting, the force of Uranus shatters convention and awakens consciousness to unseen possibilities. In myth, he is the generative vault of stars, father of Titans and the first shock of creation. Uranus governs ↓			Jan 20 *Network* Cancer	21	22 Storm Moon Leo	23 WANING
24 Virgo	25	26 *Break free* Libra	27	28 Scorpio	29	30
31 *Honor the light* Sagittarius	Feb 1 Oimelc Eve	2 Candlemas Capricorn	3	4 *Expand the field*	5 *Chines New Year* ⇨ Aquarius	6
7 WAXING Partial Solar Eclipse ⇦	8 Pisces	9 *Embrace the unexpected*	10 Aries	11 *Create a talisman*	12 Taurus	13
14 Gemini	15 Lupercalia *Reminisce*	16	17 *Expect a night shift* Cancer	18		

revolution, invention and awakening—the sudden light that shatters structure and reveals truth. In magic, he sparks insight, banishes conformity and invites the unexpected. His energy is erratic yet visionary, bringing disruption that clears space for innovation. Aquarius channels this force toward collective evolution and reimagining. Uranus rules breakthroughs, wild genius and courage to live authentically. He invites us beyond the familiar into what has never been. His lessons strike like lightning—blinding, electric, clarifying. Aligned with Uranus, we challenge patterns, question systems, embrace the future. He teaches that freedom is sacred—originality, divine.

A Traditional Tale of Old Florida

DEEP IN THE WINDING, brackish waters of the Everglades, stone crab fishermen tell tales of a mysterious mermaid who appears only on foggy mornings. She is said to be the spirit of Coralyn, a young woman who once worked with her father, a stone crab fisherman. Coralyn was known for her love of the swamp. She respected its power and beauty, learning its secrets and listening to the whispers of the mangroves. But one night, a fierce storm hit, and her boat was never seen again. Her father searched for her until his dying day, leaving offerings of fresh crab claws by the water's edge, hoping his daughter's spirit would be at peace.

Now, on certain misty mornings, fishermen claim to see her—she has an upper body like that of a beautiful woman, with a tail smooth and greyish like a manatee's, blending perfectly with the murky waters. She swims gracefully through the mangroves, and they say her dark hair is tangled with pieces of seaweed and shells, while her eyes are as green as the swamp itself.

Some fishermen claim that Coralyn's spirit is vengeful, singing haunting melodies to lure the unwary deep into the mangroves, where they lose their way and never return. These unlucky souls are said to vanish into the swamp, pulled into the depths by the mermaid's call. But others believe she is a guardian of the Everglades, there to protect the waters from those who disrespect them. Fishermen who work sustainably—taking only what they need and leaving offerings—say they've caught glimpses of her swimming by their boats, blessing them with bountiful catches and safe passage.

Old-timers share a warning for those who venture into the mangroves at dawn: if you hear singing, listen carefully. If her song is soft and gentle, it means you are safe and she is simply watching over you. But if the melody turns mournful and sad, it's a sign to leave the waters immediately, for the mermaid of the mangroves is searching for those who take more than they give, and she has no mercy for the greedy.

—MARINA BRYONY

pisces

February 19 – March 20, 2027

Mutable Sign of Water ▽ Ruled by Neptune ♆

PISCES

S	M	T	W	T	F	S
	Neptune ***Mysticism, illusion, divine union*** In mist and music, Neptune speaks—not in words, but in symbols, dreams and tides of emotion. As God of the sea , he rules the vast, formless realms of spirit, imagination and longing. In myth, he stirs both ocean and soul, dissolving boundaries and awakening the desire to merge with the divine. Neptune governs ↓				Feb 19 *Tap the force* Leo	20 Chaste Moon
21 Partial Lunar Eclipse ⇦	22 WANING Virgo ⇦	23 Libra	24	25 *Initiation reigns* Scorpio	26	27 Sagittarius
28	Mar 1 Matronalia	2 *Channel strong emotions* Capricorn	3	4 *Divine insight* Aquarius	5	6 *Take a lavender bath*
7 *Daydream* Pisces	8	9 Aries	10 *Be open minded*	11 Taurus	12 *Have self-love*	13
14 Gemini	15	16 *Play in the rain* Cancer	17	18 Leo	19 Minerva's Day	20 *Revere the owl*

intuition, mysticism, illusion and the subtle flow between worlds. In magic, he is invoked for dreams, vision work, glamour, music and trance states. His energy softens the rational and opens the heart to symbolic truth. Pisces reflects Neptune's depth and compassion, offering sensitivity, surrender and spiritual wisdom. But Neptune also warns against escapism, false light and losing the self in fantasy. He teaches that truth is not always clear—but it is always felt. Aligned with Neptune, we listen for what whispers, trust what we feel and create from the soul's tide. His gift is not certainty, but communion.

Necklace of the Gods

The Torc as Status Symbol and Cult Image

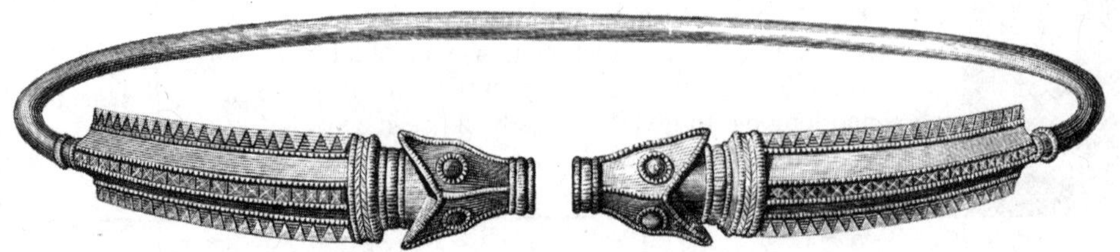

STANDING in the Capitoline Museum in Rome, the exquisite statue looks like it is about to take a breath: the pathos and clarity of this depiction of the suffering of Rome's enemies make it undeniably enigmatic. The identification as Rome's enemy is so obvious that you need not read the label on the sculpture: *The Dying Gaul*, Roman copy of a 2nd century Greek original. It's right there in the warrior's only adornment—the torc, as sure a sign of the subject's Celticness as his unkempt hair and his mustache.

From the Latin *torquere* (to twist or bend,) the torc is a decorative neck ring that was frequently worn by Gauls, Britons and other ancient Celtic peoples. They were made of gold or bronze, and could feature elegantly simple curves or elaborate twists and spirals, and ended in terminals with relief work or in discs, beads or animals heads. Unlike the golden lunulae crescent collars common in Bronze Age Ireland, which opened at the back of the neck, the torc was worn with the opening at the front.

However, torcs are neither uniquely nor originally Celtic. The ancient Thracians, who lived in the Balkan region of Southeastern Europe from the early Bronze Age until they became a Roman province in the first century CE, were renowned for their metalworking and made and wore torcs. Torcs also appear in archaeological sites from Achaemenid Persia, which thrived from 550-330 BCE. Torcs have been found at Susa, and a figurine of a chariot from the Oxus treasure shows both chariot driver and passenger wearing torcs. While the site may be Persian, the chariot itself bears the image of the Egyptian God Bes. On the steppes of what are now Ukraine and Southern Russia, Scythian men and women wore torcs as marks of aristocratic status from the 8th to the 3rd century BCE, and some burials have turned up pectoral collars similar to the Irish lunulae. None of these cultures was particularly isolated, and it is likely that the torc as both style and status symbol moved with trade, migration and conquest. They are, however, most prominent in the Celtic world from the Bronze Age through the Roman period.

In the early Iron Age, Gallic women wore torcs and were buried with them, but they were primarily (although not exclusively) masculine after the 3rd century BCE. Jewelry was a marker of status in Celtic society. Worn by Gods and monarchs, the torc was an indicator of rank, especially in gold. However, at least by the Roman era it was accessible outside the top echelons of the ruling class, being something more akin to a Birkin bag than a crown. During later periods, torcs were produced in standardized weights, suggesting that they served as portable wealth.

Like other valuables such as coins and bronze shields, torcs were sometimes presented to Gods or buried as votive offerings. While some burials of torcs outside of graves might not have been ritual in nature, but rather a way to keep them safely hidden during periods of war, ritual damage indicates that others are clearly devotional. For example, a torc from the 1st or 2nd century BCE had been broken into two pieces before being buried with a hoard of several hundred coins in Tayac in Bordeaux. Some extremely heavy examples would not have been wearable, suggesting votive offerings or decoration for cult statues. The Snettisham Great torc from the first century BCE, for example, was fashioned from 64 gold alloy strands twisted into ropes, capped with hollow cast terminals that were both embossed and chased, and it weighs in at a full kilogram.

When sized for ordinary wear, the torc was particularly prized by warriors, and the Greek historian Polybius relates that the Gallic warriors who invaded Rome wore gold jewelry around their necks and wrists. Celtic torcs were seized by the Romans as spoils in battle, and displayed in the capitol as trophies.

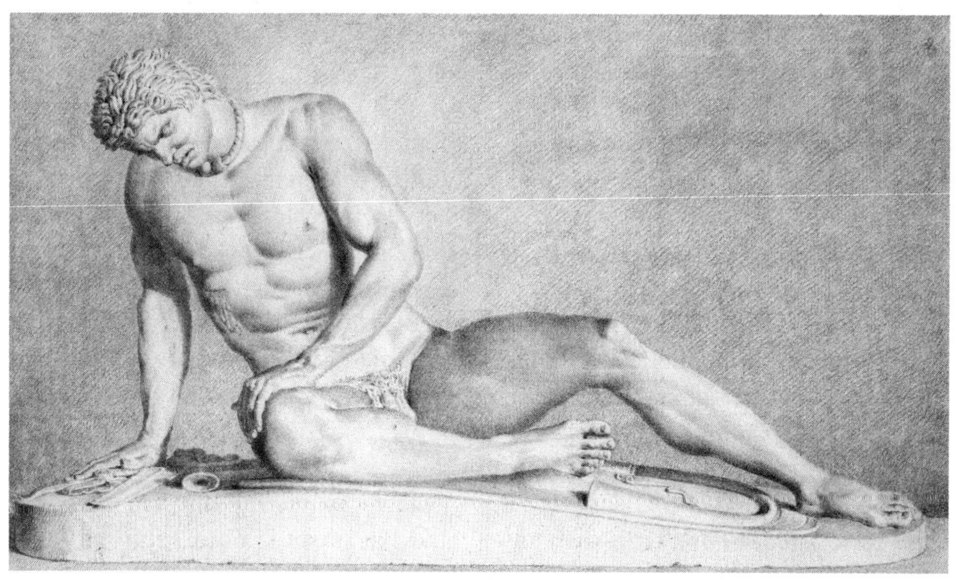

Livy tells of how the Roman general and consul Titus Manlius challenged a Gallic warrior in the 4th century BCE. Defeating him in single combat, he took the man's torc as a sign of victory and wore it ever afterwards, passing the cognomen *Torquatus* through his family. When Cassius Dio tells the tale of the revolt of a British tribe called the Iceni against the Romans—a resistance which resulted in the burning of Colchester—he includes the detail that Queen Boudicca prepared herself for battle by donning a twisted gold necklace.

In the centuries after the Gauls were thoroughly pacified (at least as Caesar put it) and integrated into the Roman empire, the torc remained a symbol of Gallic identity even within the greater Roman political affiliation. For example, Quintilian reports that a group of Gauls presented the emperor Augustus with a massive golden torc weighing 100 Roman pounds, which is roughly 33 kilograms in modern measures.

Even Roman Gods were shown with torcs as the pantheons blended: in the period after Roman conquest, the cult of Mercury in Gaul was merging with that of Rosmerta, a Goddess whose name means "great provider" and who is shown holding the purse of plenty or the cornucopia. She is depicted at times wearing the torc—and so is Mercury as he stands next to her at Trier. Hercules is depicted with the torc at Castlestead in Northumbria, as is Venus at Augst in Switzerland.

But how did the torc move from the realms of history and archaeology to modern altars? Religious values and identity are communicated implicitly through ritual aesthetics as well as explicitly through teaching, and Paganism is no exception. Go to any public Pagan ritual or gathering, and you will surely see a few torcs. Some modern Pagans and Wiccans have adopted this ancient adornment as a form of priestly regalia or personal jewelry. This is most likely because of its association with Cernunnos, a figure who has had an outsize influence on modern Wiccan and Pagan worship.

While other Gallic and Celtic deities are depicted wearing torcs, they are most strongly associated with Cernunnos in the modern Pagan mind. His name appears only one time, on a carved pillar called *Nautae Parisiaci*, or the Pillar of the Boatmen. The elaborately carved, limestone column was dedicated as an offering to Jupiter in the first century CE by sailors of the Parisii tribe of Gauls. It bears images of a number of Gallic and Roman deities, and "Cernunnos" is inscribed above an image of an antlered male figure who is sitting cross legged, with a torc hanging from each antler. These three features of his iconography are used to identify the God in other ancient images, most famously on the Gundestrup cauldron.

Unearthed in 1891 from the Raevemosen peat bog near Gundestrup in Jutland in Denmark, the gilded silver cauldron was likely manufactured in the last two centuries BCE. Its thirteen plates were dismantled before it was deposited in the bog, but when reassembled, they form a vessel fourteen inches high and twenty-five and a half inches in diameter, which could hold just above twenty-eight gallons. The primary imagery is undeniably Celtic, featuring the carnyx—a boar-headed war trumpet—along with Gallic-style shields and cult motifs. Among the images on its plates are

deities wearing torcs, including a solar wheel God, a Goddess with wheels on either side, suggesting a chariot, and a seated, antlered figure wearing one torc and holding another in his right hand. He holds a snake in his left, and is surrounded by animals, including a stag and a boar or dog. The posture, the torc and the antlers identify this figure with Cernunnos from the Pillar of the Boatmen. While at first glance, the cauldron appears quintessentially Celtic, the metalworking style—particularly the combination of embossing and punching—indicates Thracian work. Some of the imagery also points to a more Eastern and Southern origin: Cernunnos might be immediately surrounded by typically Northern European animals, but there are griffins, gazelle, leopards and elephants, as well.

Regardless of the precise location of design and manufacture of a single archaeological object, it is clear that the torc was simultaneously iconically Celtic and transnational as a symbol of wealth and prowess. This power was magnified by doubling the torc itself, as with the Pillar of the Boatmen which also showed the God with two torcs.

The torc persisted sporadically through the medieval period. Olwen is described in the *Mabinogian* as wearing a bejeweled torc, and in the 12th century CE, Gerald the Welshman described the relic Saint Canauc's Collar as a gold torc with a dog's head terminal. As jewelry, torcs resurged in popularity during the Viking Era, at which time they were primarily fashioned of silver rather than gold.

But why is the torc such a persistent symbol, even now? Are modern Pagans just cosplaying a pre-modern religious identity or playing at ancient Celt as a fashion statement? While perhaps this is true for a few, I suspect the allure of the torc arises from its original meaning as a signifier of wealth, albeit transformed into a wealth of spirit. The Horned One wears and holds it as a sign of the abundance he has to share—a promise as comforting and enticing now as when the Gundestrup cauldron was being hammered out. The early writings that influenced the modern Witchcraft movement—particularly those of Murray and Leland—emphasize the liberatory aspects of the craft as an alternative to the mainstream religion, depicting the Horned God (Murray) and Diana (Leland) as providing for their followers and freeing them from the limitations placed on them by society. Freedom, pleasure and abundance are what the Horned God has so much of to offer, and in the end, don't we all desire to live deliciously?

—MAB BORDEN

The Runes and The Zodiac

Astrology, Mercury and Woden

MORE THAN a thousand years ago early Nordic people believed that the God Woden was given a special gift from the universe. Woden shared this treasure with mortals to our everlasting benefit. That gift was a special set of symbols called the runes. The word comes from an Old Icelandic root *runar*, the Anglo-Saxon *run* and Old German *runar*. It translates to whisper, secret or mystery. The runic symbols are sketches describing every conceivable situation which can be experienced in a lifetime. These includes love, health, success, failure, prosperity, family and more. The runes offer comfort, inspiration and protection when needed. Those who know how to read them can provide answers with amazing clarity and expertise—knowledge and literacy were the real gift. Woden correlates with Mercury in the Roman pantheon of Gods and Goddesses. The deities are actually the planets, illustrating the various celestial energies, of course. Mercury (Woden) revealed how to communicate and develop intellectually. He is accredited with the invention of writing. The runes are actually the alphabet! This treasure is the tool for the sharing and documentation of knowledge, providing journeys of both the mind and body.

The runes offer much more, though. The sacred letters function as magical charms, not only describing situations and problems, but also acting as a catalyst for resolving them. Nordic mythology is rich in examples of how travelers avoided accidents, prisoners escaped from bonds, lovers evaded treachery and more through the application of these powerful symbols. Woden (Wednesday, Mercury's Day, is named for him) hung upside down for nine days and nights in Yggdrasil, the Tree of Knowledge, before receiving the runes in a trance state. In the same way that language changes from country to country and generation to generation, the runes have evolved in different ways. Like the tarot cards, the runes provide a profound key to the esoteric totality of knowledge. This includes Astrology, Numerology, Alchemy, healing and more.

What about inscribing a rune on a small piece of parchment to carry in a charm bag? Or penciling it near the entrance to your dwelling or tracing it over a beverage and then consuming it? The possibilities are infinite. Begin with the rune associated with your familiar Sun sign, then consider the symbols for your Moon and ascendant. Perhaps using runes for healing or protection to benefit a cherished animal companion or loved one could also be explored.

Here are the runes selected for the various zodiac signs. There are additional runes and also other possible astrological correlations to be discovered, but these work well to begin with.

Aries Mannaz, a rune which links to Aries, honors the higher self and personal identity. It can be helpful in learning through expanded life experience and finding self acceptance .

Taurus The Taurus rune Feoh, which translates to cattle, belongs with the sign of the Bull. Possessions, abundance and nourishment are the key notes. Feoh can help in acquiring abundance and comfort in meeting physical needs while enhancing spiritual strength.

Gemini The rune Ansuz relates to signs, speech and valuable information. Mercury, your ruler, is suggested here. Ansuz brings valuable insights offered through omens, synchronicity and coincidences. Ansuz concerns the power of factual knowledge.

Cancer Algiz, translated to mean the elk, the largest member of the deer family, is a rune suggested by the Moon and the determined Crab, emblem of Cancer. Protection, nurturing and awakening to the continuity of life are the values brought by Algiz. This rune establishes boundaries and stabilizes emotional responses.

Leo Sowelu is the rune identified with the Sun, Leo's ruler. Sowelu renews

> *The sacred letters function as magical charms, not only describing situations and problems, but also acting as a catalyst for resolving them.*

vitality, expands the light and illuminates personal power. It offers hope, guidance and a sense of direction ensuring success. It brings recognition and fulfillment by unleashing potential.

Virgo The protection rune Eihwaz is linked to Virgo. As a spiritual symbol Eihwaz relates to interpreting blockages and delays as learning experiences. It generates perseverance and the foresight to avert difficulties as well as finding alternative routes. When one door closes, Eihwaz opens another.

Libra Gebo, the rune of partnership, is associated with Libra. Preserving personal freedom while keeping a balance with cooperation and maintaining equality in significant relationships is the spiritual influence Gebo brings.

Scorpio Nauthiz, translated as the mountain ash tree, will stimulate spiritual growth and eventual added strength through learning to handle limitations and challenges. Reconsidering options when shadows arise and making needed rectifications to make way for progress is the wisdom gifted by this rune.

Sagittarius Kano, the torch or staff, is your rune, a symbol which will help to enhance spirituality. This is the thunderbolt of Thor or Jupiter, your ruler. It is an emblem of creativity, leadership and authority. It gives the ability to take charge of situations. Kano is competitive and faces challengers in order to win.

Capricorn's rune is Hagalaz. Translated as hail, with winter storms and snow, Hagalaz reveals how preparation for anticipated bad weather and difficulty to meet loss and disruption will end in gain. Hagalaz reveals that excessive focus on material security is restrictive. Balance acquisitive leanings with spiritual values.

Aquarius The rune Laguz, which means fluidity and water, is the Waterbearer's spiritual symbol. Immersion in the experiences of the sea of consciousness, flowing with circumstances that feel comfortable while heeding intuition are its message. Laguz has a cleansing, purifying influence, culminating in an alchemical transformation and happy endings.

Pisces Perth, translated as the aspen tree or dice cup, is an exclusive emblem of initiation, guarding secrets. It brings a special spiritual significance to Neptune-ruled Pisces, the sign of the unfathomable ocean depths. Perth has a transformative, phoenix-like force. Unexpected and powerful twists of fortune leading to a new dawn upon arising from the ashes, the dark night of the soul is the message. Evolutionary change attunes to this rune.

–DIKKI-JO MULLEN

2026 SUNRISE AND SUNSET TIMES

Providence—San Francisco—Sydney—London

	Sunrise				Sunset			
	Prov	**SF**	**Syd**	**Lon**	**Prov**	**SF**	**Syd**	**Lon**
Jan 5	7:11 AM	7:23 AM	5:49 AM	8:03 AM	4:30 PM	5:06 PM	8:11 PM	4:08 PM
15	7:08 AM	7:22 AM	5:58 AM	7:57 AM	4:41 PM	5:16 PM	8:10 PM	4:22 PM
25	7:02 AM	7:17 AM	6:08 AM	7:46 AM	4:53 PM	5:26 PM	8:06 PM	4:39 PM
Feb 5	6:51 AM	7:08 AM	6:19 AM	7:30 AM	5:07 PM	5:39 PM	7:59 PM	4:58 PM
15	6:39 AM	6:57 AM	6:28 AM	7:12 AM	5:20 PM	5:50 PM	7:49 PM	5:16 PM
25	6:24 AM	6:44 AM	6:38 AM	6:52 AM	5:32 PM	6:00 PM	7:38 PM	5:34 PM
Mar 5	6:12 AM	6:33 AM	6:44 AM	6:34 AM	5:41 PM	6:08 PM	7:28 PM	5:49 PM
15	6:55 AM	7:18 AM	6:53 AM	6:12 AM	6:53 PM	7:18 PM	7:15 PM	6:06 PM
25	6:38 AM	7:03 AM	7:00 AM	5:49 AM	7:04 PM	7:27 PM	7:01 PM	6:23 PM
Apr 5	6:19 AM	6:46 AM	6:08 AM	6:24 AM	7:16 PM	7:37 PM	5:47 PM	7:41 PM
15	6:03 AM	6:32 AM	6:16 AM	6:02 AM	7:27 PM	7:46 PM	5:34 PM	7:58 PM
25	5:48 AM	6:19 AM	6:23 AM	5:41 AM	7:38 PM	7:55 PM	5:22 PM	8:15 PM
May 5	5:34 AM	6:07 AM	6:31 AM	5:22 AM	7:49 PM	8:05 PM	5:12 PM	8:31 PM
15	5:23 AM	5:57 AM	6:38 AM	5:06 AM	8:00 PM	8:14 PM	5:04 PM	8:47 PM
25	5:15 AM	5:50 AM	6:45 AM	4:53 AM	8:09 PM	8:22 PM	4:58 PM	9:01 PM
June 5	5:09 AM	5:46 AM	6:52 AM	4:43 AM	8:18 PM	8:29 PM	4:54 PM	9:14 PM
15	5:08 AM	5:45 AM	6:56 AM	4:40 AM	8:23 PM	8:34 PM	4:54 PM	9:21 PM
25	5:10 AM	5:47 AM	6:59 AM	4:42 AM	8:26 PM	8:37 PM	4:56 PM	9:24 PM
July 5	5:15 AM	5:52 AM	6:59 AM	4:48 AM	8:25 PM	8:36 PM	5:00 PM	9:21 PM
15	5:22 AM	5:58 AM	6:56 AM	4:59 AM	8:20 PM	8:32 PM	5:05 PM	9:13 PM
25	5:31 AM	6:06 AM	6:51 AM	5:12 AM	8:12 PM	8:26 PM	5:11 PM	9:01 PM
Aug 5	5:42 AM	6:15 AM	6:42 AM	5:28 AM	8:00 PM	8:15 PM	5:19 PM	8:44 PM
15	5:52 AM	6:24 AM	6:33 AM	5:44 AM	7:47 PM	8:03 PM	5:26 PM	8:25 PM
25	6:03 AM	6:32 AM	6:21 AM	6:00 AM	7:32 PM	7:50 PM	5:33 PM	8:04 PM
Sept 5	6:14 AM	6:42 AM	6:07 AM	6:18 AM	7:14 PM	7:34 PM	5:40 PM	7:40 PM
15	6:24 AM	6:50 AM	5:53 AM	6:33 AM	6:56 PM	7:18 PM	5:47 PM	7:17 PM
25	6:35 AM	6:59 AM	5:39 AM	6:49 AM	6:39 PM	7:03 PM	5:54 PM	6:54 PM
Oct 5	6:45 AM	7:07 AM	6:25 AM	7:06 AM	6:22 PM	6:48 PM	7:01 PM	6:31 PM
15	6:56 AM	7:17 AM	6:12 AM	7:22 AM	6:05 PM	6:33 PM	7:09 PM	6:09 PM
25	7:08 AM	7:26 AM	6:00 AM	6:40 AM	5:50 PM	6:20 PM	7:17 PM	4:48 PM
Nov 5	6:21 AM	6:38 AM	5:49 AM	6:59 AM	4:36 PM	5:08 PM	7:27 PM	4:28 PM
15	6:33 AM	6:48 AM	5:42 AM	7:16 AM	4:26 PM	4:59 PM	7:37 PM	4:13 PM
25	6:45 AM	6:59 AM	5:37 AM	7:33 AM	4:19 PM	4:54 PM	7:46 PM	4:01 PM
Dec 5	6:56 AM	7:08 AM	5:35 AM	7:47 AM	4:16 PM	4:52 PM	7:55 PM	3:55 PM
15	7:04 AM	7:16 AM	5:36 AM	7:57 AM	4:17 PM	4:53 PM	8:03 PM	3:53 PM
25	7:09 AM	7:21 AM	5:41 AM	8:03 AM	4:21 PM	4:58 PM	8:08 PM	3:57 PM

Prov=Providence; SF=San Francisco; Syd=Sydney; Lon=London
Times are presented in the standard time of the geographical location, using the current time zone of that place.

Window on the Weather

Since ancient times, humankind has pursued knowledge of the future with a fervor rivaled only by the will to survive. Methods in this quest have ranged from the esoteric to the scientific. Predicting weather has always been part of this need. What was once the realm of priest-seers is now the domain of meteorologists, who analyze past data and current variables to anticipate future conditions. This Window on the Weather considers Earth's orbital orientation, its irregular path, cosmic disturbances like sunspots, interstellar radiation, human activity and numerous other factors.

The Sun's eleven-year cycles now number twenty-five in the modern scientific era, though informal data extends at least to the Middle Ages. Correlative behaviors in the natural world during these warming and cooling periods reveal insights into parallel activity in plant and animal life, driven by shifts in water vapor that regulate weather patterns alongside temperature changes.

Weather is never static, but adjusts to maintain a rough approximation of balance known as hydrostatic equilibrium, based on long-term temperature and precipitation data. The most variable conditions occur at mid-latitudes, both north and south of the equator—regions that also host the greatest biodiversity. This cyclical variability, as a natural state of being, defines the dynamic world in which we live and thrive.

SPRING

MARCH 2026 Mild spring weather arrives early east of the Rockies, with thawing conditions following heavy February snowfall. Temperatures are most variant from the Great Lakes to New England, where a brief late-month snowfall is possible following several weeks of above-normal temperatures. The southeastern United States enjoys generally mild weather, as spring arrives in full bloom at coastal locations from the Carolinas through Georgia and across all of Florida. The lingering remnant influence of the recent La Niña ENSO event in the Pacific Ocean increases the likelihood of several severe weather outbreaks stretching from the southern plains eastward through Alabama. A few tornadoes are likely, though they will impact a very small portion of land. Wind-swept rain across the West Coast is focused from northern Oregon through Washington state, with heavy snowfall expected from the Cascades to the Northern Rockies.

APRIL 2026 Dry weather persists through the dessert Southwest and much of the west coast. Relatively dry conditions can also be expected across growing regions from the Great Plains through the Ohio Valley. However, extreme conditions experienced during Spring and Summer 2025 are not likely. Contrasting temperature variances are felt from the mid Atlantic states through New England with several days of 70 degree warmth followed by cooling ocean breezes and misty coastal harbors. Warm weather is more consistent from Cleveland to Chicago, though a suddenly emerging late season snowfall is possible from Denver to Minneapolis. The southeastern U.S. is consistently warm and dry, though several passing and brief thunderstorm outbreaks are likely.

MAY 2026 May is the most temperate time of spring for the Deep South, southern plains and California, with warm days and pleasant evenings. Remnant La Niña conditions subdue high humidity levels for a time. Farther north, a late season frost is possible in Montana. Coastal New England remains cool with misty mornings giving way to afternoon sunshine. Seasonally normal rainfall can be expected across the Ohio Valley while below normal rainfall is evident through the plains states. The Pacific Northwest enjoys dry weather after abundant spring rainfall.

SUMMER

JUNE 2026 Summer temperatures arrive early this year through much of the nations heartland. However, a hint of Spring persists as temperatures remain pleasantly cool in the calm of night. Such conditions benefit farmers as they bring a fertile start to the growing season, with adequate rainfall at its onset. These conditions are especially notable across the Ohio Valley. Warm weather also finally arrives throughout New England, along with two days of rain that bring with them several outbreaks of passing thunderstorms. Daily thunderstorms also develop in Florida on both coasts. These occur during the morning in the East and approaching sunset on the west.

JULY 2026 The height of summer heat can be felt nationwide, coast to coast. Far from being sweltering, however, cooling sea breezes bring pleasant afternoon and evening temperatures along the coast from New England to the Jersey shore. Further west, several thunderstorm outbreaks bring a respite by briefly cooling the air across the Great Lakes states and Ohio Valley. Afternoon and evening thunderstorms are a nearly daily event on the west coast of Florida and the north Georgia Mountains. An early season brief tropical disturbance can bring heavy rain to Gulf Coast states from Texas to Louisiana. Rainfall from that system reduces crop stress across Oklahoma, Kansas and Nebraska. The West Coast is seasonably cool at the beaches. However, summer heat persists through interior California to Washington State east of the Cascades.

AUGUST 2026 Warming water continues to feed the tropical storm season, which advances steadily in August with slightly above normal activity likely this year. Such storms will be most common originating near coastal Africa before advancing across the Atlantic. Most pose little threat as they will recurve away from land, yet the southeastern United States as far north as North Carolina remains vulnerable. Throughout the month, summer heat eases steadily, beginning in the Northern Plains, as several cold fronts bring relief from dry crop conditions as far south and east as the Ohio Valley. Thunderstorms remain prevalent across Florida, while a severe thunderstorm outbreak remains a risk across interior New England. Coastal cities, however, remain safe from such activity. West coast weather remains tranquil this month while monsoon related afternoon and evening rain frequents north Arizona and New Mexico.

AUTUMN

SEPTEMBER 2026 Heralding the change of seasons from Summer to Fall, easterly trade winds bring a greater frequency of showers and gusty winds to Florida. Just to the north, Coastal Georgia experiences a similar series of squalls. That pattern initiates a flow of moisture northward, moving through the Appalachians and impacting that region in turn by bringing heavy rains. Through the Autumnal Equinox, cooler weather spreads throughout the Pacific Northwest. This cooling pattern arrives later in the high plains, where dry weather is likely to persist longer. On the coast, Santa Ana winds arrive in Southern California, bringing hot, breezy weather and elevated fire risk at the end of the month.

OCTOBER 2026 Shorter days after the Equinox cool the ocean water, bringing a welcome change as hurricane activity diminishes across the Atlantic Ocean. This quickly reduces the risk to the coastal United States, particularly the Southeast and the Gulf Coast. The season brings cool breezes, creating nearly ideal harvest conditions in the heartland. As northern Idaho and Minnesota are bracing for their first frosts, meanwhile above normal temperatures and gusty winds persist in Southern California, bringing a sense of lingering Summer even this late in the year. In the Northeast, New England enjoys fine fall weather perfect for picking apples and pressing cider. Mild days and cool nights with little rainfall create excellent conditions for a hike or drive to view peak fall foliage.

NOVEMBER 2026 Sharply colder temperatures arrive for several days across New England through the Ohio Valley and Great Lakes states. The bracing temperatures are transient, however, with several balmy days following. East of the Mississippi, generally dry conditions can be counted on at the beginning of the month. In the Pacific Northwest, the first significant rains of the fall season arrive early in the month. The same band of precipitation results in snow falling from the Sierra Nevada in California through the Colorado Rockies, just in time to kick off the ski season. After an active tropical storm season earlier in the year, Texas and Florida are pleasantly warm and dry for Thanksgiving while the mid-Atlantic states receive slightly above normal rainfall.

WINTER

DECEMBER 2026 While slightly below normal temperatures are felt across the eastern half of the country, the cold remains inconsistent. These brisker temperatures are interspersed with several light to moderate snowfall events spreading across the lower Ohio Valley and east to interior New England. However, there is no indication of major snowstorms to close the year, although the chances for a white Yule are slightly increased this year for East Coast cities as well as Chicago and Minneapolis. In the West, the central and northern Rockies return to normal snowfall. Florida turns warm and dry with consistently pleasant weather at the end of the year. After a hot, dry Autumn spent buffeted by the Santa Ana winds, California is relieved by its first beneficial rain of the winter season.

JANUARY. 2027 The new year begins with dry and cold weather throughout the eastern United States, with the greatest distribution of snowfall occurring during the last 10 days of the month. Meanwhile, temperatures are seasonably mild across the West, including California and the desert Southwest. The mercury drops as below normal temperatures can be expected again throughout the East. This change heralds a coastal storm arriving between the 20th and 25th. This storm system will bring significant snows to major cities along the Atlantic corridor. Snowfall originating from the Great Lakes is to be expected in Western New York State and parts of Michigan. A brief freeze is also possible in Florida.

FEBRUARY 2027 While most of the country will receive normal snowfall this year, above normal amounts can be expected from the great Lake states through the northern Ohio Valley. Precipitation is also elevated in central and northern New England. Blustery cold and snow opens the month in these regions, with the greatest amount of snow set to occur as a result of a series of storms in a two-week spell stretching from the first to the 14th. After Valentine's Day, much milder weather will bring relief from shoveling snow with thawing conditions accompanied by windswept rain. On the West Coast, Southern California receives heavy rain, bringing a welcome end to drought conditions.

The Shepherd and the Snow Lion

A Tibetan Folk Tale

HIGH IN the mountains where the land meets the sky and clouds cling to cliffs like silk scarves, there was a village so remote that maps marked it with only a dot. The wind there spoke in ancient voices and the people believed the mountain spirits still walked the ridges after sunset.

Among them lived a quiet man named Tenzin. He was a shepherd, neither old nor young, with eyes that held the stillness of snow. His house stood apart from the others, built from rough stones perched on a slope above the rest of the village. When smoke rose from his chimney each morning, villagers knew it was safe to rise.

Each morning, he rose before dawn, warmed a small pot of tea and shared the first sip with the earth. "For the spirits," he would say. He spoke softly—not out of fear, but because the mountain itself spoke quietly and he wished to match its voice.

He tended a modest flock—woolly, clever creatures who followed him with the trust of children. Though others used dogs, Tenzin walked alone with his staff and flute, guiding them with song. He never struck them and in return, they never strayed.

In the evenings, he sat beneath the great juniper behind his hut, carving prayer beads or mending cloth. Sometimes he played his flute—high, lilting notes that danced on the cold air and echoed through the cliffs. The villagers heard the music in their sleep and spoke of sweet dreams in the morning.

Tenzin had no family, but he did not grieve. The mountain was his kin and the wind, his friend.

One year, the snows came early. By the ninth lunar month, frost coated the fields and streams froze at their edges. The sun appeared only briefly, as if hiding behind the mountain's shoulder.

The villagers prepared for a long winter—bringing animals down from the ridges, sealing their homes with yak hide and packed earth. Fires burned day and night. Food was measured carefully.

Tenzin remained in the high pastures. "There is still grass under the snow," he said. He moved his sheep from slope to slope, watching the wind and reading the clouds. Each day, he melted snow for water. Each night, he wrapped himself in wool and shared his warmth with the youngest lambs.

The cold deepened. Ice slicked the rocks and pulled breath from lungs like a thief. Yet Tenzin endured. He gave the best of his food to the sheep and chewed the hardest bread without complaint. He hummed mantras in the dark.

By the twelfth month, his supplies were almost gone. Still, he did not descend. His sheep, though thin, were alive. He vowed not to fail them.

Then came a morning when the snow covered even the tallest shrubs and the wind roared with a voice he had never heard. It was time to climb—or surrender.

With his sheep behind him, Tenzin took the trail that wound along the cliffs above the valley—a path used only by eagles and madmen, rimmed with icicles like knives. He walked slowly, guiding the sheep one by one, whispering when the wind screamed too loud.

For hours they climbed. The world grew silent, save for the crunch of snow and the low, worried bleats. At last they reached a ridge known in old songs as the "Sky-Bone Spine." Even the sun seemed to pause, casting pale light on land untouched by time.

Then came a sound—low, thunderous, as though the mountain itself exhaled.

A creature stood ahead, where no path led. A Snow Lion—massive, radiant, its mane flowing like prayer flags in a windstorm. Its fur shimmered like stars in ice. Its golden eyes glowed, ancient and knowing.

Tenzin did not run. He placed his hand over his heart and bowed.

"You have climbed far," the Snow Lion said, its voice more wind than word. "What do you seek?"

"Only grass for my sheep," Tenzin replied.

"Many seek gold or glory. You ask only to feed others."

The lion stepped aside. "Then see what lies beyond."

The mist parted, revealing a secret valley—Beyul, the Hidden Land. There, spring never ended. Flowers bloomed. Birds sang. A stream flowed with water so clear it reflected thoughts, not faces.

"This land is beyond suffering," said the lion. "You may stay. Your sheep will never hunger. You will not age. No harm will touch you."

Tenzin stood at the edge, breathing in warmth. His bones ached. His belly was empty. Yet he looked back at his sheep—tired, trembling from the climb.

"I thank you," he said, "but I cannot stay."

The lion's eyes narrowed. "Why refuse paradise?"

"They trust me," he said. "If I leave, they are lost. What kind of shepherd enters paradise alone?"

The lion lowered its head. "Few choose love over peace. Fewer still choose duty over comfort."

It exhaled and the valley vanished like a dream. In its place stood only snow and stone.

But grass now poked through the snow. The trail home, once steep, now curved gently downward.

"Walk well, Tenzin," the lion said. "When the time comes, the gate will open again."

Then it disappeared into the mist.

Tenzin returned to his hut with the sheep close behind. The villagers, who had assumed him dead, stared in awe. Children whispered that the snow parted for him. Elders bowed their heads.

He never spoke of the Snow Lion or the valley. But the storms grew less severe around his home and the sheep flourished. Pilgrims came, drawn by stories of music in the hills that healed the heart.

Years passed. Tenzin grew old. His back bent, his hair turned white. But he still climbed each morning, still sang to his sheep. He became a legend while still alive.

One spring morning, he did not rise. They found him seated beneath the juniper, flute in hand, smile on his face. The sheep stood silent beside him.

And some say, when the wind rose that night, it carried the scent of saffron. Some say they saw a great white lion walking beside a man into the sky.

Monks later built a stupa where Tenzin had lived. Travelers still leave offerings there—flute reeds, prayer beads, bits of wool. They say the path to Beyul lies nearby and opens only to those who walk with quiet hearts and steadfast hands.

The mountain remembers those who love it.

MORAL OF THE STORY

To lead with compassion is to walk the hardest path. The one who refuses paradise for the sake of love becomes immortal in the memory of the world.

The Was Scepter

ONE OF the most evocative symbols of ancient Egyptian magic, the *was* scepter is a staff that embodies power, authority, and the ability to command the forces of chaos. For those walking the path of modern magic, the *was* scepter offers an extraordinary opportunity to connect with a lineage of spiritual mastery that reaches back thousands of years. By understanding its history, symbolic meaning and potential applications in present day practice, the magician can wield this ancient tool with purpose and insight.

In ancient Egypt, the *was* scepter was not merely an ornamental object—it was a tangible representation of divine dominion. Its elegant, straight shaft symbolized the channeling of celestial energies, bridging the realms of the Heavens and the Earth. At its apex was the carved head of a mysterious animal, often identified as the Set animal—a creature associated with the God Set. Set himself is a figure of paradox, representing both chaos and the power to master it. In the scepter this paradox was distilled into a potent tool of authority. The forked base of the staff provided balance, grounding its energy and affirming the interconnectedness of all things.

These elements combined to create a symbol that was inseparable from the concept of *hekau,* magical power. The *was* scepter was not confined to the realm of the Gods, although it frequently appeared in their hands in temple carvings and sacred texts. Pharaohs also wielded the scepter as an assertion of their divine right to rule, a reminder of their role as protectors of Ma'at—the sacred balance of the universe. Even in the afterlife, miniature versions of the scepter were placed in tombs to ensure that the deceased could carry their power and influence into eternity.

Today the *was* scepter retains its allure as a magical implement. Its beauty lies not only in its form but in its function—an object steeped in the symbolism of mastery, offering those who hold it a way to engage with forces greater than themselves. To bring the *was* scepter into a modern context, one must begin with its creation. Crafting a personal scepter is an act of profound magic in itself. A wooden staff, shaped to mimic the clean lines of the original, forms the foundation. The headpiece can be carved, molded or cast to reflect the practitioner's intention, whether you choose the traditional Set animal or another figure that resonates with your path. The addition of symbolic colors—gold for divinity, blue for celestial harmony or red for fiery strength—imbues the tool with a deeply personal energy. Traditional Egyptian colors can form a magical link to the powers conjured so long ago, gold and deep blue being two of these colors.

Once the scepter is complete, its potential uses in ritual are vast. Above all, it is a symbol of power and authority, making it ideal for rites aimed at reclaiming personal sovereignty or overcoming obstacles. Imagine standing at the heart of your sacred space, the *was* scepter in hand as you speak words of command to banish chaos from your life. Visualize its tip radiating light, channeling the energy of the cosmos as you assert your will. Hold on to the traditional use of the tool, but be creative in how it can improve your life.

In quieter moments, the scepter becomes a tool of reflection and alignment. During meditation, holding the ***was*** can center your energy, connecting you to the ancient forces it represents. Let it guide your thoughts toward Ma'at—the balance between order and disorder, between action and stillness. It is said that the scepter's forked base symbolizes duality and in meditation it can serve as a reminder to embrace the opposites within yourself.

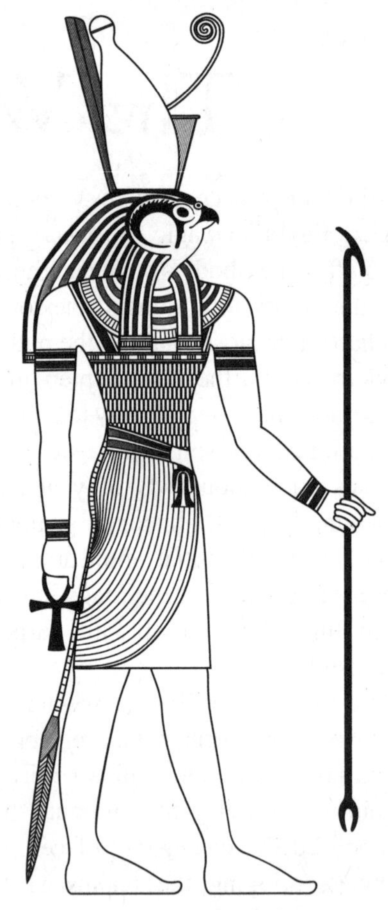

The *was* scepter is also a powerful ally in the creation of magical boundaries. Trace protective symbols in the air with its tip, visualizing a shield of energy forming around your space. Use it to bless and consecrate, directing its stabilizing force into objects or individuals. As in ancient Egypt where the scepter often stood as a guardian of the temples and tombs, it can stand vigil over your own sacred work. Treat the scepter as an extension of yourself, layered with magic from Egypt's past.

Beyond its practical applications, the *was* scepter offers a gateway into the spiritual traditions of ancient Egypt. Its use invites a deeper exploration of Egyptian magic, a system that prized harmony and alignment with the divine. Pair the scepter with an ankh to amplify life-giving energy or with a djed pillar to root your work in stability. Invoke the deities who once held the *was*, whether Set for his protective strength, Thoth for his wisdom or Osiris for his transformative power.

In many ways, the *was* scepter is a symbol of the magician's journey itself. It represents the capacity to confront chaos, to walk the edge between order and disorder and to emerge stronger and more aligned. In the hands of the modern practitioner, it becomes more than an artifact of a distant culture. It is a living symbol, one that calls you to claim your power, to command your world and to bring balance to your life.

The *was* scepter reminds you that magic is not merely a matter of tools or rituals—it is the energy of the universe, shaped by intention and wielded with authority. And in that reminder it invites each person to take up the mantle of power it has represented for millennia.

—AMELIA INGRAM

Myōken and Japan's Celestial Traditions

FOR CENTURIES, cultures across the globe have turned their gaze to the stars in search of guidance and meaning. In Japan, this celestial fascination found deep religious expression in the figure of Myōken, a deity associated with the North Star and the Big Dipper. Myōken came to embody wisdom, protection and cosmic order—a presence both divine and intimately connected to the spiritual lives of those who venerated him.

As early as the Yayoi period (300 BCE–300 CE,) the Big Dipper appears to have held symbolic significance, with images of the constellation surfacing in religious artifacts. By the eighth century, devotion to the Pole Star had evolved into a celestial cult that saw the star as a governing force over fate and fortune. From this emerged the figure of Myōken, regarded as a divine intermediary between the cosmos and human destiny.

Originally aligned with the Pole Star (Hokushin,) Myōken's influence expanded over time to include the Big Dipper (Hokuto.) Though often labeled as a bodhisattva—Myōken Bosatsu—the deity is better understood as a celestial being, or Ten, within the Japanese spiritual lexicon. Myōken became known as a protector of rulers and warriors, a healer and a guide for those in need of insight or safe passage.

The ways in which Myōken has been portrayed vary widely, reflecting the deity's diverse roles. Some traditions present him as a serene figure seated upon a dragon or turtle, both symbols of wisdom and stability. Others emphasize a more martial character, depicting Myōken with sword in hand, ready to defend and dispel misfortune. Over time, the deity has been linked with other divine figures, including Kichijōten, Goddess of prosperity and even Yakushi Nyorai, the Buddha of healing.

Stories from early religious texts recount miraculous interventions attributed to Myōken—recovering lost objects, revealing the truth in times of deception and even saving lives at sea. These tales reinforced his image as a vigilant and just protector, invested in the well-being of his followers.

By the Heian period, Myōken worship had become entwined with Esoteric Buddhism and infused with Taoist cosmology, Yin-Yang thought and native Shintō practices. This integration enriched the spiritual significance of the deity, who was often invoked for safe travel, health—especially related to vision—and the harmonizing of personal destiny with celestial forces.

Various rituals developed to honor Myōken, some of which persist today. These include imperial ceremonies recognizing his authority in the heavens, monthly observances believed to amplify the power of prayers and specific rites aligning human intention with the movements of the Big Dipper.

The Meiji Restoration in the late 19th century imposed dramatic changes on Japan's religious institutions, including the separation of Shintō and Buddhist practices. Many Buddhist deities were removed or replaced by Shintō counterparts. In this climate, Myōken was frequently substituted with Ame no Minakanushi no Mikoto, a Shintō deity also connected to cosmic origins. Nonetheless, devotion to Myōken endured—especially in temples where Buddhist traditions remained strong.

Today, Myōken continues to hold a place in Japan's spiritual landscape. Temples maintain rituals in his name and individuals seek his guidance for clarity, protection and harmony with the universe. His enduring presence is a testament to the resilience and adaptability of Japan's religious culture—one that finds continuity not by resisting change, but by integrating and transforming it.

Through the story of Myōken, we see how the heavens have long been a mirror for human hopes and fears, a realm of divine forces shaping the world below. His worship reflects a uniquely Japanese synthesis of star-lore, ritual and religious imagination—an evolving tradition that continues to bridge sky and soul.

ERINLẸ̀

River of the Wild Ones, and of healing

AMONG THE YORÙBÁ of southwestern Nigeria, the forces of nature are neither abstract nor metaphorical. They are felt in the humidity of the forest, the rush of the river after rain, the sweat of the hunter's brow and the trembling cry of the afflicted. The world is alive—conscious, responsive and governed by sacred intelligences. These intelligences, known as the Òrịṣá, represent a grand architecture of existence: forces that both create and destroy, nourish and withhold, elevate and humble. Erinlẹ̀ is among them—an Òrịṣá of depth, complexity and compassion, who walks the borderlands of the forest and the river.

Erinlẹ̀ is a hunter. Erinlẹ̀ is a healer and Erinlẹ̀ is a River.

He is among the Irúnmolè, those divine messengers or primordial emanations sent by Òlódùmaré to shape and govern the world. In Erinlẹ̀, we encounter a being of liminal power—one who stands between wild and civilized, between animal and divine, between life and death. He does not only exist within the domain of the sacred river that bears his name. He is the river, just as he is the spear, the healing root, the incantation murmured beneath the Full Moon.

The Cultural and Religious Fabric of Yorùbáland

To understand Erinlẹ̀, one must understand the context from which he arises. Yorùbáland is more than a geographical expanse; it is a spiritual terrain shaped by millennia of human interaction with the divine. Stretching across present-day southwestern Nigeria and extending into parts of the Republic of Benin and Togo, it is a cultural and cosmological heartland where the sacred and the mundane flow into one another like tributaries meeting a central river. The Yorùbá people are the stewards of one of Africa's most complex and enduring religious systems—one in which the divine is not abstract but relational, not confined to heaven but present in the forest, in the wind, in the fire and in the flowing water. To be Yorùbá, in the most ancient and complete sense, is to be engaged in a constant conversation with the unseen.

Yorùbá religion is not monolithic. It is a living tradition, a dynamic constellation of beliefs and practices expressed in royal courts, remote villages, urban neighborhoods and diaspora enclaves around the world. It adapts itself with remarkable resilience to the demands of changing times—weathering the impact of colonial suppression, the erosion of sacred groves under the weight of development, the push and pull of Christianity and Islam and the digitization of oral transmission in the modern age. The Òrìṣá are not distant, aloof Gods; they are present companions, energetic presences who may be danced into the body, spoken with through divination and offered food as one would a respected elder. The sacred texts of Ifá—its vast corpus of odu—are not only repositories of divine wisdom but practical manuals for navigating the uncertainties of daily life. Spirit possession is not entertainment but epiphany. Ancestral veneration is not nostalgia—it is continuity, protection and accountability.

The religious landscape of Yorùbá society today is layered and dynamic, marked by complexity rather than contradiction. Christianity and Islam have made deep and lasting inroads, a process accelerated by colonization, missionization and the perceived prestige of foreign religions. Yet these Abrahamic traditions have not erased indigenous spirituality; rather, they often coexist in the same household, the same heart. One may go to church on Sunday and offer yam to Ṣàngó on Monday. A devout Muslim may also consult the Babaláwo or attend an Òṣun festival. These are not betrayals of faith but expressions of a cosmology that sees no contradiction in multiplicity. In recent decades, both in Yorùbáland and throughout the African diaspora, a spiritual renaissance has taken root—a revival of Òrìṣá worship not as a relic of the past but as a blueprint for the future. This resurgence is driven by a collective hunger for ancestral knowledge, for rootedness in the face of globalization,

The sacred objects of Erinlẹ̀

for sacred narratives that reflect African aesthetics, ethics and epistemologies. It is a quiet revolution—a reawakening of the sacred rivers, groves and drums that have never truly fallen silent.

This revival is not merely religious—it is political, philosophical and cultural. It speaks to a global crisis of meaning, where the disconnection from land, lineage and language has left many spiritually adrift. In such a world, the Òrìṣá offer more than myth—they offer models of ethical agency, environmental harmony and reciprocal power. Erinlẹ̀, in particular, resonates powerfully in this moment. As a healer, a hunter and a river spirit, he represents the intersection of ecology and spirituality, tradition and transformation. His worship is not an escape into antiquity but a re-entry into sacred relationship with the Earth. In Erinlẹ̀ flowing current, one finds not only the memory of what was—but the promise of what might yet be, if we remember to listen, to offer and to praise.

The One Who Entered the Earth

The name Erinlẹ̀ invites layered interpretation. Often rendered as Erinlẹ̀,—"the elephant goes home"—it evokes both the majestic image of the elephant and the idea of a being returning to its point of origin. Other interpretations suggest "he who entered the Earth," referencing the myth in which Erinlẹ̀, once a mortal or semi-divine hunter of extraordinary power, disappeared into the river near Ilobu, becoming one with its waters and thus transcending the bounds of flesh to become a living Òrìṣá.

This sacred river—the Erinlẹ̀—is not only a geographical feature but a cosmological axis. It is believed to be a portal between worlds, a channel through

Offering made at and to Erinlẹ̀

which blessings flow and through which humans may access healing, protection and clarity. Devotees trace his passage in the flow of water, in the paths worn through forest brush and in the silence that follows a well placed arrow.

Ilobu, in Osun State, remains a principal center of his worship. There, sacred groves are maintained and rituals are performed on the banks of the river. The waters are drawn not merely for utility, but for sanctity—for bathing, healing and spiritual renewal. Here, Erinlẹ̀ is not history—he is presence.

Oríkì: The Breath of Devotion

Praise poetry, or oríkì, is among the most evocative modes of Yorùbá religious expression. It is through oríkì that Erinlẹ̀ is invoked, described and praised—not just in terms of what he does, but what he is. These chants are both biography and conjuration, dense with metaphor and mystery:

Erinlẹ̀ òde, eni tí ń bo l'ógun nítorí aláìsàn
Omo oníròko, omo pápá ń sun sùn
Òrìṣá tí ń rìn ní igbo, tí ń gún ọmi
Oun tí ń mú iko lórùn, tí ń yo èèmo kúrò l'ára

Erinlẹ̀ the hunter, the one who fights for the sake of the ill

Child of the iroko tree, child of the sleeping savannah

Òrìṣá who walks in forest, who rides the river's skin

He who soothes the cough and casts out disease

To speak these words is to draw near to the Òrìṣá, to stir his memory, to invoke his gaze. In ritual, these praises are chanted over sacred objects, over the heads of initiates, into the river as the moon reflects the gleam of the cutlass blade.

Forest and River—His Twin Domains

Erinlẹ̀ is unusual among the Òrìṣá in that he bridges two worlds not often combined: the untamed forest and the flowing river. As a hunter, he embodies the discipline of the solitary path, the patience of the stalk and the wisdom of the wilderness. He is said to know every animal in the bush by name and to walk unseen even among the most cunning prey.

But Erinlẹ̀ is not merely a killer. His arrows do not fly without justice. His strength is directed by insight and his knowledge of animals is mirrored by his understanding of humans. He is invoked not only by hunters but by herbalists and diviners who seek to know what root cools fever, what bark strengthens the womb, what leaf quiets madness.

His relationship with water is equally sacred. The river is not a backdrop—it is a living force and in Erinlẹ̀ it becomes aware. He swims not as fish but as current and it is said that when a devotee is possessed by him, they move like a man who has swallowed the river: graceful, powerful, inexorable.

Offerings and Rites of Power

Offerings to Erinlẹ̀ are made with tenderness and care. Freshwater fish, yam, cooked porridge, honey and fruits are placed gently at the river's edge, often accompanied by whispered prayers or softly spoken Oríkì. These offerings, both humble and sumptuous, are meant not only to nourish the divine presence but to establish a reciprocal relationship of gratitude and supplication. In some rites—particularly those involving healing, protection, or the lifting of taboo—animals such as rams or roosters are sacrificed. Their blood is poured with solemnity onto the stones, soil, or sacred pots that mark Erinlẹ̀'s earthly threshold, feeding the unseen current of power that flows between the human and divine worlds. It is not violence for its own sake, but rather a necessary exchange—a gesture of deep seriousness that acknowledges the living, consuming nature of spirit.

Priests and priestesses of Erinlẹ̀ are distinguished by their graceful comportment and watery aesthetic. They often wear garments dyed in indigo, sky blue, or sea green—the colors of deep water, clear skies and lush vegetation. Beads of similar hue encircle their wrists, necks and waists, forming protective and communicative circuits between themselves and the Ọ̀rìṣá. Ceremonies honoring Erinlẹ̀ may include rhythmic drumming on bàtá or dundun drums, dancing that mimics the flowing of rivers or the stalking of a hunter and moments of spirit possession wherein the Ọ̀rìṣá mounts the body of the initiate like a rider takes the back of a horse. Libations of water, palm wine and honey are poured to invoke, appease and honor. Water drawn directly from Erinlẹ̀'s sacred river is used to cleanse the ill, to cool the heads of those overtaken by spiritual affliction and to anoint the brow before major life events such as childbirth, initiation, marriage, or burial—rites of passage that mark the rhythm of life in Yorùbáland.

During the annual festival in Ilobu, one of the principal towns associated with Erinlẹ̀'s worship, devotees process through the streets in great color and devotion, singing his praises and presenting gifts both practical and symbolic. It is a time of great communal unity, where the sacred and the everyday intermingle freely. Women balance calabashes on their heads filled with offerings, young men beat drums whose rhythms seem to rise up from the soil itself and elders chant ancient verses that tether the present to the deep roots of ancestral memory. The procession winds its way to the river bank, where offerings are presented to the flowing water. Some are floated down river—ornamented gourds, bundles of herbs, cooked foods—carried, it is said, by Erinlẹ̀ himself to the unseen realms where they are received by the spirits of the deep. Others are placed into the river by the hands of priests, who kneel, chant and cast their gaze into the reflective surface as though consulting the very soul of the Ọ̀rìṣá. The river, in these moments, is not just water. It is memory. It is medicine. It is mystery incarnate.

The Diasporic Continuum

When Yorùbá people were stolen from their homeland and forced into slavery across the Atlantic, they carried their Ọ̀rìṣá with them—not always in objects or texts, but in memory, dream and devotion. In Cuba, Erinlẹ̀ is known as Inle and in Brazil, as Inlè.

Inle in Cuba is regarded with a distinct elegance. He is often described as beautiful androgynous and serene. His association with healing and marginalized communities—especially queer and gender-nonconforming individuals—is deeply respected. He is said to have been rendered mute after being taken by Olókun to the bottom of the sea, where he remained in contemplative silence, learning secrets hidden from the surface world.

In Brazil, particularly within the Ketu nation of Candomblé, Inlè is linked to health and hunting. His worship may intersect with that of Oxóssi, Òsanyìn and Omolu, all of whom deal with aspects of the body, the forest and the unseen. His symbols include the fish, snake and staff and his rites are performed with deep solemnity beside flowing water.

These diasporic expressions are not diluted versions of the Yorùbá originals—they are evolutions, born of necessity and shaped by the trauma of displacement. They stand as testament to the endurance of Yorùbá cosmology and to the adaptability of the Òrìṣá themselves, who refuse to be forgotten.

Continuity and Change

In the 21st century, the worship of Erinlẹ̀ continues to evolve. In Yorùbáland, there is a rising interest in reclaiming indigenous spirituality, particularly among youth who see the traditions of their ancestors as a form of cultural empowerment and spiritual decolonization. While global Pentecostalism and Islam exert strong influence, there is also a renewed pride in Òrìṣá worship and many urban devotees maintain shrines in their homes, travel to sacred rivers and study Ifá with both scholarly and devotional rigor.

Meanwhile, across the diaspora, Òrìṣá traditions are experiencing a renaissance. From the urban temples of Havana and Salvador to the quiet altars in New York, Paris and Johannesburg, Erinlẹ̀ is called upon with increasing frequency. Academic interest, artistic exploration and spiritual seeking all intersect in this revival, yet the challenge remains: how to preserve the depth and integrity of the tradition amid the distractions and commodifications of modern life.

Nevertheless, the river flows on.

He Who Waits at the River

Erinlẹ̀ is not a deity of spectacle. He is not always loud or flamboyant. His miracles are subtle—an illness resolved, a path cleared, a heart soothed. He teaches that strength can be silent, that justice need not be cruel and that healing is the most profound of all transformations.

May Erinlẹ̀ guide your feet into the forest, where wisdom waits in shadow. May his river cleanse your spirit and restore your balance. And may his spear, should it ever fly in your defense, strike true and without hesitation.

We who remember must continue to praise, to pour water, to sing the names that our ancestors sang. Erinlẹ̀ has not left us. He is the whisper beneath the surface, the ripple that follows no wind.

Let us walk to the River.

Let us listen.

—IFADOYIN SANGOMUYIWA

Erinlẹ̀, omo igbo tó wo inú omi,
Okùnrin tó ń gún omi bí eja,
Olùkó èwe àti egbo,
Ajànàkú tí kò mo pé ó tóbi,
Onígbeyin alâìlera, akoni onírele.
Mo júbà fún Erinlẹ̀,
Omo aláráyé, Olóòóto ni pátápátá,
Kí omi re má bàje, kí irin re má bàje

Erinlẹ̀, child of the forest who entered the water,
Man who rides the river like a fish,
Teacher of roots and leaves,
The elephant who does not boast of his size,
Guardian of the weak, humble champion.
I pay homage to Erinlẹ̀,
Child of the vast world, wholly truthful one,
May your waters never be troubled, may your iron never rust.

–traditional praise poetry for Erinlẹ̀

The Witches' Stang

Influences From Medieval European Witchcraft

As Craft practitioners, the stang is the Horned God, the Great Father, made manifest. Through the stang we experience symbolic connection of Earth to Sky, each to another, and recognize the universality of human myth and experience in the intertwining branches and leaves of the World Tree—sprung from a single seed and existing as the divine and primordial Source.

Loren Crawford

THE WITCHES' STANG is thought to have been incorporated into contemporary Craft practice by the late Robert Cochrane in the 1960s, yet historical evidence of a bifurcated staff used by accused Witches can definitively be traced to central Europe toward the end of the Medieval Period (late 1400s.) Depictions of items resembling the stang can be traced to earlier historical periods, but the congruity of use and intent becomes clouded with time and cultural diffusion. Acknowledging central Europe as a major documented locus for the Witch hunts of the Early Modern Period provides a unique perspective in tracing the origin of the stang as an implement of Witchcraft

Woodcut illustrations from Ulrich Molitor's (1442–1507) De lamiis et pythonicis mulierbus. *Considered to be the earliest known woodcuts of witches transversing on bifurcated staves instead of brooms.*

practice as evidenced in period manuscripts and artworks.

With the invention of the printing press by Johannes Gutenberg in 1455, images of Witches and demons taking to flight or engaged in malefic magic would now find their way into print and distribution to much of the general population. This mass availability of printed material, the long term combined impacts of plague and disease, religious, economic and political turmoil, climate change and crop failure, were catalysts in fueling the first embers of persecution in continental Europe—and especially those areas under direct influence of the Holy Roman Empire.

It is significant that German speaking peoples comprised roughly 50 percent of all those accused and executed for Witchcraft, despite constituting only 20 percent of the population of Europe during the centuries encompassing the Witch hunts. The areas directly affected by Witchcraft accusations were typically agrarian, and it is believed that even as late as the 16th century CE, 75 percent of the population was heavily dependent on agriculture. With the general population intimately connected to the working of the land, those most acutely impacted by adverse climate and economic shifts were instilled with preternatural beliefs and superstitions associated with the need for continuous protection of the harvest—and survival. Here, the tools of the Witch would be considered innocuous—items that would be commonplace when installed at the hearth or used in the field—yet simultaneously and adversely subject to scrutiny in the face of accusations of magical misdeeds.

Of Distaffs, Forks, and Brooms... Shovels, Rakes and Oven Crutches

The period between the 15th and 18th centuries saw significant climatic cooling across Europe, which is believed to have contributed to regional food shortages and related social stressors. The successful cultivation of hay was necessary to guarantee fodder for cattle and other farm animals, which in turn provided meat and dairy for the farmer, manure for soil fertilization and the raw power for ploughing the fields. During periods of wetter, colder weather, hay would be subject to rot—resulting in hardship and often disaster for the largely agrarian population. Spiritual help was often sought to ensure a successful harvest, while drought, hailstorms and other misfortunes tied to weather were considered the acts of supernatural forces or malevolent Witches.

The introduction of the fork (or *gabeln*) into popular concepts of witchcraft of the time is evidenced by Hans Sachs's 1556 publication *Das Unholdenbannen* (*The Fiend Banishing.*) In this work, Sachs notes the prevalence of superstitious belief by the common man that witches and demons would "ride on distaffs, forks and brooms, on shovels, rakes and oven crutches" on their way to the Sabbat or to wreak malicious mischief, and writes:

> *So many a man is still deceived and led around by the nose by magicians and vagabonds,...incensing their art with praise; And yet their magic is a blue haze and fantasy, Fabricated and miserable, As one can see every day. From this follows much trouble (adversity;) Beware of them.*

In agricultural practices, the pitchfork was instrumental in harvesting hay by tossing it in the air to aerate and dry it, and for pitching it into a stack or onto a hay wain (wagon.) While men were typically engaged in cutting and scything, the tossing and pitching were typically the responsibility of women. The two-pronged pitchfork, brandished largely by women who were characterized as vain, covetous and capable of evil deeds due to their inherent sinful—and oft vengeful—nature, thereby became the tool by which alleged Witches could summon up a storm to destroy the crops of their neighbors and wreak havoc on the community at large.

In this artwork, women are using two-pronged forks to bale hay onto a hay wain. Atop the stack, two figures are seen in intimate repose, tying together the theme of women as provoking, enabling or engaging in carnal activities which were contrary to the nature of godliness.'

Detail of central panel of the Haywain Triptych, *1516. Hieronymus Bosch, Dutch.*

Wind, Wild Witches, and Weather-Wrangling

Since ancient times, the wind was conceived of as being a living force whose capricious nature was to be feared and respected. In Europe, Druids and the priestesses of many Celtic tribes were believed to possess the ability to control the winds. Tempestarii was a general Latinized term for common village Witches or magicians—who lived among the common people and professed the ability to cause thunder and hailstorms. Even while Christianity overtook Europe during the centuries following, the conflict between priests and Pagan or non-Christian weather magicians (typically deemed charlatans) persisted:

> *...these half-faithful of ours, who, as soon as they hear thunder, or when there is a breath of light wind, say 'a gale is raised' and curse, saying, 'Cursed be the tongue that did these things, and may it be dried up and now be cut off.'*
>
> *–Bishop Agobard of Lyon, 815 AD*

While the Tempestarii largely left the greater scene or had otherwise gone underground, the practices believed to control and manipulate weather were still retained through the era of the Witch hunts and in some locations into the 18th century.

Classical Influences on the Depiction of the Witch's Staff or Stang

Knowingly, artists and historians are likely to draw their inspiration from symbolic or classical sources, not

Illustration of Witches engaged in weather magic from Ulrich Molitor's Von den unholden oder hexen, *1508. Three bifurcated staves are seen in the upper central part of the image. The far-right figure appears to be using one to summon a storm, while two other Witches brandish theirs while sitting astride a goat or using directly as a means of flight.*

necessarily provincial ones. Just as pagani were considered with derision and country folk deemed provincial and largely ignorant of the greater world, more cosmopolitan populations sought to reinterpret those aspects based on classical or romantic influences.

The association of Witchcraft and sorcery with the darker elements, the Underworld and foreign and mysterious places in the world provided artists and scholars of the time with perspectives that included syncretism with other well known, often more acceptable and palatable forms. It is not difficult to envision Hades' or Pluto's tridents as being representative of the dark Underworld and thus evoked a tool of the Witch or magical practitioners.

In L'Envoûteuse (see next page) the sorceress is wielding a stylized stang reminiscent of classical depictions of Hades' bident and a poppet or effigy impaled with a knife is seen lying on the ground in front of her. There is no identification nor description known for this work, but the author posits that the representation is that of a German-Jewish sorceress: the effigy's clothing is distinctly German or Bavarian, complete with period-appropriate Houpplelande and Miesbacher hat.

In Conclusion: The Contemporary Stang

The interpretation of the Witches' stang as being representative of masculine and feminine principles may be considered a 20th century neo Witchcraft construct. Prior to the late 19th

L'Envoûteuse (The Sorceress)
Georges Merle, 1883

century's scientific and technological advancements, the role of the male principle in the process of procreation was essentially unknown. Historical perspectives suggest that the woman, as Witch, was the typical user, by social default, of the agricultural pitchfork and oven crutch as tools that identified and delegated her to a domestic role in society. 21st century feminist and gender diversity/equality movements have continued to influence Craft and Pagan practices and ephemera.

The contemporary concept of the stang borrows extensively from other Pagan, Neopagan and classical sources. Interpretations of the stang as directly evolved from European mythology—including it being representative of the horns of animal deity or deities, the bident of Hades (Pluto) or symbolic of the World Tree as part of the universal world mythos—may be largely based on the syncretism of diverse, continually evolving belief systems in a world based Pagan community.

It is significant that the contemporary Witches' stang is reminiscent of the tool employed by Germanic peoples during the Medieval period—and well into the Early Modern period—in central Europe. The prevalence and influence of Germanic peoples in Europe and the association of the pitchfork or bifurcated staff as a tool or utility of Witch and wayfarer would have provided for its endurance during a period of persecution of alleged Witches and outcasts. While I cannot testify with any degree of certainty regarding the motivation to employ the stang in mid 20th century practice, it is reasonable to presume the historical basis for its use in Witchcraft is definitive.

–LOREN CRAWFORD

Engraving of Pluto

Vulcan vs Venus

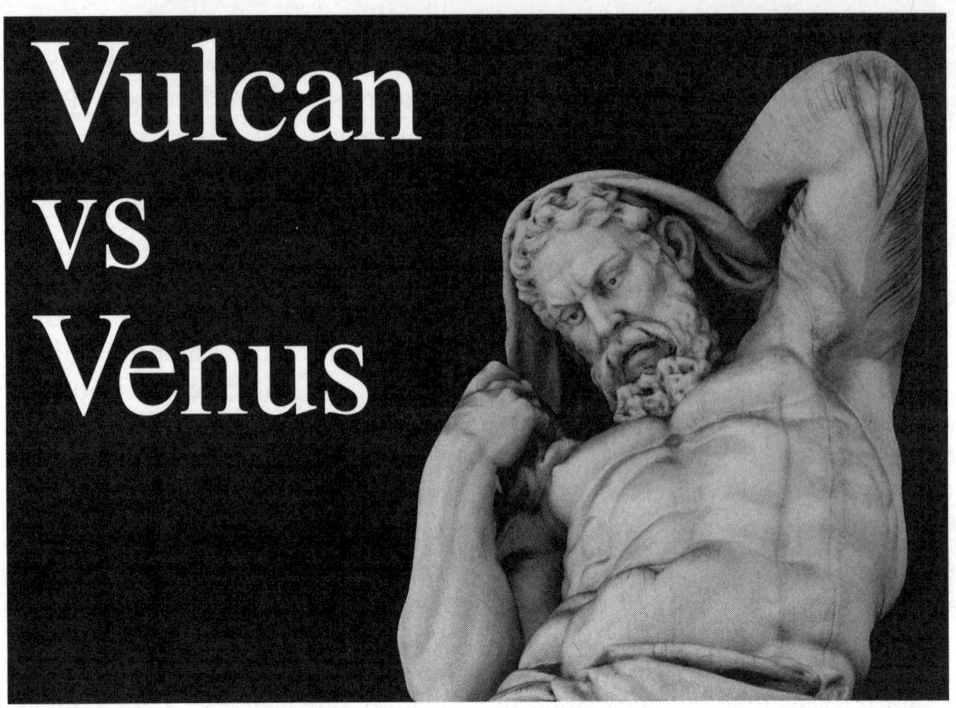

ADULTERY is not necessarily limited to the mortal world; Greek and Roman divinities fell into rather frequent marital lapses. Perhaps the most notorious is the case of Vulcan and Venus, the odd couple of Mount Olympus.

From the birth of Vulcan—known as Hephaestus to the Greeks—things went badly. His mother Juno considered her son misbegotten, an unattractive baby with a deformity. The feet of the unfortunate infant were on backward, heels front, toes back. In a fit of revulsion the heartless mother cast the child from the mountain. His fall took nine days and nine nights, injuring his legs at landing on the isle of Lemnos. Nourished by nereids and grown to manhood, Vulcan spent his time in the abyss of a nearby volcano, its fiery crater providing a smithy for metalwork.

And what work! Vulcan's creations, gifts for the Gods, were exquisite beyond describing. He made a golden thunderbolt and scepter for Jupiter, a magical shield for Minerva, arrows for Eros, the trident of Neptune and the wondrous chariot that Helios the Sun God drove across the sky. For Hades he devised a Helmet of Darkness that made the God of the Underworld invisible. Vulcan then made glorious golden thrones for the Gods of Mount Olympus, but the one presented to Juno exacted revenge on his unnatural mother. When she sat, the throne trapped her and she was unable to arise. The Gods pleaded with Vulcan to return and release their queen, but he refused.

Bacchus took charge. He plied Vulcan with divine wine, and when the smith was drunk Bacchus took him up the mountain slumped over the back of a mule. When Vulcan recovered consciousness, he demanded godly status on Mount Olympus and Venus as his bride in exchange for freeing Juno.

The Olympian Goddesses were renowned for their beauty, but the Goddess of Love outshone them all. To see Venus was to fall passionately in love—the Gods, one and all, were mad for her. Sooty Vulcan, limping on his crutch, dressed in a ragged sleeveless tunic and woolen hat, was as ugly as Venus was gorgeous. But to the surprise of the Olympians she agreed to the marriage for the best of tricky reasons. Vulcan was busy day and night at his forge and would leave the love Goddess free to do what she did best. In addition, he promised to build her a golden palace, the most splendid ever conceived.

Of all her lovers, Venus most adored Mars, the God of War, handsome, brawny, vain, cruel. Homer enjoyed the irony of the tale and wove it into the *Odyssey*. When Vulcan heard of his wife's adulterous lust, the vengeful husband "pondered evil in the deep of his heart and set on the anvil block the great anvil and forged bonds which might not be broken or loosed, that the lovers might bide fast where they were." He crafted a net "fine as spiders' webs" and threw it over the couch where the lovers lay, and about them "flung the cunning bonds." Venus and Mars, clinging in love, could not "in any wise stir their limbs or raise them up."

Then Vulcan cried out, "Ye blessed Gods that are forever, come hither that you may see a laughable matter and a monstrous." The Goddesses came, fled and "abode for shame each in her own house. But the Gods stood in the gateway and unquenchable laughter arose." Vulcan swore to keep the couple in this disgraceful position until her father repaid all the "gifts of woo that I gave him for this shameless girl." Negotiations proceeded with Father Jupiter, the bonds were loosened and the two "sprang straightaway." Mars departed in humiliation to Thrace. But the laughter-loving Venus, unabashed by her nudity, made way to her favorite altar. There the Graces, "bathed her and anointed her with immortal oil such as gleams upon the Gods that are forever. And they clothed her in lovely raiment, a wonder to behold."

The exposure of the guilty pair still reverberated on Mount Olympus. One God asked Mercury how he would feel in such a snare. Mercury answered with words in the hearts of all, "I would suffer thrice the number of bonds if only I could share the bed of Venus the Golden."

–excerpted from *Greek Gods in Love*

WATER WITCH

A romance of the passive elements

Water is life's matter and matrix, mother and medium. There is no life without water.
–Albert Szent-Gyorgyi

Let the salt of Earth admonish the Water to bear the virtue of the Great Sea. Mother, be thou adored.
–Aleister Crowley

MY FATHER wasn't a Witch. He was, in my opinion, however, a real magician—not a Merlin-type magician but, in his own ordinary way, a true magician. If he were alive today, I'm sure he would eschew the title. But in every sense of the word, it is absolutely true, because for a large portion of his life he was master of the spirits of the *passive Elements* of Water and Earth.

Earth

Dad was a geologist and possessed the visionary power of the hourglass. He could scan the topography of most any vista and read it like a history book. He could tell you how the present landscape looked millions of years ago, as the floor of a primordial sea teaming with strange creatures and weird forms of prehistoric life. With his time machine mind's eye, he watched as eons of evolving lifeforms died and settled layer-upon-decaying-layer on the ocean floor, then formed (under immense pressure) strata of rocks and minerals and pools of oil.

Pushing his super-vision forward in time, he witnessed the Earth cool and the polar waters freeze into solid ice, causing sea levels to drop and exposing vast expanses of dry Earth teaming with evolving terrestrial lifeforms with their own time-doom. He followed the drama of the Gods of

Water and Earth clashing in titanic combat as whole continents of glacial ice—two and a half miles thick—shaved and gouged the rocky surface of the Earth as they advanced.

For a geologist, millions of years pass in a blink of an eye. In a heartbeat, the Earth rewarmed and the subarctic glaciers melted, pooling into great freshwater lakes and rivers, some of which filtered down through the earthen skin to create vast underground oceans of fresh, sweet, ice-cold water.

One such subterranean freshwater sea was of particular interest to him—the Ogallala Aquifer. In the 1950s she rested peacefully just a few hundred feet beneath the rich topsoil of the Great Plains of North America. Experts of the day, including my father, estimated that the Ogallala Aquifer was so vast that, if wisely tapped, could supply farmers an abundant source of clean irrigation and drinking water for many hundreds of years.

Water

Dad was not merely a geologist—he was also a professional well driller. On an oil rig crew, the driller is the engineer responsible for creating the day's protocols and making the myriad calculations of deep level drilling. The driller was foreman of the crew and responsible for the entire process from beginning to end. In the early 1950s, Dad and his drilling crew in the Huntington Beach California Oil Fields drilled a well that was at the time one of the deepest holes ever drilled on Earth. It was a good job, a responsible job, and he was good at it. But it was dirty and dangerous, and he would come home each day dead tired, covered in dusty crude oil and smelling of cigarettes, black coffee and sweat.

Dad desperately wanted out of the oil business. In 1955, when he was 44 years old, he moved our family from sunny Southern California to drought-parched Nebraska to seek his fortune drilling for the water that was at the time desperately needed. For over a century, small farmers in the area lay at the mercy and caprice of violent seasonal thunderstorms for the water needed to irrigate their crops. Many of them could not survive two consecutive years of drought . It seemed like a good time to be in the water well drilling business.

Witch

One sweltering Nebraska summer afternoon when I was eight or nine years old, I overheard a phone conversation Dad was having with a farmer client. They were discussing the terms of the standard well drilling contract. It sounded like pretty dull stuff until I heard him say,

"No, you will have to pay the Witch yourself. I can suggest somebody, but if you want to use your own Witch, you'll have to have them confirm the drilling site before we break ground for the slush pit."

Witch? My dad hires Witches? When he got off the phone, he explained that most Midwestern farmers insisted on having a dowser (whom everyone called a "Witch") confirm the best location to drill. I was amazed, to say the least. Dad was a very scientific and un-Witchy kind of guy.

"But you're a geologist. You already know where to drill, don't you? Why would you trust a *Witch* to tell you where to drill? Are they ever wrong? If you disagree with a Witch, aren't you afraid of they'll curse or hex you or something?"

He laughed and explained that water Witches are hardly ever wrong, and most of the time they even predict how many feet down he'd have to drill to strike water. He assured me. "It's not too amazing. Around here all you have to do is poke a stick in the ground and you'll find water."

Still, I wanted to see for myself, and I begged him to take me with him next time the Witch showed up to do her thing. (I assumed the Witch would be a "she" because Witches on TV are all cool-looking women with long black hair, hourglass figures and great cleavage.) I was terribly disappointed when, after shivering for a pre-dawn hour in Dad's truck, the Witch arrived, not on a broom, but in an ancient pickup truck. "She" was a "*he*" and he looked just like all the other farmers that had gathered to watch the *Witchin'*.

Dad and the Witch chatted for a couple minutes over cigarettes and cups of hot thermos coffee. Then the Witch went to work. He waddled over to the cab of his truck and got out what appeared to be two wire coat hangers bent into two large Ls. With a hand-rolled cigarette dangling from his lips, he grasped a hanger in each hand and pointed them forward. He puffed away as he paced back and forth around small section of the field. Then he stopped. The coat hangers slowly bent downwards and pointed straight at his feet. He took one final drag off his disintegrating cigarette, then threw it down on the ground and spat directly where the hangers had pointed.

"Here! 'Bout a hundred ten feet, I reckon."

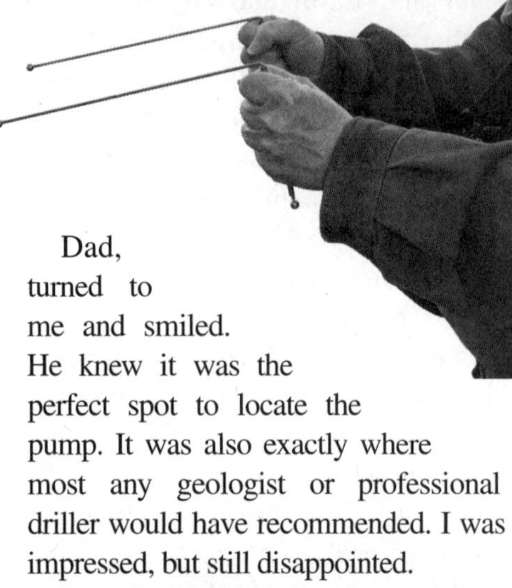

Dad, turned to me and smiled. He knew it was the perfect spot to locate the pump. It was also exactly where most any geologist or professional driller would have recommended. I was impressed, but still disappointed.

Three consecutive years of above-average rainfall and bumper crops dampened the perceived need for new irrigation wells. DuQuette Drilling Company eventually faltered and died. Dad's deteriorating health soon brought an early end to his entrepreneurial dreams. He passed away in 1973 at the age of 62, without learning the true facts about the health and life expectancy of the Ogallala Aquifer. (We now know that this once-great resource is polluted with chemical fertilizers and pesticides and will be completely depleted before the end of this century.)

Who knows the full ends of all our acts?

Codependent elemental spirits

What does this bitter-sweet childhood memory have to do with the magical significance of Water? Maybe nothing, except perhaps as a metaphor of life's dependency upon the Four Elements (and the Four Elements' codependency upon each other.)

I'm not a geologist or a well driller like my father was, but I am a magician. And an important part of *my* work deals with the powers and mysteries of the four classic Elements: Fire, Water, Air and Earth, and the spiritual forces (beings) that inhabit them. Please understand that these Elementals are more than just the flames in your fireplace or the water in your bathtub or the air in your tires or the soil in your garden. Everything in the universe has elemental characteristics to its existence. Even four great forces of physics (strong force, weak force, electromagnetism and gravity) can be viewed as the Four Elements. Indeed, all things, all concepts, attitudes, potentials and qualities are either Fire-ish, Water-ish, Air-ish, or Earth-ish in nature. Everything visible and invisible, real or imaginary, manifest or unmanifest has been created by and is composed of a combination of these Four Elements.

The Four Elements are grouped into two polarized subcategories according to their basic natures and characteristics: two active/positive (Fire and Air) and two passive/negative (Water and Earth.) There is also the all-important fifth Element, Spirit, that pulls them together in different combinations and proportions to make absolutely everything in the cosmos, and, at the same time, keeps the individual Elements pushed apart so they don't meld into a soupy mush.

In my opening words about my father, I spoke of him visualizing a time when Water covered Earth, then later when Earth covered Water. It's a crude but highly illustrative demonstration of the symbiotic romance of the two passive elements. The dynamics of their interaction are obvious, and all the Elements are similarly engaged.

Conjuring an undine

One of the most important magical books of the 19th century is Eliphas Levi's *Transcendental Magic: Its Doctrine and Ritual*, translated into English by A.E. Waite in 1896. Levi devoted an entire chapter of his classic text to the "Conjuration of the Four" Elemental Spirits of Fire (Salamanders,) Water (Undines,) Air (Sylphs) and Earth (Gnomes.)

Perhaps the most helpful aspect of Levi's work is that he establishes a step-by-step basic formula of a ceremony to conjure the elemental spirits. Because this little article concerns the spiritual significance of Water, I will share parts of Levi's conjuration of a water elemental—an *undine*. But in order to properly conjure an undine of Water, we must first get Water's passive lover—Earth—in on the act. Here's Levi's basic technique on how to do that:

To call forth the Undines, a small amount of Water is ceremonially charged by wedding it to its passive element counterpart, Earth. This is done by dissolving ashes from the magician's incense censer (the ash is itself the product of the marriage of the Active elements of Fire and Air,) and then to this adding some Salt of Earth to the Water. This Earth-alized Water will be then sprinkled upon the

Circle and the other temple accoutrements and then used for the material basis for the undine to manifest.

All this is of course accompanied by prayers (in Latin to be fancy) and invocations of specific qabalistic angels, intended to elevate a 19th century magician's consciousness.

Here's part of what the magician recites as he or she prepares the Salt of Earth. (It must be remembered that Levi was a mystic Roman Catholic qabalist magician.)

> *May wisdom abide in this salt, and may it preserve our minds and bodies from all corruption, by Hochmael and in the virtue of Ruach-Hochmael! May the phantoms of Hyle depart herefrom; that it may become a heavenly salt, salt of the earth and earth of salt; that it may feed the threshing ox, and strengthen our hope with the horns of the flying bull! Amen.*

A similar prayer is recited before the ashes are added to the Water. When the ash and salt have been mixed in the Water, the magician concludes this part of the ceremony with these words:

> *In the salt of eternal wisdom, in the water of regeneration, and in the ash whence the new earth springeth, be all things accomplished by Eloim, Gabriel, Raphael and Uriel, through the ages and aeons! Amen.*

All this might seem archaic and ponderously wordy and complex just to conjure up an undine or two. After all, undines are already alive and well within every wet little cell of our bodies and in everything else around us. What makes Levi's procedure magically interesting is the fact that it mirrors in profound simplicity the dynamics of the cosmic partnership of the passive elements of creation. What self-respecting undine could resist being attracted to such an eloquent passion play of its own ancestry?

Once the salt solution water has been properly prepared as the material basis for the undine's appearance (or arrival,) the magician restates in no uncertain terms his or her justification and reason for performing this act of magick.

Exorcism of the Water

> *Let there be a firmament in the midst of the waters, and let it divide the waters from the waters; the things which are above are like unto things which are below, and things below are like unto things above, for the performance of the wonders of the one thing: The sun is its father, the moon its mother, the wind hath carried it in the belly thereof. It ascendeth from earth to heaven, and again it descendeth from heaven to the Earth. I exorcise thee, creature of water, that thou mayest become unto men a mirror of the living God in His works, a fount of life and ablution of sins. Amen.*

The climax of the entire ceremony is the magician's direct address to the undine itself. It must be pointed out that this "prayer" (as with all prayers recited with full magical intent) is only as effective as the magician's level of spiritual exultation at the time the prayer is delivered. In other words, at the pinnacle of the operation, the magician's consciousness must be highly expanded.

Prayer of the undines

Notice that at the very beginning of the prayer of the undines the King of the Sea confines the waters of the Underworld in the caverns of Earth—the same Water/Earth codependent (even combative) dynamic at work on all levels of manifest existence.

> *Dread King of the Sea, Who hast the keys to the floodgates of heaven and dost confine the waters of the underworld in the caverns of earth; King of the deluge and the floods of the springtime; Thou Who dost unseal the sources of the rivers and fountains; Thou Who dost ordain moisture, which is like the blood of earth, to become the sap of plants: Thee we adore and Thee we invoke! …Speak unto us also in the murmur of limpid waters, and we shall yearn for Thy love! O immensity into which flow all rivers of life, to be continually reborn in Thee! O ocean of infinite perfections! Height which reflects Thee in the depth, depth which exhales Thee to the height, lead us unto true life by intelligence and love! Lead us to immortality by sacrifice, that we may be found worthy one day to offer Thee water, blood and tears, for the remission of sins! Amen.*

Traditional qabalists often use familiar biblical fables to illustrate cosmic principles and universal truths, and the story of Noah and the flood is one that is often used to illustrate the mystical significance of the Element Water. One Noah story tells that after the flood, when the Earth once more rises above the waters, Noah hops out of the ark and plants a vineyard in the dry Earth and immediately gets good and drunk. Aleister Crowley, in his comment on the Tarot card, The Hanged Man and the Hebrew letter Mem (which means "water",) wrote the following. I can think of no better blessing and benediction to end this little essay on the romance of the Passive Elements of Water and Earth.

> *Let not the waters whereon thou journeyest wet thee. And, being come to shore, plant thou the Vine and rejoice without shame.*
>
> *–Aleister Crowley,* The Book of Thoth

–LON MILO DUQUETTE

Twelve Dancing Princesses

A Brothers Grimm fairy tale retold

ONCE UPON A TIME, in a kingdom nestled between deep forests and silver rivers, there lived a wise and aging king. He had twelve daughters, each more beautiful and full of life than the last. The people of the land adored the princesses, who were known not only for their beauty but for their grace, wit and joyful spirits. Every evening they dined with their father, laughing over golden plates and sipping sweet wine from goblets of cut crystal and then they would retire to a grand chamber filled with carved oak beds and velvet hangings, where a tall guard locked the door behind them.

But the king was troubled by a strange mystery. Every morning, the shoes of his twelve daughters were worn through—as if they had danced all night. And yet, their door was locked from the outside and no one had seen them leave.

Disturbed and perplexed, the king made a proclamation: "Whosoever can discover where my daughters go each night shall have his choice of them for a bride and shall one day inherit my crown. But be warned—he shall have three nights only. If he fails, he shall lose his head."

This promise, though grand, was not without danger. Many young noblemen came to try their luck. One by one, they were welcomed, fed and lodged next to the princesses' chamber. Each was given

a cup of wine at night—and each fell into a deep, dreamless sleep. In the morning, the shoes were once again worn through. And one by one, the suitors met the headsman's axe. Rumors spread far and wide and soon only the bravest dared to try.

Now, far from court, a soldier was making his way through the land. He had served many years in war and though he bore the scars of battle, he still had a sharp eye, a steady hand and a curious mind. Hearing of the king's challenge, he decided to try his luck. What had he to lose? He had no family, no land and little gold. But he had his courage—and his cleverness.

As he walked along a wooded path toward the palace, he came upon an old woman. Her back was bent with years and her face was lined like the bark of an ancient tree. She leaned on a walking stick carved with strange symbols.

"Where are you bound, soldier?" she asked, her voice like rustling leaves.

"To discover the secret of the twelve princesses," he replied.

The old woman gave a knowing smile. "It's not an easy thing. But take my advice and you may yet succeed. Do not drink the wine they offer you. And take this cloak—it will make you invisible. Use it wisely and observe everything."

He thanked her, tucked the cloak beneath his coat and continued on.

At the palace, the king welcomed him. That evening, the eldest princess brought him a goblet of spiced wine. He thanked her with a smile, but when she turned away, he poured the wine into a potted plant and lay down, feigning sleep, his breaths long and even.

As the Moon rose, the chamber stirred. The soldier cracked open one eye and saw the eldest rise from her bed. She clapped her hands three times. The floor creaked, then slid open to reveal a hidden stairway lit by flickering torches.

"Are you sure he's asleep?" whispered the youngest.

"He drank the wine," said the eldest confidently. "He won't wake."

The soldier, now wide awake, pulled on the magic cloak and followed silently as the princesses descended the stair.

They passed through a forest of silver trees. Their branches clinked like wind chimes and the leaves glowed in the Moonlight with a soft, ethereal sheen. The soldier snapped off a branch as a token. Deeper in, they passed through a golden forest that shimmered like Sunlight and then a diamond one, glittering with cold fire. From each forest, the soldier took a branch, tucking them beneath his cloak.

At last, they came to a lake where twelve boats waited, each rowed by a prince in dark finery. The princesses stepped in. The soldier quietly boarded the boat of the youngest, making it rock slightly.

"Something feels different," she said, looking around nervously.

"The wind, perhaps," said her prince. "Or the Moon."

They crossed the still water to a great castle of crystal and colored glass. Lights blazed from every window. Inside, musicians played enchantments on silver flutes and golden harps. The floor shimmered with inlaid gems and the walls pulsed with magic. The princesses danced with their suitors, laughing and twirling beneath the spellbound ceiling. Their gowns sparkled like starlight and their feet flew over the floor.

The soldier watched, invisible and when one princess set down a golden goblet, he took it. Then he waited, unmoving, as they danced through the night until their shoes were nearly in tatters.

At dawn, they returned across the lake. The soldier followed again, hiding behind the trees and slipping back into his bed just before they returned to their chamber.

"Still asleep," whispered the eldest, peeking in.

The second and third nights followed the same pattern. Each time, the soldier followed, collected tokens and returning unnoticed. On the final night, he gathered a silver goblet and a braid of golden hair that had fallen from one of the princesses as she danced. He even pressed his ear to the wall of the

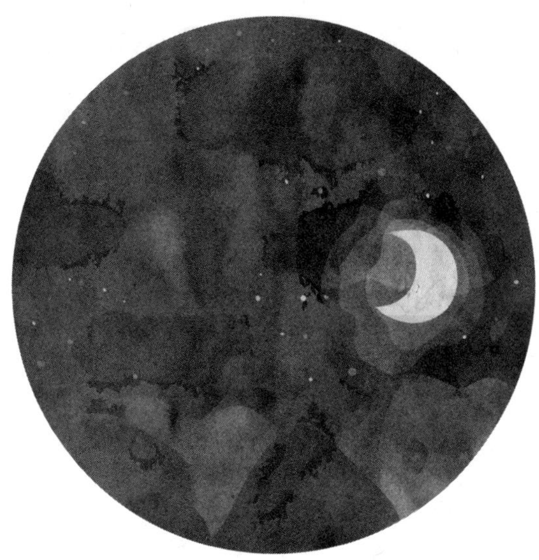

crystal ballroom and heard the princes whispering in strange tongues.

On the fourth morning, the king summoned him.

"Well, have you discovered my daughters' secret?" the king asked, his eyes heavy with worry.

"I have, Your Majesty," the soldier replied. "They descend through a trapdoor in their chamber and pass through enchanted forests of silver, gold and diamond. They cross a lake in boats rowed by shadowy princes and dance until their shoes are worn thin in a castle made of crystal."

He laid out the silver and gold branches, the diamond twig, the golden goblet and the strand of hair.

The twelve princesses stood silent, their faces pale.

The king turned to them. "Is it true?"

The eldest lowered her eyes. "Yes, Father. We were under a spell to keep it secret. But now, it is broken."

The king sighed, more relieved than angry. The spell had been powerful indeed.

The soldier was offered his choice of bride. He chose the youngest, for her honesty and kind heart. Their wedding was splendid, with guests from far and wide. The bells rang for three days. In time, the old king passed and the soldier ruled with wisdom and courage.

The soldier's wedding was the grandest celebration the kingdom had seen in a generation. Lanterns floated into the sky like stars and the people cheered for days. Bards sang of his courage and children reenacted the tale in the market squares. The youngest princess, once quiet and cautious, grew radiant with happiness and together they brought peace to the realm.

He built schools and libraries, repaired bridges and roads and listened to the people. The memory of the dancing mystery faded, replaced by years of prosperity. And though the forest still whispered of ancient magic, none ever found the hidden stair again.

The Journey Beyond

How Different Cultures View Death and the Afterlife

THE MYSTERY of what happens after death has continually fascinated humanity. Across cultures, the afterlife is seen as a place of judgment, transformation, rebirth or, in some cases, eternal rest. Some traditions envision a structured journey—crossing rivers, climbing mountains or facing trials before reaching a final destination. Others describe a seamless merging with cosmic forces, where the soul dissolves into the universe itself. For many, the afterlife is a reflection of earthly deeds, rewarding virtue and punishing wrongdoing. Whether guided by Gods, carried on the wings of an eagle or sailing across celestial waters, the deceased embark on spiritual voyages that mirror the beliefs of the living. Below are 24 unique ways different civilizations have imagined this transition, offering insight into the fears, hopes and philosophies that shape human perspectives on life and death.

1. Ascending to Heaven (Christianity, Islam, Judaism)

In many monotheistic traditions, the righteous ascend to *Heaven*, a divine paradise where they are reunited with God. The concept varies, from Christianity's Kingdom of Heaven to Islam's *Jannah*, where believers experience eternal bliss. In Judaism, some interpretations describe *Olam Ha-Ba* (the World to Come) as a spiritual reward for the faithful, although Jewish beliefs about the afterlife vary considerably because they are not a focus of the faith.

2. Descending to Hell (Christianity, Islam, Zoroastrianism)

In contrast, sinners are condemned to *Hell*, where they face eternal punishment. Christianity describes Hell as a fiery realm ruled by Satan, while Islam's *Jahannam* has multiple levels of suffering. Zoroastrianism also includes a concept of Hell as a place for those who have lived wicked lives, though it is seen as temporary purification akin to **Purgatory**.

3. Crossing the River Styx (Ancient Greece & Rome)

The Greeks believed souls must *pay Charon*, the ferryman, to cross the *River Styx* into Hades, the Underworld.

Without proper burial rites and a coin for passage, the dead would be doomed to wander the riverbanks forever.

4. Traveling to Mictlan (Aztec Mythology)

In Aztec tradition, the souls of those who died natural deaths journey through *nine levels of Mictlan*, an underworld filled with obstacles. The deceased must pass challenges like fierce winds, mountains crashing together and a jaguar that eats hearts before reaching final rest.

5. Entering the Bardo (Tibetan Buddhism)

The Tibetan *Bardo* is an *intermediate state* between death and rebirth, lasting 49 days. Here, souls face visions of wrathful deities, illusions and karmic reflections. If they recognize the true nature of reality, they may achieve enlightenment instead of reincarnation.

6. Passing into Yomi (Shintō, Japan)

Yomi is the Japanese land of the dead, depicted as a dark and shadowy realm. Unlike Hell, it is not necessarily a place of punishment but one of stagnation and impurity. Once a person eats food in Yomi, they can never leave.

7. The Spirit Path and the Great Eagle (Lakota Sioux, Native American)

Among the *Lakota Sioux*, the soul walks the *Spirit Path* toward the land of the ancestors. A *Great Eagle* helps the worthy cross safely, while those who fail are cast down into oblivion.

8. The Hungry Ghost Path (Chinese Folk Belief, Buddhism, Taoism)

Some spirits, burdened by *bad karma or unfulfilled desires*, become *hungry ghosts*—restless beings unable to move on. They are depicted as having tiny mouths and bloated bellies, symbolizing their insatiable hunger.

9. ***Reincarnation (Hinduism, Buddhism, Jainism)***

In the *cycle of Samsara*, souls are reborn in different forms based on *karma*. A person's actions in one life determine whether they are reborn as a higher being, an animal or even into suffering.

10. Becoming an Ancestral Spirit (African Traditional Religions)

In many African cultures, the dead do not truly leave but instead become *ancestral spirits* who guide and protect their descendants. Regular offerings and remembrance ensure they remain benevolent.

11. Sailing Across the Duat (Ancient Egypt)

The deceased must journey through the Duat, the Egyptian underworld, where their hearts are weighed against the *feather of Ma'at*. If the heart is lighter, the deceased reach eternal paradise; if not, the soul is devoured by a monstrous being called *Ammit*.

12. The Bridge of Chinvat (Zoroastrianism)

Zoroastrians believe in the *Chinvat Bridge*, which the dead must cross. For the righteous, it is wide and welcoming—for sinners, it becomes razor-thin, causing them to fall into torment.

13. The Fires of Muspelheim (Norse Mythology)

Those deemed unworthy of *Valhalla* or *Fólkvangr* might end up in *Muspelheim*, —a world of fire and destruction ruled by the giant Surtr—or in *Helheim*, where souls linger in shadow.

14. Transformation into a Star (Many Indigenous Traditions)

Various cultures, including Native American tribes and Australian Aboriginals, believe that deceased ancestors *become stars*, watching over the living.

15. Absorption into the Void (Taoism, Zen Buddhism)

Some Taoist and Zen traditions teach that death is simply a *return to the Tao*, where individual consciousness dissolves into the cosmic whole.

16. Merging with Brahman (Hinduism, Advaita Vedanta)

Rather than being reborn, those who achieve enlightenment *merge with Brahman*, the ultimate reality.

17. Burial with Earthly Possessions (Ancient China, Viking, Egyptian, Mongol)

Various civilizations buried the dead with *gold, weapons and even servants*, ensuring they were prepared for the afterlife.

18. Entering the Elysian Fields (Greek & Roman Mythology)

Reserved for heroes and the virtuous, *Elysium* was a paradise where souls enjoyed eternal bliss.

19. The Dreaming (Australian Aboriginal Beliefs)

Death is a transition to *The Dreaming*, a realm where ancestors live on through the land.

20. Becoming a Wandering Ghost (East Asian Traditions, Hinduism, Buddhism)

Spirits who die *violently or with unfinished business* may become restless ghosts, haunting the world of the living.

21. Returning to Mother Earth (Pagan, Wiccan, Druidic Traditions)

In many *Neo-Pagan* traditions, death is seen as a return to *nature*, where the soul cycles through the Elements.

22. Joining the Wild Hunt (European Folklore, Norse Mythology)

The dead may join the spectral *Wild Hunt*, riding through the sky with spirits and deities.

23. Journeying Through the Nine Worlds (Norse Mythology)

The deceased may be sent to various realms, depending on their deeds in life.

24. Awakening in the Pure Land (Buddhism—Pure Land Sect)

Devout Buddhists are reborn in the *Pure Land*, a celestial realm where enlightenment is easily achieved.

Merry Meetings

A candle in the window, a fire on the hearth,
a discourse over tea…

Few figures have contributed as prolifically—and as impactfully—to the world of Western esotericism as Dr. Stephen Skinner. A scholar, author, translator and practicing magician, Skinner has spent more than five decades reviving and clarifying the practical dimensions of the magical arts. From his groundbreaking early work on *The Complete Magician's Tables* to his pioneering translations of grimoires such as *The Veritable Key of Solomon* and *The Ars Notoria*, he has helped reintroduce authentic, operable magic into the hands of contemporary practitioners. With a background in classical languages, a deep understanding of the Hermetic tradition and an abiding respect for the efficacy of ritual, Stephen Skinner stands as a bridge between scholarship and lived magical practice. Join us as we explore his lifelong dedication to magical realism, the spirits who walk with him and the ever-evolving landscape of ceremonial magic in the modern age.

In your extensive research, what do you see as the core principles that unite most magickal traditions, whether they follow a formal ceremonial approach or a more intuitive path?

The need to announce, invoke or evoke out loud the objectives of the operation and what is required. The presence of spirits, Gods, etc., to answer those invocations.

Your work on classical grimoires has shed light on many ancient practices. How might someone new to magick begin exploring this rich tradition without feeling overwhelmed?

Maybe attempt divination by Tarot, Geomancy or I Ching, before attempting magick. Then start with a simple and easily verifiable request, to see that it is working.

For those starting out, how would you suggest balancing practical spell work aimed at results with practices that focus more on personal spiritual development?

In fact, those two things are quite different. Spell work is focussed on achievable results, mostly on the physical plane, whereas personal spiritual development is more allied to mysticism rather than to magick.

Many magickal traditions use ritual tools like the wand, chalice and knife. From your perspective, how important is the specific design or consecration of these tools for effective practice?

The making of tools ties the magick to the physical plane, which is where you wish to see changes. The actual design is not so important, provided it reflects the intention or desired outcome. The consecration of those tools is important as it ties the magical realms to the physical plane.

Creating sacred space is a common theme across spiritual practices. What, in your view, makes a space truly "sacred," and how might a beginner approach this aspect of ritual?

A sacred space is essentially a location of purity and purity is important for the manifestation of spiritual presences.

Working with spirits can be daunting for beginners. What foundational practices would you recommend for someone interested in safely exploring spirit communication?

Keeping the boundaries clear and functional, just as the magical circle must be cleanly drawn with no breaks.

The practices of incensing a space and consecrating a tool are important foundational practices, along with the memorisation of invocations and relevant poetry.

Planetary influences are central to many magickal systems. Are there particular planetary energies that you think are especially useful for those just beginning their practice?

It is important to understand the seven planetary energies, as they penetrate most of magick and are used extensively in time allocation and the categorisation of particular magical objectives.

Many modern practitioners adapt historical practices to fit contemporary lifestyles. How do you personally approach the balance between traditional authenticity and modern practicality?

I try to do as much as possible 'by the book' rather than attempting to simplify things for my own convenience. It is important when invoking to feel that the whole weight of tradition is behind you and the power of the words you are calling.

Some magicians focus on personal spiritual ascent (theurgy,) while others aim for tangible results (thaumaturgy.) How would you advise someone new to magick in choosing which path to emphasize, if either?

Try first for tangible results. Then you can clearly see if the method you are using is working or not. Spiritual ascent is not so easily measurable and you can fool yourself about your degree of ascent.

In many traditions, divine names hold significant power. How important is it for a beginner to understand the historical and cultural context of the names they might encounter in rituals?

It is sufficiently to understand their holiness and to treat them with the respect they deserve.

You've witnessed how Western magick has evolved over the years. Are there

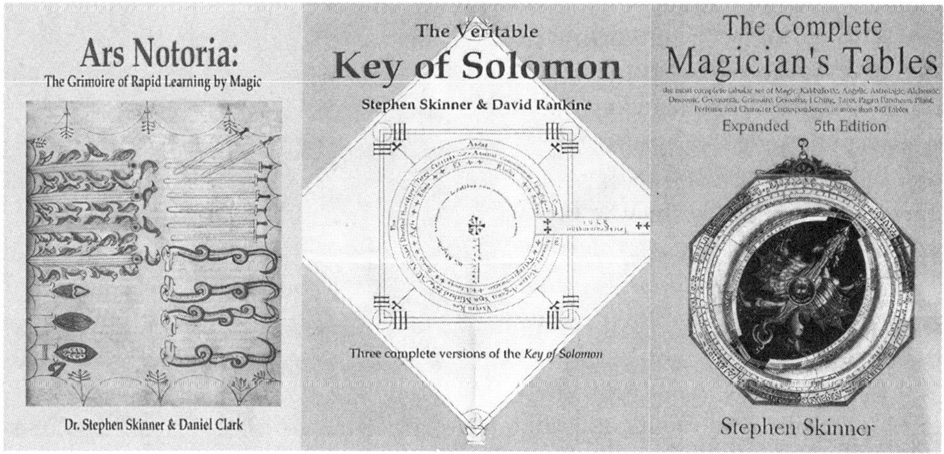

any recent trends or approaches that you find particularly promising for new practitioners?

The trend towards oversimplification should be avoided. Magick is serious and complicated and so should be treated as such.

Different traditions approach magickal ethics in varying ways. From your perspective, is there a common ethical framework that new magicians should consider adopting?

The ethics of the hero, where honesty and support of others is most important.

Astrological timing is emphasized in many classical texts. How critical do you think it is for modern magicians to observe planetary hours and alignments, especially when they're just starting out?

Essential.

With so many books, online courses and forums available today, how can someone new to magick discern trustworthy sources of knowledge from less reliable ones?

One can only trust experience, yours or that of someone you trust.

Looking forward, how do you envision the future of magickal practice evolving? Are there any developments you hope to see in how magick is taught or practiced?

I would hope to see it evolve as a technology which clearly establishes specific provable methods for specific outcomes. There can of course be multiple methods, but then each should be tested and only retained if regularly proven effective.

We die with the dying;

See, they depart, and we go with them.

We are born with the dead:

See, they return, and bring us with them."

–T.S. ELLIOT 1888–1965
excerpt from *Little Gidding*

WILLIAM BUTLER YEATS

Poet, Dramatist, Occultist, Nobel Laureate

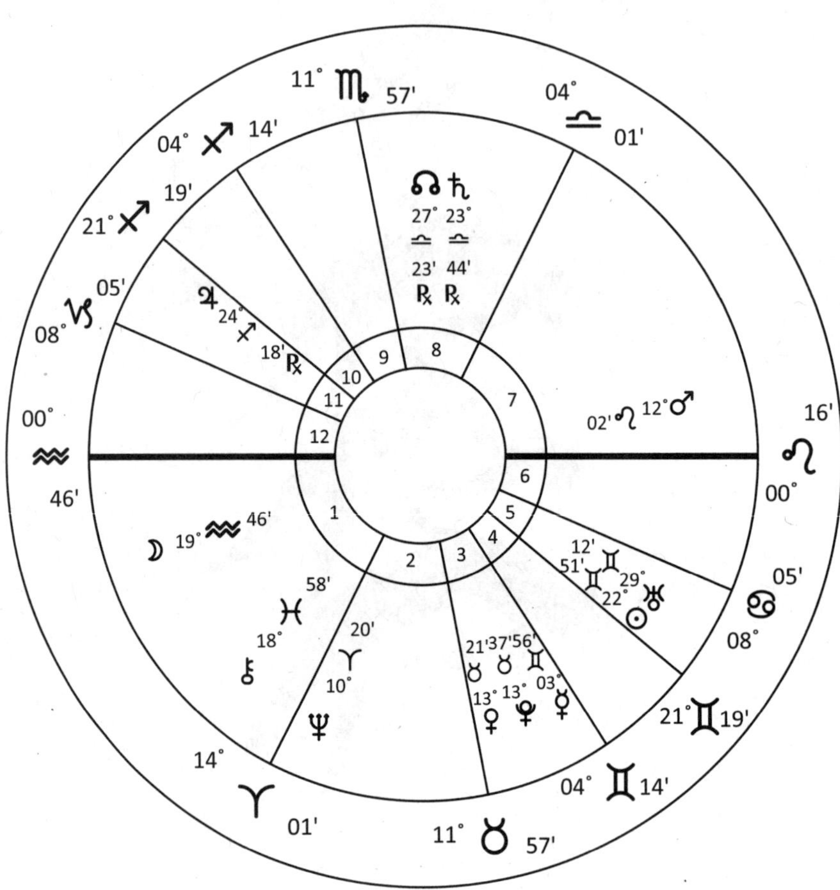

Each year *The Witches' Almanac* features a celebrity horoscope. The choices explore the lives and times of intriguing people who have influenced the world of spirituality, Witchery and the occult. This year's selection is the Irish poet, political activist, actor and mystic William Butler Yeats. Mr. Yeats was a Gemini born on June 13, 1865 at 10:40 am in Dublin, Ireland. He was certainly true to his birth sign, the Twins. Dual faced and multi faceted, those born with the Sun in Mercury ruled Gemini are mercurial in nature. A Gemini will often seem to be more than one person at a time, capable of living multiple lives simultaneously. Gemini is the zodiac's storyteller. This is the birth sign of the master magician wordsmith. Throughout his life William Butler Yeats pursued varied interests. These included a fascination with magic and the supernatural, literature, the theater and politics. His life was woven like a tapestry threaded with complexities and paradoxes.

Looking at the natal horoscope of William Butler Yeats, a close Sun-Uranus conjunction in Gemini is prominent. This aspect shows originality, nonconformity and eccentricity. His Mercury was also in Gemini indicating curiosity and great intellectual capacity. He led what seems to be a truly charmed life. The Moon and ascendant (rising sign) are in Aquarius. The North Node and Saturn are in Libra. The Moon, Sun and Saturn placements together form a fortunate grand trine aspect in the three air signs. This suggests freedom, ease, luxury and opportunity. Mr. Yeats was born into an upper class and talented Protestant family. His father, John Butler Yeats, left a career as a barrister to become an acclaimed artist. This choice on the part of John Yeats brought a Bohemian quality to the family environment. Yeat's mother, Susan Mary Pollexfen, came from a wealthy merchant family. While vacationing as a child at her family home in Sligo, Ireland Yeats was allowed to run wild. He considered Sligo, Ireland his home. Overall he had many advantages during his formative years. He grew up living with his parents in London. There he received a good education, studied art and encountered many key figures in the literary and metaphysical circles of the 19th Century. Venus and Pluto are conjunct in Taurus in his third house. Mercury is also in the 3rd house. This planetary grouping describes his affinity for the arts and his exceptional intellectual inclinations. These gifts became apparent during his early school years.

Metaphysical interests also developed early, as revealed by his Saturn in the 8th house. Saturn is exalted by sign and was conjunct the favorable fixed star Spica. This positive influence is strengthened by Saturn's proximity to the North Node in Libra. As a young man Yeats encountered Helena Blavatsky and the Theosophical Society in London. He was inspired to become a Theosophist. This led to his embracing the popular 19th Century Spiritualism. Katharine Tynan, a writer and scholar who was active in metaphysical circles, invited young Yeats to a séance. This sparked his lifelong interest in the world of the paranormal and supernatural. Fairyland

Portrait from Ireland 20 PuntPounds

was a common theme in his stories and poems. The Aquarius influence as well as the Sun-Uranus conjunction also shows his interest in and talent for astrology. In March of 1890 Mr. Yeats joined a mystery school, The Hermetic Order of the Golden Dawn. During the next 32 years he remained active in the Golden Dawn, attaining a high grade of membership. Astrology, scrying, Tarot, ritual and related topics were all a part of his studies. His personal motto within the Golden Dawn was "Daemon est Deus inversus" which translates "Devil is God Inverted."

Yeats was a key figure in the Irish literary revival of the late 19th and early 20th Centuries. He co founded the famous Abbey Theater in Dublin where he acted in and produced plays. His Mars in Leo shows his theatrical flair. Mars is trine Jupiter in Sagittarius and Neptune in Aries, forming a grand trine in fire signs. This is the second grand trine in his natal chart. Although the orb is wide, the two grand trines together in air and fire signs create an especially auspicious Star of David pattern. The Star of David indicates the celebrity status Yeats achieved during his lifetime. The elevated Jupiter is the planet closest to his midheaven. This shows his international connections. Mr. Yeats enjoyed much travel throughout Europe and the United States.

Yeats also became a leading political activist. He supported the Irish separatist movement. Eventually he served as a senator in the newly established Irish Parliament after Ireland achieved independence from England in 1923. That was the same year that Yeats won the Pulitzer Prize for his poem "Easter, 1916," a political work about the Easter Sunday uprising against English rule.

True love came Yeats' way through his involvement in politics. He met a woman named Maude Gonne, a fellow activist. Maude Gonne was a vibrant and exceptionally brilliant, beautiful woman, by all accounts. Yeats fell hard. It was his first and deepest love. His affections were not reciprocated. His natal Venus and Pluto are exactly conjunct in the fixed sign of Taurus, near the unfavorable fixed star Algol. This deeply passionate conjunction is square Yeats' Mars in his 7th house of marriage. He became obsessed with Maude Gonne and proposed marriage at least three times over a period of several years. When she turned him down for the final time he turned his attention to Maude's daughter. She also refused him. Eventually Yeats transferred his attentions to Georgie Hyde-Lees whom he met in 1917. Georgie came from a vaguely Bohemian lifestyle similar to his own upbringing. Yeats was intrigued by her and admired her psychic talent with her gift in automatic writing. Yeats was 52 and Georgie was 25 when he proposed. The marriage was a surprising success. They had two children and remained together until his death. Georgie never remarried. She lived until August 23, 1968 when she passed away at the age of 76.

Yeats was heavily influenced by the mystical and occult, topics which found their way into his poetry and prose. His writing often explores the relationship between the physical world and the spiritual realm. It draws upon on sources like Irish mythology, Theosophy and Spiritualism.

In this verse, considered to be one of Yeats's finest short poems, he compares man's awareness that he will die with an animal's lack of awareness of death:

Nor dread nor hope attend
A dying animal;
A man awaits his end
Dreading and hoping all;
Many times he died,
Many times rose again ...

William Butler Yeats passed away on January 28, 1939 in Roquebrun-Cap-Martin, France. Years later his remains were returned to his beloved Sligo, Ireland. His career was a long one, dating from the late 1800's until his passing, a period of about half a century. There is a Yeats museum in Sligo which displays an interesting collection of memorabilia honoring this literary giant. The contributions he made to the world of poetry and drama are celebrated each year during at the Yeats festival which takes place near his birthday in June. It is the longest running summer academic camp in the world. The popular event has presented programs and tributes to Yeats for more than 65 consecutive seasons. Readings of his poetry and stories are offered. Throughout the year, the Yeats Museum facility in Sligo poetry reading and themed teas can be booked by appointment. Those interested in attending these events can contact the official Yeats Society in Sligo for details at http.//www.yeatssociety.com.

–DIKKI-JO MULLEN

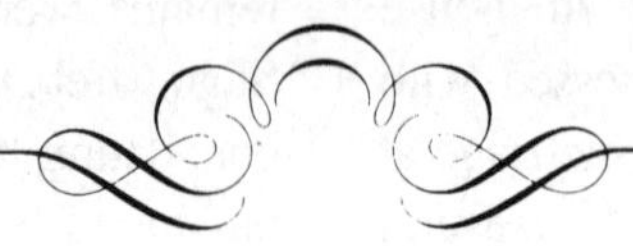

William Butler Yeats

Born June 13, 1865

10:40 pm LMT

In Dublin, Ireland

Data Table

Tropical Placidus Houses

Sun 22 Gemini 51—5th house

Moon 19 Aquarius 46—1st house

Mercury 3 Gemini 56—3rd house

Venus 13 Taurus 21—3rd house

Mars 12 Leo 02—7th house

Jupiter 24 Sagittarius 18—11th house (retrograde)

Saturn 23 Libra 44—8th house (retrograde)

Uranus 29 Gemini 12—5th house

Neptune 10 Aries 20—2nd house

Pluto 13 Taurus 37—3rd house

Chiron 18 Pisces 58—1st house

North Moon Node 27 Libra 23—8th house

Ascendant (rising sign) 00 Aquarius 46

Midheaven 4 Sagittarius 14

Who Will Speak for the Frogs?

Chief Seattle's 1854 Speech

THE MODERN environmental movement began just over half a century ago in 1970. Since that time, concern has deepened and the movement has gained momentum. The key factor involves addressing the explosive impact human beings are continuing to have on every aspect of life on Earth, humanity's only home. Long before the first Earth Day, though, there were those who recognized an impending problem, a conflict with nature which had to be addressed and resolved to assure survival at all. Prominent among these was a Native American from a powerful family of the Duwamish and Squamish tribes of the Washington Territory, now Washington State. Chief Noah Seattle was born between 1780 and 1786. He died on June 7, 1866. In 1854 the Chief delivered a speech which, it is said, was transcribed and translated into English as a letter which was sent to President Franklin Pierce in Washington, DC. The speech has become legendary.

At the age of six, young Sealth—whose name was later changed to Seattle—had an encounter which affected him for the rest of his life. He was present at a trade meeting with George Vancouver and tribe members. It was then that he first recognized the need to cooperate with and befriend the white settlers who were flooding into the region. Young Sealth converted to Christianity and was baptized Noah. Years later Noah under-

went a coming of age ceremony which led to a vision quest. He received a spiritual awakening from a spirit being, the Thunderbird. It is thought that the insights Noah Seattle expressed years later may have germinated during that vision quest.

The earliest known version of the speech comes from the pen of Dr. Henry A. Smith, a settler and amateur writer who was present and took notes at the time. Elders who later saw the transcribed notes supposedly verified the words for authenticity. The occasion was the arrival of Governor Stevens, who had been appointed in charge to oversee what was then Washington Territory.

Henry Smith's account of Chief Seattle's Speech, as published on October 29, 1887 in The Seattle Sunday Star:

> *"When Governor Stevens first arrived in Seattle and told the natives he had been appointed commissioner of Indian affairs for Washington Territory, they gave him a demonstrative reception in front of Dr. Maynard's office near the waterfront on Main Street. The Bay swarmed with canoes and the shore was lined with a living mass of swaying, writhing, dusky humanity, until old Chief Seattle's trumpet-toned voice rolled over the immense multitude like the startling reveille of a bass drum, when silence became as instantaneous and perfect as that which follows a clap of thunder from a clear sky.*
>
> *The governor was then introduced to the native multitude by Dr. Maynard, and at once commenced in a conversational, plain and straightforward style, an explanation of his mission among them, which is too well understood to require recapitulation.*
>
> *When he sat down, Chief Seattle arose with all the dignity of a senator who carries the responsibilities of a great nation on his shoulders. Placing one hand on the governor's head, and slowly pointing heavenward with the index finger of the other, he commenced his memorable address in solemn and impressive tones."*

The Chief spoke in his native Lushoot seed tongue which was then translated into the Chinook Indian trade language, then finally into English. It is likely that some liberties were taken with the translation. The excerpts here present the gist of what the Chief's message to the Governor was and what might have been sent as a letter to President Pierce. The quotes reflect Chief Seattle's deep respect for nature and his belief for living in harmony with the planet. They continue to inspire the many people around the world who support the environmental movement.

"Yonder sky that has wept tears of compassion on our fathers for centuries untold, and which, to us, looks eternal, may change. Today it is fair, tomorrow it may be overcast with clouds. My words are like the stars that never set. What Seattle says, the great chief, Washington...can rely upon, with as much certainty as our

pale-face brothers can rely upon the return of the seasons...

...The son of the White Chief [a reference to Terr. Gov. Stevens] says his father sends us greetings of friendship and good will. This is kind, for we know he has little need of our friendship in return, because his people are many. They are like the grass that covers the vast prairies, while my people are few, and resemble the scattering trees of a storm-swept plain...

...The great, and I presume also good, white chief sends us word that he wants to buy our lands but is willing to allow us to reserve enough to live on comfortably. This indeed appears generous, for the red man no longer has rights that he need respect, and the offer may be wise, also, for we are no longer in need of a great country...

...There was a time when our people covered the whole land, as the waves of a wind-ruffled sea cover its shell-paved floor. But that time has long since passed away with the greatness of tribes now almost forgotten. I will not mourn over our untimely decay, nor reproach my pale-face brothers for hastening it, for we, too, may have been somewhat to blame...

...When our young men grow angry at some real or imaginary wrong, and disfigure their faces with black paint, their hearts, also, are disfigured and turn black, and then their cruelty is relentless and knows no bounds, and our old men are not able to restrain them...

...But let us hope that hostilities between the red-man and his pale-face brothers may never return. We would have everything to lose and nothing to gain...

...The Earth does not belong to us: we belong to the Earth. If all the beasts were gone, men would die from a great loneliness of the spirit...

...Humankind has not woven the web of life. We are but one thread within it. Whatever we do to the web, we do to ourselves. All things are bound together. All things connect. If we do not own the freshness of the air and the sparkle of the water, how can you buy them? Who will speak for the frogs?...

...Only when the last tree has died and the last river has been poisoned and the last fish has been caught will we realize that we cannot eat money...

...We do not inherit the earth from our ancestors; we borrow it from our children. Take only memories, leave nothing but footprints."

Princess Angeline (1820–1896,) the eldest of Chief's Seattle's eight children, became a respected member of the community. Angeline sold handmade baskets and did laundry. She is buried in Seattle's Lake View Cemetery and it is said that her coffin is shaped like a canoe. Angeline's grave is marked by a commemorative plaque. The Princess remains a well-known figure in the records of historic Seattle.

–LAURIE BELL

The Energy of Sacred Spaces

ENERGY LINGERS. Like fingerprints (or nose or paw prints) from past entities' lives, energy from long ago can still be found if we are quiet enough to sense it. Some energy is new and alive, or perhaps sent from a distance. The space can be anywhere—outdoors, in a forest, in a room, a dark basement, cemeteries, anywhere. You will know it if you sense it, sometimes in varying manners. A cold feeling in a specific area. A tingling feeling or slight goosebumps. A weak or strong feeling of comfort, fear, anxiety, sadness, grief, protection or something undefinable. Sometimes a smell, sound, taste or even flashes of visual images if the area is strong enough. Déjà vu, feelings of reliving a scene or life event, or even a claustrophobic anxiety to leave in an open space may be the trigger that makes you realize that the area you are in is just...different.

Some people feel these ways in hospitals, at funerals, spooky places or other high-stress locations which may very well be full of residual energies, or from learned personal experiences and a desire to avoid repeating them. The sensation may be from both, and while it is certainly understandable, it may be worth trying to feel what is there, if that is possible. Probably everyone at some point in their lives has felt something like this, whether it is that spooky house you used to walk past going to school, that creepy old tree in the dark part of the woods, that old, dangerous looking factory that has been closed forever or thunderstorms.

As a small child, I have distinct memories of several old New England houses that I just knew were haunted. I refused to go into the front room of the house next door, especially during thunderstorms. I later discovered that this house was part of a farm that rendered (slaughtered) animals, although there was nothing to indicate anything actually occurred in that front parlor area or sitting room. Perhaps that was where the farmer of the family sat and considered the details of the work and this energy still lingered over one hundred years later and was felt by my younger self. An old but still used cemetery was also located right behind my house growing up, which I visited almost daily. This was a vast, meandering place with many trees, hills and streams flowing through it, and there were a few areas that felt different—they still do. The feeling was not foreboding or sad, but slightly uneasy and old. It was also used for hunting by early Native Americans, along the stream with a very long ancient name—Shumatuscacant River. The combined energies are still there.

My travels have taken me to the Southwest, where one of the first visions I ever encountered was one of a distinctly clear ancient village, while visiting deep off the beaten path in Utah's Valley of the Gods. This was brief but overpowering, as I witnessed a large ancient Native American type of village. The people were all dressed in rough, white fabrics and seemingly looking directly at me from another time. This was followed by a calming presence of a Native American Grandfather embracing me and telling me that everything will end up being ok. This was incredibly real, brief, completely sober and under the watch of a massive pillar of a rock outcropping.

A different feeling of energies was felt on the same trip, this time from the Redwoods Forest and Giant Sequoia in California. The energy from the Redwoods forest was all encompassing, as it is given off from these ancient but still living trees. The Redwoods felt comforting and primeval, like all life was respected and welcomed there. This is a place I would want to be unassumingly interred someday, to become a part of this ancient life, which radiated an intelligence throughout the ecosystem. In contrast, the energy at the Giant Sequoia was harsh, as fires have decimated and severely damaged these massive trees. The feeling was one of mistrust, pain and defense. I did not feel welcomed there, and it was not subtle.

An expedition to visit the ancient Mayan sites in Mexico's Yucatan Peninsula brought two more visual experiences. The first was very brief—a flash really—when walking through a vacant area behind one of the major ruins at Chitzen Itza. I could clearly see a large crowd from ancient times, and what appeared to be a sacrifice about to happen. The feeling was energetic, uneasy and foreboding. Something was about to happen and the energy reflected the anticipation. A much different location during the expedition was in a little-known site that is very well preserved and sees few tourists. We were in a courtyard of several large structures, almost completely overgrown from the jungle, when I saw a very brief but terrifying result of a battle, one which probably was the last time this site was home to the inhabitants. The feeling was one of great sadness very similar to American Civil War battlefields, but this included the complete populace as well as soldiers. I recall only one other person in our group feeling something there, as all the rest were engaged in a lecture about the site, a talk which did not mention any battles or similar occurrences. These feelings of the residual energy are strong and stay with you as though that is the reason they are still there—as ancient messages to future people.

Six months after the Mexico expedition, I visited Egypt on a similar tour. I expected at this point to find or feel something in the massive pyramids and temples, but ancient energy has other plans. There was certainly the feeling of ancient and mysterious memories in these locations, however, the strongest was felt in two unexpected places—on the Nile River and in a small, out of the way ancient temple. Part of the trip included several days on a Nile cruise to reach the many sites along

the River's course. The Nile Herself absolutely radiated ancient energy, as I was inundated with a multitude of energies felt from the bow of the ship over several days. The smell is ancient, earthy, smoky and dirty, but it carries the combined energies of countless lives and lifetimes. I had never felt such a connection to the Earth and time, and I experienced past lives flashing through me. These were my past lives, I believe, and they were from all possible walks of life—ship's captain, cabin boy, sailor, female passenger, impoverished mother in the city on the bank, prisoner—I felt all of these very clearly while standing alone on the bow of the ship. Time was not a barrier, but was fluid and traversable—it is difficult to explain how this felt.

The second place I felt very strong energy was in the Temple of Sekhmet, the lion-headed Goddess. Her energy was off the charts, and the only divine presence I felt during the entire trip. The feeling was of a fierce but protective mother, timeless and a true Goddess. This was in a small group of about six people, alone in the temple. We each had a chance to make a brief but personal connection to Her, and I felt a reciprocation or acknowledgement. Her energy is both ancient and alive, unlike anything I have encountered before or since, and it was completely unexpected. This was a last minute side trip, and not a main attraction, but it became one of the highlights of the entire expedition.

I share these experiences because I realized that one does not have to travel to ancient and faraway places to feel energy, nor does it exist in only famous places. Anywhere energy can be felt is a sacred space, and it is a connection to another place in time or to a still-living entity. The comforting place under the tree in your yard where you feel safe is a sacred space. The walk through the woods where you feel a connection to something is a sacred space. The spooky house down the street is a sacred space. Your altar is a sacred space, and you can create your own sacred space to invite energies to enter it. The energy is everywhere, if you seek it.

—CASTOR

Hans Christian Andersen

The Snow Queen

First Story: Which Treats of a Mirror and of the Splinters

Look, now we are about to begin. When we have got to the end of the story, we shall know more than we do now, for it was an evil troll!—one of the very worst! It was the devil.

One day he was in a very good humor, for he had made a mirror which had the power of making everything good and beautiful that was reflected in it shrink to almost nothing, but everything that was worthless and ugly was shown up magnified in a horrible way.

The most beautiful landscapes looked like boiled spinach, and the best people appeared hideous, or stood on their heads without bodies. Their faces were so distorted that they were not to be recognized. And if a single good thought passed through a man's mind, it showed itself in the mirror in such a way that the troll grinned at his clever invention.

All the little trolls who went to his troll-school—for he kept a troll-school—told everybody that a miracle had happened. Now they could, they said, see for the first time how the world and mankind really looked. They ran about with the mirror, till at last there was not a country nor a person who had not been distorted in it.

Then they wanted to fly up to Heaven itself to scoff at the angels and the Creator. The higher they flew, the more slippery the mirror became. They could hardly hold it. Up they flew, higher and higher, nearer and nearer to Heaven. Then the mirror trembled so terribly with writhing and mocking, that it flew out of their hands and fell to the earth, where it was dashed into hundreds of millions, billions, and more fragments.

And now it wrought more mischief than before. Some of the fragments were scarcely so large as a grain of sand, and they flew about in the wide world. But wherever they went into people's eyes, they remained fixed there, and those people saw everything perverted or only had eyes for that which was evil.

The smallest splinters of the glass had the same effect. Some people even got a splinter of the mirror into their hearts, and then it was horrible—their hearts became like a lump of ice.

Some fragments were so large that they were used as window panes; others as spectacles. But the wickedest of all was a tiny grain that got into people's eyes or hearts. And this caused many evils. The troll laughed till his sides ached, and still the fragments of glass flew about in the air.

Now we shall hear what happened.

Second Story: A Little Boy and a Little Girl

In a big town where there are so many people and so many houses that there is not room enough for everybody to have a little garden, and where therefore most persons are obliged to content themselves with flowers in pots, there lived two poor children who had a garden somewhat larger than a flower-pot.

They were not brother and sister, but they loved each other as much as if they were. Their parents lived in houses opposite each other. The two children often played together. In the winter, when the windows were frozen over, they used to warm copper pennies and lay them on the frozen panes. Then they could see each other quite well.

In summer they could go out and sit on their little chairs under the rose trees, which grew beautifully in both windows. They had learned to climb over to each other's windows, and very often they would sit with each other reading or playing.

The boy's name was Kay; the girl's name was Gerda. In summer they played happily. But one day, Kay said, "Something has got into my eye! It hurts!"—and it was one of the splinters from the wicked mirror. Poor Kay!

Now everything that was beautiful and good seemed to him ugly and worthless. He could no longer see the beauty in the roses, or Gerda's kindness. Soon, he grew cold toward her and began to play with other boys and make fun of her.

One day, when snow was falling and big white flakes were drifting down, Kay took his little sled to the town square. Suddenly a large, white sleigh drawn by white horses appeared. In it sat a tall, beautiful lady all in white—The Snow Queen.

She nodded to Kay, and he hitched his sled to her sleigh. Then they sped away, faster and faster, out of the town, into the great white world. The snowflakes became larger and thicker; Kay was frightened and tried to say a prayer, but all he could remember was multiplication tables. Then the Snow Queen kissed him on the forehead—and he forgot everything: Gerda, his grandmother, everything.

Third Story: The Flower Garden of the Woman Who Could Conjure

What became of little Gerda when Kay did not return? All the people in the town thought he must have drowned in the river that ran nearby. Gerda cried and wept.

At last, in springtime, she decided to go and look for him. She set off in her red shoes down the riverbank. When she could not find him there, she got into a boat and floated far away, looking for her friend.

She came to a little cottage, where an old woman lived. The woman was kind and gave her cherries and brushed her hair. But she was also a sorceress, and she wanted to keep Gerda with her. She made the roses in her garden disappear, because they reminded Gerda of Kay.

But one day, Gerda saw a painted rose on the woman's hat and suddenly remembered her mission. The roses in the garden were gone, but she cried so much that the bush burst up through the ground, and the flowers spoke to her: "We have not seen Kay."

So Gerda continued her journey.

Fourth Story: The Prince and the Princess

Gerda wandered far and wide, and finally came to a great castle. She was told that a young prince lived there who resembled

Kay. She went into the castle, and the prince and princess received her kindly, but he was not Kay.

They gave her a carriage of gold and fine clothes and provisions. Once more she set off to look for her friend.

Fifth Story: The Little Robber Girl

As she traveled through the woods, robbers attacked her carriage. A fierce little robber girl wanted to keep Gerda for herself. But when she heard Gerda's story, she took pity on her.

The robber girl had a reindeer who came from Lapland. She told Gerda that Kay had been taken to the Snow Queen's palace, far to the north in Spitsbergen.

The reindeer agreed to carry her there.

Sixth Story: The Lapp Woman and the Finn Woman

The journey was long and hard. The reindeer took Gerda to a wise Lapp woman, who wrote a message for a Finn woman. The Finn woman read it and told the reindeer that Gerda had no magical powers—only her pure, loving heart.

"She must not be told this," said the Finn woman, "for if a human being cannot obtain power from herself, nothing can help her."

So Gerda went on to the Snow Queen's palace.

Seventh Story: What Happened in the Snow Queen's Palace and Afterwards

The palace walls were of drifted snow, with windows of cutting winds. Kay sat frozen in a great hall, blue and nearly black with cold. The Snow Queen had left him there to try to complete a puzzle made of shards of ice. If he could form the word "Eternity," he would be free and master of the world.

But he could not.

Then Gerda came in. She ran to Kay, weeping hot tears. One of her tears fell on his chest and melted the ice around his heart. He cried, and the glass splinter came out of his eye.

He recognized her and was full of joy.

They danced, and the pieces of ice formed the word "Eternity" by themselves. The Snow Queen's power was broken.

Kay and Gerda returned home together, hand in hand. When they reached the town, they saw everything was the same—but they were grown-up children now, grown through sorrow and joy.

And the roses on the roof bloomed again.

The End.

The Mora, Sweden Witch Trials1670

The Sorcerous North

Abode of Witches, Conjurers and Demons

TO THE ANCIENT peoples who inhabited the lands of the Mediterranean Rim (Near East, Southern Europe and Northern Africa,) the regions to the North were typically considered to be the realm of chaos and misfortune. These largely unexplored, sparsely populated, darker and colder regions were believed to harbor all forms of disaster and evil which could be unleashed upon the world in opposition to divine or cosmic order.

The Hebrews, like many other ancient peoples, oriented themselves relative to the rising of the Sun where it was established that right meant South and left implied North. The concept of direction assumed other aspects in addition to spatial orientation, where right symbolized strength and left implied weakness or even defect. The Abrahamic faiths similarly contain many references to the "right hand of God" overcoming adversaries, or the right eye or hand being considered more valuable than the left.

The Unfinished Corner of the World

An early version of the Hebrew creation myth tells how the northern corner of the world was left unfinished by Yahweh and became the dwelling place of demons, bitter winds, earthquakes and all manner of evil which sought to hide from the light. Schwartz describes this in 2004:

> *All of Creation had been completed except for the north corner of the world. There, in that unfinished corner, demons, winds, earthquakes, and evil spirits dwell...When the Sabbath departs, great bands of evil*

spirits set out from there and roam the world.

Archetypes of Evil

To the early Israelites, the land of Canaan (ancient Syria) which lay directly to the North was known as the stronghold of the warrior storm God Baal, whom they took for an enemy of Yahweh. The divine mountain where Baal held council lay north of Ugarit. It was called Tsaphon or Zephon and both mountain and deity respectively assumed the toponym and title Baal-Zephon, or Master/Lord of the North. In the Semitic language tree, *tsaphon* צָפוֹשׁ is defined as "hidden" or "North" while the archaic Hebrew word *smol* implied left. The latter term is related to the Arabic word *šimāl*, meaning left hand or North—and bad omen. One of Baal's epithets was "Prince, Lord of the Underworld," which denoted his connection to the spirit world and realm of the dead.

The belief in evil originating in or coming from the North was well established during biblical times. References allude to the prophet Isaiah (14:12–13) writing of the fallen Lucifer taking up a stronghold in the North and the fear that a great enemy (Gog and Magog) would be unleashed from the heights of the North to wreak apocalyptic destruction upon Christianity, Judaism and Islam.

The representation of Gog and Magog as being an enemy "from the uttermost parts of the North" in Christianity, Judaism and Islam may be conceived as a reference to incursions by nomadic peoples of the Eurasian Steppes, who appeared on the northern borders and swept across Europe and the Near East wreaking havoc and leaving destruction in their wake. Coupled with fear and ignorance of the vast and still largely unknown places beyond known civilization, these accounts of nomadic waves of barbarians—and in later times, plague and other calamitous misfortunes—would have been interpreted as godly punishments against mankind through manifestations of evil being released and spreading across the world.

In Egypt, the Canaanite God Baal became conflated with the God Seth (earliest attestation as *Satesh.*) Seth, who was referred to in the Egyptian Book

The People of Gog and Magog, Perverted by Evil
The Rising of the Lucky Stars and the Sources of Sovereignty by Mehmed al-Su'ûdî, 1582

of the Dead as "Lord of the Northern Skies," was associated with the circumpolar stars—specifically the *septentriones* (seven) stars of Ursa major—the great bear. He transformed into an increasingly malevolent God of chaos, warfare, darkness, storms and turbulent sea waters—attributes in opposition to light and order. In his 1899 *History of the Devil*, Paul Carus characterized Seth as an inversion of other Egyptian Gods:

> *As an enemy to life, Set is identified with all destruction. He is the waning of the Moon, the decrease of the waters of the Nile, and the setting of the Sun. Thus, he was called the left or black eye of the decreasing Sun, governing the year from the Summer Solstice to the Winter Solstice, which is contrasted with the right or bright eye of Hor, the increasing Sun, which symbolizes the growth of life and the spread of light from the Winter Solstice to the Summer Solstice.*

> *Seth is alternately identified in the works of several ancient Greek and Roman historians , including Plutarch (46-120 CE,) who associated the deity with Typhon, the serpentine storm entity and father of all monsters, who was symbolic of evil and destruction.*

The seven-star circumpolar asterism Mesekhtui, associated with the Egyptian deity Seth.

Septentrion: the Abode of Satan

During the Early Modern Period in Europe, the North was reputed to be teeming with Witches and demons who wreaked havoc with their sorcery and wicked intentions. At the height of the Witch hunts during the 16th and 17th centuries—spurred by civil unrest from disease and climate change leading to harvest failures—accounts of the northern sorcerers and Witches of Scandinavia and Scotland preoccupied the rest of Christianized Europe.

One of the key sources for accounts of northern sorcery and Witchcraft came from Olaus Magnus, a Swedish Catholic clergyman displaced to Italy during the Reformation, who wrote a highly influential treatise entitled Historia de Gentibus Septentrionalibus (*History of the Northern Peoples*) in 1555. Olaus reported that the "demons were so numerous in the far North that they even perform menial tasks—like cleaning the stables," detailing accounts of their abilities with wind-summoning, divination, and other sorcerous endeavors:

> In the regions under the Seven Stars, that is to say, the North, where in quite literal sense the abode of Satan lies, demons with unspeakable derision and in diverse shapes express their encouragement to people who live in those parts.

The French philosopher and theorist Jean Bodin similarly declared in *La Démonomanie des Sorciers* (1580) that the North was intensely populated with Witches because the devil's power was more concentrated in that region.

A Hellish Landscape

The bitter cold, dark and barren landscape of the North was believed to be the domain of the Underworld. During the Middle Ages, Mount Hekla volcano in Iceland was deemed the entrance to Hell and the abode of Satan—a myth propagated by Cisternian monks following the 1100 CE eruption. It was on Hekla that Witches were thought to converge on its slopes while doomed souls were cast into its fiery depths. In the *Book of Wonders* penned in 1180 CE, Chaplain Herbert of the Clairvaux monastery wrote that while Sicily was called Hell's chimney, Mount Hekla made it seem almost insignificant.

The Great Deceivers

The divination skills of Finnish conjurers and *noaidi* (Sámi magic workers) were renowned for centuries throughout Europe. Written during the 13th and 14th centuries, the Icelandic Sagas told of the northern sorcerers who could divine the future and envision events transpiring in distant parts of the world, while encounters with seafarers continually brought imaginative accounts of their prowess with weather and wind magic back to European home ports.

By the 18th century, the northern indigenous sorcerers and practitioners of magical arts had all but disappeared in the aftermath of the Witchcraft persecutions and through cultural eradication—leaving naught but charlatans and tricksters in their wake. Many practitioners had otherwise gone underground or absorbed their Pagan and folk beliefs into the prevailing Christianized culture.

The Devil's role as the "Great Deceiver" heavily influenced European views of the North and the peoples who inhabited it. In his Old French–English Dictionary, Alan Hindley notes that in Old French, the archaic term *Norois* meant "a Norse, Norseman," and also "action worthy of a man from the North, i.e. usually considered as deceitful."

Old English references considered Northern peoples as *wærlogan*—deceivers, those who broke oaths or religious-based covenants—a term that came to apply specifically to the devil as early as the 11th century. Accounts of early Pagan peoples who were forcibly converted and who had subsequently forsaken their baptisms and covenants with the Church were not unusual. Those who occupied more isolated areas in the North would often revert to their original beliefs after Christian missionary efforts largely withdrew—or continue to oppose the new religion after forced conversion.

Many of the beliefs of the North as being a place of evil and a dwelling place for Satan, Witches, devils and their ungodly activities are known to have persisted in areas of Europe until the 1800s. References from historic accounts of the Witch hunts, persecution of indigenous peoples and their beliefs and the remains of folklore and myths were passed down through generations of northern peoples and in the spurious accounts of their oppressors.

> *The ritual of Witchcraft is the ritual of an oppressed people. The religion of ...the conquered has often become the magic of societies formed as a result of conquest.*
>
> *–Georges Bataille, 1928*

–LOREN CRAWFORD

ÆSOP

Now you see him, now you don't

I MUST REPORT that I am very, very disappointed in the *Encyclopedia Britannica.* Yes. Usually so reliable for kick-starting research, the entry for Aesop *dithers.* I am not on firm ground here. I learn that Aesop, beloved creator of wondrous fables, is a "supposed author," a "legendary figure." All that I can establish is that a slave is shrouded in shadows and that the tales started circulating around the mid-sixth-century B.C.

I turn to other sources and encounter more confusion. Aesop's place of birth provides a good starting point. Now I have it—Thrace. No. Phrygia. Wait a minute. Egypt. What, Samos? Perhaps Athens? Maybe Ethiopia? All proposed, all disputed. One authority favors Ethiopia, deducing that the name Aesop derives from Aethiopian, the Greek term for dark-skinned people. He also points out that African animals populate many of the fables, beasts unknown to the Greeks. Sounds reasonable, but he seems to be howling alone in a historical wilderness.

What is operative here obviously are ages so bygone as to leave Aesop in obscurity akin to, say, Homer, King Arthur or Merlin. We are curious about them and pick over such historical bones as we unearth. We can do no less for Aesop and offer what we find where consensus seems convincing.

Beastly mentors

The integrity, beauty and comedic swagger of Aesop's work is where solid agreement exists. He is synonymous with the form of the fable and its concealed aim—the improvement of human conduct. Neither teachy nor preachy, fables are rollicking little fantasies written with maximum economy, their morality aim concealed by an animal cast of characters. Actual people sometimes turn up, usually rural folk—shepherds, woodcutters, hunters, although an occasional king or God appears. But denizens of a teeming literary zoo have mouths or beaks ready with sassy speech and are generally favored. They serve as iconic symbols for human behavior and also display the attributes of particular species. The

fables are, according to one authority, "intentional travesties of human affairs." Hundreds of fables are accredited to Aesop, although not the same hand created them all. But beyond doubt Aesop created the form as we know it and is the master fabulist. In the whimsical realm of Aesop, foxes are sly; ants, industrious; wolves, cruel; hares, timid; asses, stupid. A lion is brave, even with a thorn in its paw.

The fable's tight, bright narrative flows into the only possible conclusion, the moral. In "Mountain Delivered of a Mouse," for instance, the Mountain moans and groans in labor, attracting a crowd of onlookers. Finally a little Mouse runs out. The payoff—"much ado about nothing," is surely no stranger to Shakespeare. I look in vain for "all's well that ends well," a moral that seems Aesopian. In the fables, unlike in life, rascals suffer and the virtuous prevail.

Reality and murky stories

That he was a slave under two masters seems established. The second, Jadmon, freed Aesop in honor of his wisdom, wit and the pleasure of his company. Like Socrates, Aesop was considered ugly and sometimes even

The beautiful Rhodope in love with Aesop. Engraved by Francesco Bartolozzi after a painting by Angelica Kauffmann.

described as deformed, although no details about any particular infirmity have ever emerged. In the Villa Albani in Rome exists a grotesque marble figure deemed to be Aesop. Athenians disputed the account of his deformity and commissioned a noble statue in his honor by the noted sculptor Lysippus. Like a "he said, she said" legal controversy, we seem to have confusion compounded in marble—this one depicts Aesop, that one depicts Aesop, what statue do you credit?

In the ancient republic, a freedman had permission to play a role in public life. Aesop engaged in civic affairs and raised himself from his servile early life to a position of consequence. Apparently, he traveled widely and at last settled in Sardis at the court of King Croesus, patron of artists and philosophers. Here Aesop shone in discourse, holding his own in mental jousting with Solon and other sages. The ex-slave also served the king with commissions to lesser Greek republics, his persuasiveness often reinforced by the soft sell of fables. In Athens during the reign of Pisistratus, for instance, Aesop recounted "The Frogs Asking for a King" to discourage the discontented populace from agitating for a new ruler. In the fable the Frogs so annoyed Jupiter that he sent them a new monarch, a Heron who "preyed upon the Frogs day by day until there were none left to croak upon the lake."

The Man Aesop by Diego Rodriguez de Silva y Velázquez

Wrongful death in Delphi

In his guise as ambassador for Croesus, Aesop met a violent death in Delphi. That much is factual. He was entrusted with a delicate commission—a large sum of gold for distribution. Aesop was so appalled by the greed he encountered that he refused to disburse the money and sent it back to the king. The furious Delphians, ignoring the sacred status of ambassador, accused Aesop of impiety. Some murky story also emerges about sacrilege with a silver chalice, perhaps the "impiety," intriguing but unexplained. Other sources, other versions of his offense: according to one, he insulted the townspeople with sarcasm. According to another, he embezzled the gold entrusted to him. Whatever the story, we do know that Aesop was sentenced as a common criminal. He warned that great misfortune would follow his unjust death. Unheeding, the enraged Delphians threw him over a cliff. Shortly after the execution, a pestilence followed which the Oracle of Apollo confirmed was punishment for the wrongful killing of Aesop.

Moral: Don't believe everything you read, including this.

—BARBARA STACY

TAROT'S THE TOWER

TRUMP NUMBER SIXTEEN depicts a tower with its battlements set ablaze by a lightning bolt. Early decks show bodies falling from the battlements. Our depiction is based on a woodblock design from an uncut page of Tarots created in 15th century Venice or Ferrara. In a poem about the Tarot written around 1550, the Tower is identified as "la Casa del Diavolo," the Devil's House, so the lightning bolt may indicate the Devil's defeat as dramatized in the once popular medieval liturgical play known as The Harrowing of Hell. "The Harrowing," which means "plundering," occurs just before the drama of the "Last Judgment" in the religious play-cycle. It recounts the story of Jesus' descent into Hell after his crucifixion to smash its gates and release the souls of good Pagans and unbaptised innocents that had been consigned to Limbo, a place considered by theologians to be situated within Hell's domain and under the Devil's control. The story was well-known and used extensively by medieval poets and playwrights, and it forms a vital part of the Christian liturgical drama-cycle. In readings the Tower signifies the downfall of tyranny or a tyrant, maybe one who has the subject of the reading in his or her grasp, unless of course the subject of the reading is the tyrant (which may be something worth tactfully investigating.)

Excerpted from Dame Fortune's Wheel Tarot—A Pictorial Key *by Paul Huson, published by The Witches' Almanac.*

Alcyone

The Hen

EACH YEAR *The Witches' Almanac* features a different fixed star. Alcyone (pronounced al-sigh-on-ee) is this year's selection. The fixed stars twinkle from the vast reaches of outer space. They are far outside of our solar system located beyond the planets which are interpreted within the familiar horoscope. The fixed stars actually do move slowly, though. This is due to the precession of the equinoxes. The stars shift barely a zodiacal degree within a span of 72 years. Scientists estimate the age of Alcyone to be about 100 million years old. This star is about 440 million light years away from our Sun, yet it is so large and bright that its influence is significant and obvious.

The Danish astronomer and scientist Tycho Brahe made important discoveries and observations in the development of measuring and fixing the positions of various significant stars, and he lived from December 14, 1546 to October 24, 1601.The relevance of certain stars has been noted much longer, though. About 130 BCE Hipparius of Nicaea, a Greek astrologer and scientist, mentioned influential stars. Later, about 140 CE, Ptolemy of Egypt expanded upon that earlier work.

Alcyone is the brightest star in Pleiades, a well-known constellation identified with the seven daughters of Atlas and Pleione

in mythology. Alcyone was a princess of Thessaly and the wife of Ceyx, who was a son of Venus, the morning star. In China Alcyone is the 6th star of Mao Xiu, a constellation dubbed "The Hairy Head," because the grouping of stars in Pleiades can resemble a circle of streaming, hair-like lights. The Pleiades constellation has inspired many myths. One is that the stars symbolize a flock of hens. This is where the name Alcyone, interpreted to mean The Hen, comes from. Alcyone has recently shifted away from the zodiac sign of Taurus to 00 degrees of Gemini. This rare sign shift is very important astrologically. The planet Uranus transits the Taurus-Gemini cusp in 2025–2026. Uranus will move all of the way into Gemini on April 26, 2026 where it will remain until August of 2032. The influence of Alcyone will become especially apparent when Uranus completely activates the early degrees of Gemini. This transit last occurred during World War II. Cultural and political events which took place at that time, during the 1940's, have shaped global situations ever since. Alcyone combines the qualities of the Moon and Mars. "Truth is the daughter of time." Events which occur in 2026 will offer insight into the specifics of what the transit of Uranus conjunct Alcyone will mean in the long run.

The fixed stars have very small orbs. Most astrologers will only allow a degree or two from the exact conjunction. Other aspects aren't considered to be significant. However, if the Sun, Moon or a planet does conjoin a fixed star, the impact has proven to be profound. If a conjunction with a fixed star occurs in a natal chart it can impact an entire lifetime. When interpreting future trends a planet conjunct a fixed star often correlates with significant events and life experiences. Those born from May 19–22 of any year will have Alcyone conjunct the Sun. This can indicate great determination, strong opinions and a desire to assume positions of leadership.

Here are some keywords for the Moon and planets when they are within orb of a conjunction with Alcyone. This is at about 29 Taurus to 2 degrees of Gemini.

Conjunct the Moon Challenges are many. Don't procrastinate, it is important to stay active and fulfill obligations.

Conjunct Mercury Analyze situations. Strategize to overcome disappointments, a child has special needs.

Conjunct Venus Passions are exceptionally strong. Caution with and careful management of finances is needed.

Conjunct Mars Be aware of and avoid accident hazards or accelerating arguments. Be careful with fire.

Conjunct Jupiter Legal matters need attention, follow rules. A relative might become estranged.

Conjunct Saturn Health issues must be addressed promptly. Chronic sickness or tumors might need treatment.

Conjunct Uranus Faith and fidelity issues surface. Avoid hazardous weather, environmental or political conditions.

Conjunct Neptune Military honors are won, helpful friends are of value. A surprise regarding heritage or parentage can twist fate.

Conjunct Pluto Secrecy is present, truth seeking is important. Uphold the highest values and ethics to enjoy success and peace.

A New Moon rises with the Sun,
Her waxing half at midday shows,
The Full Moon climbs at sunset hour,
And waning half the midnight knows.

NEW	2027	FULL	NEW	2028	FULL
Jan 7		Jan 22			Jan 11
Feb 6		Feb 20	Jan 26		Feb 10
Mar 8		Mar 22	Feb 25		Mar 10
Apr 6		Apr 20	Mar 26		Apr 9
May 6		May 20	Apr 24		May 8
June 4		June 18	May 24		Jun 7
July 3		July18	Jun 22		July 6
Aug 2		Aug 17	July 21		Aug 5
Aug 31*		Sept 15	Aug 20		Sept 3
Sept 29		Oct 15	Sept 18		Oct 3
Oct 29		Nov 13	Oct 17		Nov 2
Nov 27		Dec 13	Nov 16		Dec 1
Dec 27			Dec 15		Dec 31**

*A rare second New Moon in a single month is called a "Black Moon."
**A rare second Full Moon in a single month is called a "Blue Moon."

Life takes on added dimension when you match your activities to the waxing and waning of the Moon. Observe the sequence of her phases to learn the wisdom of constant change within complete certainty.

Dates are for Eastern Standard and Daylight Time.

presage

by Dikki–Jo Mullen

ARIES, 2026–PISCES, 2027

EVERYTHING is the same, yet nothing is the same. Day–to–day life, priorities, the seasons and circadian cycles illustrate the rhythms marking the hours of the days and nights with predictable sameness, but beneath brews a sense that a new destiny is emerging.

Unusual astrological patterns offer insights for the year to come. Pluto has moved into Aquarius where it remains until January 2044; transformative impacts involving technology are on the horizon. Artificial intelligence and aviation, including space travel, assuming new significance reflect the Pluto transit. In April of this year Uranus will move into Gemini. This last took place during World War II. Uranus brings surprises, related especially to democracy. Gemini is about duality; new situations develop regarding communication, education and shifts in government. Neptune will join Saturn in Aries; spiritual concepts can dissolve and redevelop differently. The spirituality segments in this year's Presage present birds as spirit guides for each birth sign as revealed in the Pancha Pakshi, an early zodiac which comes from India's ancient Tamil literature.

There will be four eclipses this year, in Leo, Pisces, Aquarius and Virgo. Pivotal events are frequently related to eclipses. The Leo eclipse suggests new leadership involving world powers, the Pisces eclipse might involve water and rainfall as well as religious figures. The Aquarius eclipse points to technology and human rights issues. Health care and wellness concerns are illustrated by the Virgo eclipse. Read about what these means to you in Presage. Begin with the forecast for your familiar zodiac sign to understand the general direction of your year. Consider next the forecast for your Moon sign for insight into your emotional direction and hereditary factors. Your ascendant (rising sign) illustrates your physical environment and outward interaction with others.

ASTROLOGICAL KEYS

Signs of the Zodiac

Channels of Expression

ARIES: fiery, pioneering, competitive
TAURUS: earthy, stable, practical
GEMINI: dual, lively, versatile
CANCER: protective, traditional
LEO: dramatic, flamboyant, warm
VIRGO: conscientious, analytical
LIBRA: refined, fair, sociable
SCORPIO: intense, secretive, ambitious
SAGITTARIUS: friendly, expansive
CAPRICORN: cautious, materialistic
AQUARIUS: inquisitive, unpredictable
PISCES: responsive, dependent, fanciful

Elements

FIRE: Aries, Leo, Sagittarius
EARTH: Taurus, Virgo, Capricorn
AIR: Gemini, Libra, Aquarius
WATER: Cancer, Scorpio, Pisces

Qualities

CARDINAL	FIXED	MUTABLE
Aries	Taurus	Gemini
Cancer	Leo	Virgo
Libra	Scorpio	Sagittarius
Capricorn	Aquarius	Pisces

CARDINAL signs mark the beginning of each new season — active.
FIXED signs represent the season at its height — steadfast.
MUTABLE signs herald a change of season — variable.

Celestial Bodies

Generating Energy of the Cosmos

Sun: birth sign, ego, identity
Moon: emotions, memories, personality
Mercury: communication, intellect, skills
Venus: love, pleasures, the fine arts
Mars: energy, challenges, sports
Jupiter: expansion, religion, happiness
Saturn: responsibility, maturity, realities
Uranus: originality, science, progress
Neptune: dreams, illusions, inspiration
Pluto: rebirth, renewal, resources

Glossary of Aspects

Conjunction: two planets within the same sign or less than 10 degrees apart, favorable or unfavorable according to the nature of the planets.

Sextile: a pleasant, harmonious aspect occurring when two planets are two signs or 60 degrees apart.

Square: a major negative effect resulting when planets are three signs from one another or 90 degrees apart.

Trine: planets four signs or 120 degrees apart, forming a positive and favorable influence.

Quincunx: planets are 150 degrees or about 5 signs apart. The hand of fate is at work and unique challenges can develop. Sometimes a karmic situation emerges.

Opposition: a six–sign or 180º separation of planets generating positive or negative forces depending on the planets involved.

The Houses — *Twelve Areas of Life*

1st house: appearance, image, identity
2nd house: money, possessions, tools
3rd house: communications, siblings
4th house: family, domesticity, security
5th house: romance, creativity, children
6th house: daily routine, service, health
7th house: marriage, partnerships, union
8th house: passion, death, rebirth, soul
9th house: travel, philosophy, education
10th house: fame, achievement, mastery
11th house: goals, friends, high hopes
12th house: sacrifice, solitude, privacy

Eclipses

Elements of surprise, odd weather patterns, change and growth are linked to eclipses. Those with a birthday within three days of an eclipse can expect some shifts in the status quo. There will be four eclipses this year, one is total and three are partial.

August 12, 2026—New Moon—total solar eclipse in Leo, South Node

August 28, 2026—Full Moon—partial lunar eclipse in Pisces, North Node

February 6, 2027—New Moon—partial solar eclipse in Aquarius, North Node

February 20, 2027—Full Moon—partial lunar eclipse in Virgo, South Node

A total eclipse is more influential than a partial. The eclipses conjunct the Moon's North Node are thought to be more favorable than those conjunct the South Node.

Retrograde Planetary Motion

Retrogrades promise a change of pace, different paths and perspectives.

Mercury Retrograde

Impacts technology, travel and communication. Those who have been out of touch return. Revise, review and tread familiar paths. Affected: Gemini and Virgo

February 26–March 21, 2026
in Pisces

June 30, 2026–July 24, 2026
in Cancer

October 25, 2026–November 14, 2026
in Scorpio

February 10, 2027–March 4, 2027
in Pisces and Aquarius

Venus Retrograde

Venus retrograde influences art, finances and love. Affected: Taurus and Libra

October 4, 2026–November 14, 2026
in Scorpio and Libra

Mars Retrograde

The military, sports and heavy industry are impacted. Affected: Aries and Scorpio.

January 11, 2027–April 1, 2027
in Virgo and Leo

Jupiter Retrograde

Large animals, speculation, education and religion are impacted. Affected: Sagittarius and Pisces

December 13, 2026–April 12, 2027
in Leo

Saturn Retrograde

Elderly people, the disadvantaged, employment and natural resources are linked to Saturn. Affected: Capricorn and Aquarius

July 27, 2026–December 11, 2026
in Aries

Uranus Retrograde

Inventions, science, electronics, revolutionaries and extreme weather relate to Uranus retrograde. Affected: Aquarius

September 11, 2026–February 9, 2027
in Gemini

Neptune Retrograde

Water, aquatic creatures, chemicals, spiritual forces and psychic phenomena are impacted by this retrograde. Affected: Pisces

July 8, 2026–December 13, 2026
in Aries

Pluto Retrograde

Ecology, espionage, birth and death rates, nuclear power and mysteries relate to Pluto retrograde. Affected: Scorpio and Aries

May 7, 2026–October 16, 2026
in Aquarius

ARIES

March 20–April 19

Spring 2026–Spring 2027 for those born under the sign of the Ram

Moving onward while carving out a new and very individual life path appeals to this Mars-ruled cardinal fire sign. Aries, you are the zodiac's courageous optimist. Your enthusiasm and generosity of spirit often will inspire and motivate others.

March 20–30 Venus will conjoin your Sun. Your charm and charisma will attract admiration and the support of others. As April begins you will be influenced by Saturn, an awareness of responsibilities and a need for greater stability and security develops. April 10–May 18, Mars transits your birth sign. This generates energy and promotes a competitive urge. Much can be accomplished if you control anger and impatience. Focus on peace and forgiveness while celebrating May Day. Late May favors planning a family vacation or home improvement projects.

Throughout June financial issues will be in your thoughts. Pay attention to managing and budgeting your earnings. The New Moon on June 14 highlights the specifics. Your inner child surfaces at the Summer Solstice. Incorporate a favorite game or hobby into ritual celebrations as you welcome the Summer season. July highlights repeating cycles directly related to family life. Take time to understand your heritage. A relative who has been out of touch may visit. At Lammas, August 1, your sector of love and leisure is highlighted by both Jupiter and the Sun. The growth and accomplishments of a loved one will delight you. A favorite hobby or entertainment brightens the mellow Summer days. The solar eclipse on August 12 brings insights concerning creative projects.

September 1–10 a Venus opposition strengthens relationships. Teamwork and group efforts set the pace through the Autumn Equinox. The Full Moon in Aries on September 26 promises recognition and appreciation. On September 28 a favorable Mars influence begins which lasts through Halloween. At a Halloween celebration, prepare a ritual fire of sacred wood. Include oak and pine. A cosmic warrior theme can inspire your perfect costume this year. Your energy level and vitality will intensify during the colorful weeks of Autumn. You will welcome a new challenge. Business and pleasure will meld together from mid October through November 25.

December brings positive influences from the Sun and Mercury. Travel December 7–25 provides refreshing new perspectives. Both Saturn and Neptune complete retrograde cycles in Aries during December. This deepens your awareness regarding situations and associations which you've outgrown. At the Winter Solstice the mood is one of looking toward the future unencumbered by obsolete patterns.

January 1–13, 2027 is an excellent time to update your job skills. Consider what is current and innovative regarding your interests and field of expertise. The last half of January through Candlemas on February 2 brings spiritual insights involving the fine arts and poetry. Accept invitations then. Attending an event or gathering enriches your life. There is a sense of making up for lost time during early February. By February 9, Uranus completes its retrograde in your 3rd house. Transportation issues are resolved during late February and March. A cycle begins which facilitates better communication in all ways, including electronic means, conventional mail, face to face meetings and conversations. February 2–March 19, Mars joins Jupiter to create a favorable aspect involving your sector of recreation and pleasure. An enjoyable avocation can become a more important part of your life as the Winter ends. Rapport with someone you love and admire deepens then too.

HEALTH

November 26, 2026–February 21, 2027, Mars will make a long transit through your 6th house of health. This entire time favors overcoming past health challenges and forming good health habits. The eclipse on February 20, 2027 starts a time to pay close attention to what your body is indicating. Health changes can surface then. Usually your body will respond well to regular exercise. In general Aries can be prone to depression because your birth sign rules the head and brain. It is always important for you to avoid negative and redundant people and uncomfortable or wearisome surroundings.

LOVE

The eclipse on August 12 promises some changes in love. A current connection can move in a new direction near that date. Jupiter, the most fortunate of planets, begins a year long transit through your sector of romance on July 2. Love prospects will be bright and promising, on the whole, from early July throughout the remainder of the year.

SPIRITUALITY

2026 begins a 14 year long transit of Neptune through Aries. You are starting an important cycle which will enhance lifelong spiritual growth. In the Pancha Pakshi zodiac, your spirit bird is the hummingbird. The quick, energetic, impatient and territorial hummingbird relates to the planet Mars, ruler of Aries. In the Andes mountain cultures humming birds are linked to happiness. When seeking a spiritual experience, recall this legend about the hummingbird. "Long ago when the world was younger, a demon was gambling with the Sun and lost. Angered, the demon caused a volcano to erupt. Other birds and animals were paralyzed with fear and many perished. However, a group of brave hummingbirds flew in all directions away from the flames and called upon the clouds to bring cooling rains. The fires were extinguished. Forever afterward the hummingbirds were colored in red, yellow, orange and other beautiful shades."

FINANCE

Near your birthday this year, Venus will brighten your sector of finance during the period March 31–April 23. Pursue promising financial opportunities and strategies at that time. Meditate at the Full Moon on October 26. Insights and guidance regarding your finances are likely to develop then.

TAURUS

April 20–May 20

Spring 2026–Spring 2027 for those born under the sign of the Bull

Symbolized by The Bull, this Venus ruled fixed Earth sign accents stability, comfort and abundance. Loyalty and reliability are constants in your life.

A yearning for peace and privacy envelopes you as the Springtime begins. Quietly, you will be drawn toward involvement in volunteer work, especially if there is an opportunity to facilitate charitable deeds. April 1–23, Venus brightens your birth sign—both finances and social prospects will be promising. Late April through May Day, disruptive Uranus finally exits Taurus, completing a seven year cycle which has been quite chaotic. A sense of order and clarity builds as your celebrate your birthday. Travel plans can be discussed and decisions made by May 17. Mars enters Taurus from the end of May through June 28. This generates enthusiasm and motivation. You can attain goals and successful competition. Midsummer's Day brings confidence and strength. On July 1, Jupiter begins a year long transit through your sector of home and heritage. You will have many thoughts about improving your residence and HEALING troubled family dynamics. Deep patriotic feelings touch the July Fourth holiday. Plan a picnic or attend a parade to celebrate the beauty and promise of America.

Mid July through August 7 Venus affects your 5th house of creativity and pleasure. Enjoy music and the visual arts as well as sports and games. Lammas, on August 1, is a time to socialize. There is genuine camaraderie. August 10–25 a family member or close associate will feel the need to share both concerns and joys. Take time to listen and comment. September 1–30 health and fitness goals are accented. Planning wholesome meals and an exercise regime would be beneficial for both you and your loved ones. A beloved pet can need extra attention near September 21–23, at the Autumn Equinox. Venus, your ruler, turns retrograde in October, where it will impact your relationship sector until November 14. A close partnership can be stressed; cope by analyzing repeating patterns. Seek fairness and balance in resolving any differences. Careful budgeting and seeking the best price in purchasing expensive items is advisable from early October until mid November. The Full Moon in Taurus on October 16 highlights the specifics. A Mercury aspect during October and November generates some controversy and debate. Listening and compromising rather than maintaining your usual bullish stubbornness allows you to resolve differences by December 7.

The Winter holiday season is highlighted by a favorable influence from Mars. Enjoy Winter sports and other activities outside the home. Natural decorations, especially including live plants, would be good choices for Yule decor. At the Winter Solstice, make a wreath or other decorative arrangements of pine cones and fragrant branches. Add a bayberry or beeswax candle to your altar or dinner table. December 26–January 13 your mental outlook will be optimistic. Communication of all kinds as well as travel plans will succeed because a harmonious Mercury aspect creates serenity.

In late January through the first part of February an eclipse combined with a stellium of transits, including Pluto, in your career sector can bring about changes in your job situation. Adapt. Think of a disruption or a new professional picture as an opportunity to learn and grow. Bless gold and white tapers at Candlemas on February 1–2 and add an appropriate affirmation for success. February promises to be a month of turning points in many avenues. A new direction for a child or other loved one can be a part of this near the partial eclipse on February 20. During March strong aspects from both Mars and Jupiter indicate choices to be made regarding both your home and work environments. Patience and the willingness to consider new perspectives will restore peace and productivity during the last days of Winter.

HEALTH

On June 19, 2026, Chiron will enter Taurus. This transit will last until July of 2033. This entire time emphasizes learning about maintaining both physical and emotional well-being. You might also find yourself facilitating the healing of others or becoming more interested in the field of health. Taurus has a spccial link with thc hcalth of thc ears and throat. Avoid exposure to loud noises. Protect the throat and ears during cold weather, too.

LOVE

April is bright with the promise of a Springtime of love. Venus will transit Taurus then. The Venus retrograde during October—November can revive the flame of an old or waning love. The eclipse on February 20, 2027 impacts your sector of romance. There can be a sudden change of heart or a new love connection at that time.

SPIRITUALITY

Charity and care giving are about to become key factors in your spiritual path for the future because Neptune starts a long transit through your 12th house this year. In India's Pancha Pakshi bird zodiac the bullfinch is your spiritual guide. Feeling most secure when close to the ground, this tiny and determined nest builder enjoys frequenting bushes which have juicy and delicious berries. It reflects the Taurean need for stability and fine cuisine. Bullfinch also is legendary for its exceptionally sweet singing voice.

FINANCE

The past seven years have been a financial rollercoaster because erratic Uranus has been in your birth sign. Taurus has a strong link to monetary matters so the fluctuations have affected you especially. A favorable aspect from Jupiter from the Spring Equinox through June promises good financial opportunities. At the New Moon in Taurus on May 16, writc a financial wish list and chant prosperity affirmations.

GEMINI

May 21–June 20

Spring 2026–Spring 2027 for those born under the sign of the Twins

This mutable, Mercury ruled air sign adapts easily to changes and variety. Expanded possibilities and multi–tasking delight the dual nature of the Twins. You revel in all types of communication, especially if stimulating word plays are involved. You are a clever independent thinker. Gemini is characterized by an energetic imagination which always keeps life interesting.

The Spring Equinox arrives just as Mercury completes its retrograde. A sense of relief and release engulfs you—the mood is upbeat and optimistic as the new season begins. March 22–April 9 brings a strong Mars aspect which inspires a competitive spirit. Your strong motivation supports attaining success and excellence. The last three weeks of April bring invitations from others. A group or organization can become a bigger part of your life. Community concerns or humanistic and charitable goals can be a part of this. On April 24, Venus enters Gemini where it remains until May 18. May brings improvement in finances as well as relationships. On May Day, create an altar decorated with fresh flowers to honor true love. May 19–June 1 Mercury will conjoin your Sun; pursue travel opportunities and focus on meaningful communication. Throughout June Jupiter is completing a passage in your 2nd house of income and valued possessions. A long desired purchase can be finalized and the financial picture is promising. Include a prosperity affirmation as you observe the Summer Solstice on June 21, the longest of days.

During July, Mars moves through Gemini. A more assertive side to you emerges. You might assume a position of leadership near Lammastide on August 1. If differences accelerate with others, focus on finding constructive solutions to problems rather than giving way to anger. Offer hospitality to create good will at a seasonal gathering. Serve delectable platters of bread and fruit. Late August through September brings several favorable transits through the air signs. Challenges and tensions will ease by the Autumn Equinox. Creative ideas which you communicate will win you admiration and support from others. An enjoyable hobby or favorite sport adds pleasure to the late Summer and early Autumn days. During October both Mercury and Venus will be retrograde in your financial sector. Be aware of repeating patterns involving your budget to find greater financial success. Use care if considering signing a contract or making other commitments. A déjà vu helps you to make wise decisions near All Hallows. A nostalgic theme or historic costume would be a good choice while celebrating Halloween.

After November 14 a more dynamic energy develops. The Full Moon on November 24 reveals the specifics. Your focus will turn toward the future, perhaps involving plans and purchases related to celebrating the Winter holiday season. From mid November through December 4 your personal charisma opens doors of opportunity. Business and pleasure combine well during this time. The Winter Solstice can bring some serious considerations to address involving your family dynamics and residence. Mars will be affecting your 4th house. A relative can need extra support and understanding or there could be an issue involving a home repair and maintenance coming to the forefront. Include a house blessing or affirmation for domestic harmony and peace while observing the longest of nights on December 21.

January brings suggestions and plans from others. A Venus opposition indicates that these ideas are positive and will have your best interests at heart. Listen carefully and be receptive to considering what is presented. As February begins, business related travel can be productive. Light a blue candle to assure a safe journey at Candlemas. The eclipse on February 6 promises to be very interesting. Its influence opens new horizons and wider perspectives. The remainder of February evokes a contemplative mood. Loving memories of friends or relatives who have passed away bring comfort as the month ends. March highlights Mars and Jupiter influences in your 3rd house. Transportation concerns can be resolved. During the last days of Winter, communication, especially with a neighbor or sibling, improves, providing you with worthwhile answers and insights.

HEALTH

On April 26 Uranus will begin a seven, year transit in your first housc. Innovative health care and a change in personal habits can have a long term impact on your wellness picture. Your birth sign is often prone to seasonal allergies, stress related illnesses and respiratory concerns. Care of the hands and arms is also an important consideration. When Uranus completes its retrograde on February 9, 2027, health concerns can be successfully addressed. The late Winter begins a promising cycle of renewed strength and well being.

LOVE

April 24–May 18, August 7–September and the last half of November are promising for attracting happiness in love. Mental stimulation and enjoyable communication will always be supportive factors in nurturing true love. Above all, Gemini must avoid boredom within close relationships.

SPIRITUALITY

Neptune's presence in your 11th house this year shows spiritual growth through enjoying meditation and other spiritual activities involving a circle of like minded friends. The Full Moon on September 26 is a time when spiritual awakening and insights can develop. In the Pancha Pakshi bird zodiac, the mischievous and curious woodpecker relates to Gemini. This association goes way back to Roman times. It was Woodpecker who helped Romulus and Remus, the infant twins, by guiding the wolf who rescued them to find food.

FINANCE

From the Spring Equinox until June 30, lucky and benevolent Jupiter will transit your 2nd house of money and property. Pursue financial opportunities then to establish long-term prosperity.

CANCER

June 21–July 22

Spring 2026–Spring 2027 for those born under the sign of the Crab

The Crab, enclosed in its protective shell, is always surrounded by its home. Maintaining that place of safety and belonging characterizes those born under this Moon-ruled, cardinal Water sign. Naturally gentle, hospitable and a caregiver, you are likely to find that close family relationships are often at the core of your life. Cancerians are generous, sensitive and sentimental. You appreciate keepsakes and collectibles that preserve memories and honor your heritage.

Throughout the Springtime, benevolent Jupiter blesses your birth sign. A wide range of activity and possibility is present. March 20–April 8 a supportive Mars aspect provides confidence and initiative—much can be accomplished. From mid to late April your thoughts will focus on business travel and new developments related to career goals. On May Day reflect upon ways you can ease the worries and concerns of those in need. May 17–31, thoughts and conversations will center upon business and managing resources. June 1–13, Venus will brighten your 1st house. All that is artistic and beautiful will captivate you. Attend the theater, visit an art gallery or experiment with creative crafts. Mercury affects you from shortly before the Summer Solstice through August 9. Travel, especially along or over the water, highlights your birthday. Because Mercury will be retrograde in your birth sign during most of July, you will be in the mood to reminisce. A visit involving people or places linked to your past can bring much pleasure. At Lammas, assemble an album or scrapbook to record precious Summertime and birthday memories. Appreciate all that you have achieved.

During August, a hectic cardinal sign pattern promises a busy schedule. Prioritize. Pace yourself to avoid feeling overwhelmed. Retrograde Saturn will square your Sun. An ambitious goal tantalizes you. Mars will conjoin your Sun in September. Your motivation will be high and challenges will be exhilarating. Sports and other competitive activities can interest you near the Autumn Equinox. Celebrate Fall by appreciating nature and savoring the rewards of your efforts. After September 27, it will be easier to diffuse anger and stress. On October 4, Venus turns retrograde in your sector of romance and pleasure. A loved one needs understanding, kindness and support from you. Celebrate Halloween with simple, comfortable and traditional treats and decorations. Can you recycle a costume from yester–year? During October and the first half of November, review your budget. Seek the best price if shopping for costly items. November 15–30 Venus highlights your home and family sector. You can take pride and find pleasure in the accomplishments of a loved one. Decorating your dwelling and hosting a holiday gathering would be especially successful and enjoyable. During

December both Saturn and Neptune will complete retrograde cycles in your career sector. Long-term projects related to your professional efforts conclude on a high note shortly before the Winter Solstice. Express gratitude on the longest of nights. On December 23 meditate on the Full Moon which will be in Cancer. Feelings and insights stirred by this lunation can reveal the presence of a benevolent spirit guide. Welcome it and the guide will remain with you through the end of December.

January 1–7 brings a favorable Venus aspect. Accept invitations. Cultivate the company of someone you care about. Relationships of all kinds are favored. Mars will turn retrograde in your 3rd house by mid January. Be diplomatic regarding all communication throughout the remainder of the month. Soften an angry response during an annoying conversation or email by adding a bit of humor and offering a constructive suggestion. Address transportation needs during January. At Candlemas, on February 2nd, dedicate altar candles in beautiful shades of blue to facilitate understanding as well as safe, easy journeys. February 3–18 Others might request your participation in a volunteer project. Take this opportunity to win affection and do a good deed. February 19–March 4, Pluto and Mercury will both impact your 8th house of mysteries. There could be a puzzle to solve. There are important facts to uncover. Throughout Winter's last days, be aware of current trends involving economic factors. There might be worthwhile business opportunities to explore. Timing will be important.

HEALTH

A sensitive digestive system often is the source of your health concerns. Consume wholesome foods in several small meals during the day. Avoid eating when you're upset or stressed. From the Spring Equinox through June 30, Jupiter, the zodiac's healer, will transit your birth sign. That time favors healing and meeting wellness goals.

LOVE

Venus will highlight your love and romance sectors September 11–October 25 and again December 5–January 7. Heartwarming love connections can develop at those times. The Full Moon on May Day also favors love. Plan either a cozy evening at your house including a home cooked meal or a romantic day at the beach near May 1.

SPIRITUALITY

On August 28, the lunar eclipse awakens spiritual potentials. In the Pancha Pakshi bird zodiac the Swan is your spiritual messenger. This graceful bird is at ease in Water, your element. Its feathers form crescent shapes, suggesting the lunar phases. The tale of the Ugly Duckling, an ugly hatchling who grows into a beautiful swan, parallels the challenging path Cancerians must tread toward spiritually awakening.

FINANCE

A working from home situation, or a home based or family owned business will often be lucrative for you. A very promising financial cycle occurs for you this year starting on July 1 and continuing through the end of Winter.

LEO

July 23–August 22

Spring 2026–Spring 2027 for those born under the sign of the Lion

Dignified, confident and ruled by The Sun, this fixed sign of Fire is symbolized by the magnanimous Lion. Quality and generosity are your hallmarks. You are creative and will set the stage of your life as a journey to be approached with a theatrical flair.

From the Spring Equinox through early April, the focus of conversations and priorities will center upon gathering information involving financial management. April 10–May 18, Mars favorably aspects your Sun. Your enthusiasm and motivation will be high. Much can be accomplished. On May Day meditate on and visualize a cherished goal. From late May through the Summer Solstice your 11th house is highlighted. Friends will be a source of encouragement and inspiration. Long range goals can be a topic of special interest. On the longest of days, invoke the light of the Sun for guidance concerning paths you might follow and connections which can be nurtured. Jupiter enters Leo as July begins. Your natural charm and charisma are in evidence during the weeks before your birthday. The Summer can bring promising career opportunities as well as stellar social connections. The scope of your life widens during July and August. At Lammas reflect upon potentials and prospects. The total solar eclipse on August 12 reveals how the direction of your life is shifting. Be flexible. Mercury moves rapidly through Leo during mid August. Valuable insights and information comes along which helps you to make the best decisions and choices.

During September family life and events within your neighborhood will attract your attention. Conversations and meetings about making needed improvements will be the focus as the Autumn Equinox nears. A compromise can smooth over a volatile situation. On September 28, Mars enters Leo, a transit which sets the pace through November 25. A competitive spirit arises. Be considerate. Maintain a sense of humor so you can reach a truce if any situations become volatile near Halloween. Design a costume featuring a favorite mythological figure. Emphasize the color orange. A solar deity or a divine feline, perhaps a sphinx or a cat, would be good costume options. Venus and Mercury both complete retrograde cycles on November 14. An ease will envelope relationships of all kinds after that. A former adversary becomes a friendly supporter by early December. A favorable Mercury transit December 7–25 promises good mental rapport with young people. A child's achievements can be a source of pride. The weeks near the Winter Solstice also favor planning holiday travels and visits. Share a toast of hot mulled cider with kindred spirits on the longest of nights. Plan a gathering around a blazing fire to make the Winter holiday celebrations especially memorable. From late December through mid January health considerations are important. Collect information related to fitness and wellness. Select wholesome foods and maintain good health habits during this time. The Full Moon in Leo on January 22 promises a shift in focus. Insights will develop then concerning your personal priorities and the goals you would benefit from pursuing during the year ahead. At Candlemas on February 2nd dedicate a silver or gold candle to illuminate the path ahead.

By February 4 a Venus transit begins which will generate a desire to promote camaraderie, goodwill and an upbeat atmosphere in your workplace. Focus on making the daily grind more pleasant. This Venus influence also points to deeper connections with a beloved animal companion. Your heart can be warmed in mid February by connecting with a new pet. During March, Mars will be retrograde in Leo. This favors keeping the peace with any difficult people. An old disappointment can be viewed from a new perspective as Winter fades into Spring. Winter's last days promise much personal growth.

HEALTH

The back and spine, with a focus on maintaining good posture, are likely to be at the center of any health concerns. A yoga practice with a focus on these areas might be beneficial to your overall health. From July 1 throughout the remainder of the year, Jupiter, the healer and greater benefic among the planets, will be in Leo. This entire time period indicates enhanced health of the body, mind and spirit.

LOVE

This year Pluto is in the midst of a very long and intense transit through your relationship sector. Past life contacts and other karmic factors can transform love connections in your life. Leo, you will always want a partner to feel proud of. Favorable situations regarding true love are likely to develop June 14–July 9 and again January 8–February 4. The eclipse on February 6, 2027 can mark an important choice regarding a significant relationship.

SPIRITUALITY

Neptune's impact in your 9th house this year favors spiritual growth through attending metaphysical classes, discussion groups and meditation circles. In the Pancha Pakshi bird zodiac, your spiritual messenger is the large and magnificent eagle. The protector of the king in ancient Egypt was linked with this noble bird. The Aztecs also related the eagle to the celestial realm. Soaring high, the powerful eagle seems to exude confidence and superiority.

FINANCE

July 10–August 6 brings a favorable Venus transit to your financial sector. Cultivate monetary opportunities which are available then. February 20, 2027 a partial lunar eclipse will affect your sector of income and finance. Be flexible concerning your financial plans near that time. Changes in your source of income can develop which will require an adjustment in the status quo.

VIRGO

August 23–September 22

Spring 2026–Spring 2027 for those born under the sign of the Virgin

The Virgin supports the quest for perfection and purity. Eliminating confusion and disarray, organizing while maintaining wholesome, healthy living and working conditions is your focus. This mutable Mercury ruled sign of Earth is helpful and reliable. Your intelligence attracts awe and wins respect.

At the Spring Equinox Mercury, your ruler, is completing a retrograde cycle. The start of the new season brings a renewed sense of direction and purpose. Mercury and Mars oppose your Sun during the first part of April. Compromise to maintain good working and personal relationships. A competitive mood is present. April 8–23, Venus creates a pleasant influence. Schedule vacation travel to celebrate Spring break. By May Day career aspirations occupy your thoughts. Dedicate a ritual, meditation or affirmations to open new professional horizons. May 1–18 messages from the afterlife and happy memories of loved ones who have passed away bring a sense of peace and closure. It's a good time to decorate a gravesite memorial or create a legacy.

Throughout late May and June, Jupiter completes a long transit through your sector of long term hopes, wishes and social connections. "Go for it," regarding a cherished secret dream which you've been nurturing. A dream can easily become a reality this year. By July 10 Venus enters your birth sign. This upbeat transit lasts through August 6. A promising new relationship blossoms and the financial situation improves. At Lammas choose either love or money as a theme for the ritual of the early harvest. Others expect much from you during the remainder of August. Pace yourself to avoid getting overwhelmed. The extra efforts you make will advance your position with both business and professional contacts. August 26–September 10, Mercury moves quickly through your 1st house. Travel can be very productive then. This time is also favorable for communication. Discuss concerns and be a good listener. Helpful answers emerge. The eclipse on August 28 marks a time of revelation. Uranus turns retrograde on September 11 in your sector of public recognition and success. This trend lasts until early February. The status quo changes. Expect the unexpected from colleagues. Be receptive to new trends impacting your career. At the Autumn Equinox dedicate rites to promoting prosperity. The colors and fragrances of Fall will carry healing qualities and attract spirituality .

At the end of September, Mars joins Jupiter in your 12th house. Until the end of November you will feel a need for some quiet time and solitary reflection. You could find solace in charity work, perhaps helping the homeless or hungry. At Halloween decorate to honor the humor of the season. Provide treats to bring smiles to the very young or the disadvantaged. On November 14 both Mercury and Venus complete retrograde cycles.

Throughout the remainder of November, you can release old regrets. A long term obligation draws to an end. A past trauma dissolves. December arrives as a strong Mars transit through Virgo commences. You will experience increased motivation and enthusiasm. This vibrant cycle lasts until late February of 2027.

Challenges and adventures will attract you throughout the Winter holiday season. Consider attending a new holiday event with friends. Travel to explore and enjoy the natural beauty of the Winter landscape.

December 26–January 12, Mercury affects your sector of hobbies and leisure. Your skill in all modes of communication will be especially impressive. This is a favorable time for making decisions. On January 11, Mars will turn retrograde in Virgo. This lasts until the end of Winter. Avoid expressing anger during this entire time. Seek a positive outlet to release stress. A light exercise program or arts and crafts projects would be good choices.

At Candlemas, on February 2, light pale pink candles dedicated to love and forgiveness. February 5–March 1, Venus will aspect your Sun. A playful and child-like quality touches all social connections. A friendship deepens into a romance near Valentine's Day. Business situations combine nicely with pleasure during mid February. Winter's final days, the first three weeks of March, find Mercury, Venus and Pluto all in your 6th house. Progress can be made in addressing any health challenges then, especially if they are stress related. March 1–20 accents connections with animal companions. You might welcome a new pet, perhaps a kitten, bunny or bird, into your life.

HEALTH

Pluto is moving through your health sector and will quincunx your Sun. Hereditary and environmental factors can impact your overall health. Try doing health related research in order to unravel the source of any mysterious health situations. The eclipse on February 6, 2027 puts you in touch with a treatment plan.

LOVE

Sharing mutual concerns and interests stimulates your love connections. Try gardening or cooking together. The lunar eclipse on August 28, 2026 affects your sector of close partnerships. A relationship can take a new twist near that time. July and February bring positive influences from Venus, the celestial love Goddess.

SPIRITUALITY

Places of natural beauty, especially forests and well manicured gardens, can provide an environment which will stimulate spirituality. In the Pancha Pakshi bird zodiac, dove is your spiritual messenger. An emblem of serene simplicity, the dove represents the purity of the Holy Spirit. Doves also are linked with the Goddess Aphrodite as well as to Saint Columba, whose name means dove.

FINANCE

Over the past several years a difficult aspect from Saturn has probably brought you financial challenges. That trend is drawing to a close now. The first three weeks of August can be especially profitable.

LIBRA

September 23–October 23

Spring 2026–Spring 2027 for those born under the sign of the Scales

Balance, justice and artistry are Libra's values. Maintaining harmony and fairness are your priorities. You're a natural diplomat. However, make sure that you don't lose sight of your own objectives in your efforts to please others and help put their situations at ease. This Venus ruled cardinal Air sign is attracted to all that is beautiful. Artistic appreciation and perhaps artistic talent, can feature prominently in your life.

Venus opposes your Sun at the Spring Equinox. This generates complex interactions and controversy. This trend lasts through March 30 when tranquility is restored. Mid April through May 2 sees a strong Mercury influence. Others will offer worthwhile suggestions and ideas. Dedicate May Day rites to nurturing both business and personal connections. During May a strong Mars aspect brings an unsettling competitive situation. Cope by drawing inspiration from others. June 1–13, Venus joins Jupiter in your career sector. Colleagues seek your professional expertise regarding work projects. By the Summer Solstice your efforts will generate profits as well as satisfaction. . On the longest of days, June 21, draw down the Sun with a meditation and invocation to honor the brightest and the best. As July begins, cardinal sign transits are strong. The pace is hectic. You can be impatient. Address concerns promptly. Delays can add to stress or frustration. By Lammas, on August 1, your sense of balance and perspective is restored. Create an early harvest altar of seasonal fruits and blossoms in appreciation for all the bounty that is available to you. Throughout August your days will be busy. You will find satisfaction by developing a deeper sense of community.

Venus will glide through your 1st house mid August–September 9. You will win the approval and acceptance of others. Compliments come your way. As the Autumn Equinox approaches, a Mercury influence accents travel opportunities. Accept and issue invitations September 10–30. During October favorable Mars and Jupiter aspects to your Sun bring help and advice from a friend or neighbor. Dedicated time and effort to a favorite charity near your birthday. At Halloween enjoy seasonal poems and stories. Select a comfortable traditional costume. During the first half of November, Venus will be retrograde in your financial sector. Budget carefully. Compare as a way to trim expenses. After November 14 a more prosperous cycle begins. Financial obligations are met by December 4. In mid December Saturn completes its retrograde in your section of partnerships. Someone close to you overcomes a health challenge or other troublesome issues. Trust your instincts. Your insight concerning a vulnerable person is especially on target after December 13. By the Winter Solstice hope and optimism are renewed regarding a loved one's well being. On December 21 quietly honor the longest of nights with restful destressing.

The new Moon on January 7 promises improved family dynamics. As January commences, redecorating your residence or even seeking a new home becomes a priority. By Candlemas, on February 2, new health goals are of interest. The eclipse on February 20 favors making wholesome changes regarding your menu choices. Allow more time for rest during the remainder of February. On March 2, Venus changes signs and forms a favorable trine to your Sun. This pleasant aspect remains in effect through the rest of the month. Your vitality will improve. Enjoy hobbies, games and other recreational activities as Winter draws to a close.

HEALTH

Saturn and Neptune will oppose your Sun all year. Avoid close contact with those who are unwell. Environmental factors can impact your health too. Your kidneys and lower back tend to be vulnerable. Therefore it is beneficial for you to drink plenty of fresh water. Take care not to risk injury to your lower back when engaged in demanding exercise or other physical activities.

LOVE

Pluto is making a long transit through your sector of love and romance. A past life attraction can add a new and intense yet unsettling dimension to your love life. The eclipse on February 26 reveals the specifics about the future direction of an intimate relationship. Favorable times for love include April 24–May 18, November 14–December 3 and the entire month of March, 2027.

SPIRITUALITY

Mystical Neptune, an important indicator of spirituality, is crossing the cusp of your section of partnerships this year. Contacts and connections with spiritually inclined people promise deeply spiritual experiences. In the Pancha Pakshi bird zodiac of India, the condor is Libra's sign. It directs your path toward spiritual growth. The condor, the largest member of the vulture family, glides effortlessly on wind currents for long distances. This reflects Libra's urge to avoid struggles and seek ease. As a scavenger, Condor clears away debris, adding beauty to the landscape and restoration of nature's balance. Condors mate for life, echoing romantic Venus ruled Libra's support of commitments.

FINANCE

October is an ideal time to study financial trends. Gather information then to gain insight into events which can impact your financial plans. The eclipse on August 28 affects your sector of inheritance, investments and financial settlements. Events which unfold near that date can shape your long term security. Make conservative and low risk choiccs this year. Patience pays off in the long run.

SCORPIO

October 24–November 21

Spring 2026–Spring 2027 for those born under the sign of the Scorpion

Forever seeking depth and intensity, the Scorpion remains inscrutable and secretive. The profound mysteries of life and death concern this passionate fixed sign of Water. Ruled by Pluto, transformation and renewal can be important themes in your life. Your approach is dynamic and resourceful. Insight and intuitive talent are present.

At the Spring Equinox both Mars and Mercury are favorably placed in your sector of romance and creativity. Add a note of artistry to your spiritual observances upon welcoming the new season. A journey linked to art appreciation or to attend a sporting event in early April can lead to romance and inspiration. April 15–30 promises a busy schedule and unusual pressure. Make time for self care and focus on healthy habits. Meditate on the Full Moon in Scorpio on May Day. Profound inspiration and prophetic dreams are likely. The first half of May can bring some sudden shifts in your familiar surroundings. Adapt. Associates will support new priorities regarding your everyday routine of work and service.

June 1–13 finds Venus moving in tandem with Jupiter in your 9th house. Expanding your horizons will become a priority. Enjoy imported items or educational travel. By the Summer Solstice on June 21 you will have outgrown some familiar activities. Your curiosity is piqued as July begins. The world news as well as anecdotes and ideas shared by a neighbor or coworker can encourage you to do some fact finding and analysis. By Lammas on August 1, a mystery is solved. August 1–11 after life connections are strengthened, prepare a seasonal altar to honor the fruits of your personal experiences. The eclipse on August 12 brings a comforting message from a spirit entity regarding a cherished ambition. During the last half of August through September an upbeat aspect from Mars generates renewed enthusiasm and motivation. At the Autumn Equinox on September 22 your confidence impresses an influential colleague. Bask in the warmth of the good reviews and positive notoriety which follows you through the end of the month.

October 1–25, Venus influences you. Purchasing items you've longed for as well as attending interesting and enjoyable events can be on your agenda as your birthday approaches. The Full Moon on October 26 attracts invitations. A relationship blooms, becoming a bigger part of your life. Networking opens doors of opportunity. Bright and beautiful accessories added to a plain and comfortable ritual robe would be a good choice for your Halloween costume. November 1–24, Mars and Jupiter will square your Sun. An ambitious and competitive edge develops. Your aspirations blossom. A new business or community project can propel you forward.

During December both Neptune and Saturn will complete their retrograde cycles. This affects your health sector. Faith and intuition guide you to select the wisest choices concerning wellness. A health challenge or concern can be resolved in a positive way near December 12. By the Winter Solstice on December 21 party invitations, greeting cards, decorations and other seasonal delights will be in abundance. Express gratitude for both long time friends and new acquaintances. During January, Mars affects your 11th house. Involvement within your social circle can become more of an effort than expected. You might feel inclined to step away from activity within an organization. The New Moon on January 7 reveals the specifics of this trend.

From late January through Candlemas, on February 2, connections with animal companions strengthen. Adopting a special cat, dog or other pet could brighten your life. Mid February–March 1 a Venus influence draws approval and encouragement from others. Suggestions you offer, perhaps at a meeting or gathering, are favorably received. By March 3 Venus joins Pluto in your sector of home and heritage. During the final weeks of Winter, home life and living arrangements are improving. A rift or misunderstanding with a relative can be healed. Reminisce while flipping through photo albums or rearranging collectibles to calm turbulent emotions and dispel regrets.

HEALTH

Your ruler, Pluto, forms several significant aspects involving your sector of residence and heredity. Health conditions can arise from inherited tendencies. Be alert to any potential health hazards around your home or neighborhood. These can be addressed and corrected near the time of the Full Moon on July 29. Improved vitality return during the Autumn. .

LOVE

Your birth sign often senses a past life connection regarding love. Undergoing a hypnotic regression or meditation session to address this can help you understand your feelings, therefore making the wisest choices regarding love. Venus makes two long transits through your birth sign September 11–October 25 and again December 5–January 7. Prospects are promising for nurturing romantic bliss at those times.

SPIRITUALITY

Neptune, the indicator of spirituality, is quincunx your Sun all year. This indicates that spiritual awakening can be affected by synchronicities and fate. In the Pancha Pakshi bird zodiac, the corvids—the ravens, crows, jackdaws, magpies and blackbirds are your spiritual messengers. In true Scorpio fashion corvids are mysterious and haunting shapeshifters. Clever and suspicious, these birds are thought to be able to speak as well as being able to secretly hoard and hide items which appeal to them.

FINANCE

Lucky Jupiter favors your birth sign from the Spring Equinox through June 30. Promising financial opportunities appear then. Plan a prosperity ritual at the Summer Solstice to attract good fortune. This year, on April 26, Uranus changes signs. This lessens the financial burdens brought by others in recent years.

SAGITTARIUS

November 22–December 20

Spring 2026–Spring 2027 for those born under the sign of the Archer

This Jupiter ruled mutable sign of Fire is symbolized by the Archer who forever aims high at distant and challenging targets. Your quest for complete freedom is approached with optimism and good cheer. Upbeat and entertaining, you impress and attract others with your warmth and confidence. The Archer is actually a Centaur, a half human and half animal creature. Animals, especially horses, are especially dear to you. Teaching, travel and trouble shooting are activities you'll gravitate toward.

At the Spring Equinox Mercury forms a tense aspect to your Sun. Bless a citrine crystal to improve communication skills. Conversations can be rather terse and blunt. Soften impatience with humor and empathy to smooth over any differences of opinion or misunderstandings. This lasts until April 14. April 15–28 a coworker or business associate seeks your assistance and advice. Lend a helping hand and make a new friend. Your vitality is excellent as May begins. May 1–18, Mars supports your health goals—your energy level is high. Late May through mid June, Venus joins Jupiter in your 8th house. Financial strategies brighten—a payment you're expecting can arrive. There is also a sense of helpful afterlife connections present. A spirit guide sends an omen. By the Summer Solstice connections with animal companions are accented. Spend quality time with a favorite pet or focus on wildlife rescue on the longest of days. During late June–July 9 recreation and pleasure are highlighted. Plan a vacation or attend sporting events. The growth and accomplishments shown by a younger person please you.

Mid July–August 11, a Mars opposition generates highly competitive situations. Try to understand the viewpoints of those who challenge you. Near the Full Moon on July 29 don't let an argument escalate. Compromise instead. At Lammas, on August 1–2, dedicate a meditation to celebrating peace. Share loaves of freshly baked bread as a gesture of friendship. The solar eclipse on August 12 highlights your 9th house. You'll long for adventure and new experiences. Enrolling in classes or visiting places of historical interest and natural beauty could appeal to you throughout August. September 1–22 Your career sector sets the pace. New developments affect your profession. Publications can offer helpful information and insights. Business travel, perhaps to attend a conference or seminar, can attract worthwhile connections. Throughout October, Mars will trine your Sun. This aspect brings the ability to take needed actions. This is also an excellent time to focus on exercise programs. For Halloween select a costume portraying a gypsy, traveler or superhero.

During November, Venus activates your sector of future plans and cherished dreams. A friend's offer can lead you to your heart's desire. You will find that camaraderie offers a source of valuable encouragement near your birthday. December 7–25 Mercury races through Sagittarius. You might find yourself speaking in public or writing important letters. On December 8 the New Moon in your birth sign is an excellent time to write a wish list or to set intentions using positive visualizations and affirmations. Holiday travel near the Winter Solstice motivates and uplifts you. Visitors who arrive near the Winter solstice on December 21 brighten and cheer the longest of nights.

January finds Mars squaring your Sun. This generates both stress and enthusiasm. Set boundaries in order to avoid becoming overwhelmed. Celebrate Candlemas on February 2 by lighting a circle of white votive candles symbolizing the brightest and best coming from all directions. February brings a favorable financial pattern. Heed creative inspiration and combine business with pleasure to contribute to financial security. The lunar eclipse on February 20 brings changes related to teamwork and partnerships.

March welcomes supportive influences from Mars and Jupiter in Leo as well as Saturn and Neptune in Aries. Both sets of these fire sign planets will trine your Sun. Your workload eases as Winter draws to a close. The New Moon on March 8 emphasizes family dynamics. A home decorating or repair project can make your residence more comfortable then.

HEALTH

A service animal or the companionship of a beloved pet can often add to your well being. Uranus exits your health sector on April 26. This ends a seven year cycle during which stressful situations have affected your health.

LOVE

A love connection which offers a challenge as well as permitting you to have plenty of freedom is ideal for you. You might be intrigued by someone from a foreign land or who is from a different ethnic background. Love connections are favorable March 20–30, June 14–July 9 and again January 8–February 3.

SPIRITUALITY

Your 9th house of spirituality is favorably influenced by Jupiter from July 1 through the Winter. Travel to spiritual sites as well as study and discussion groups linked to spirituality can widen your perspectives then. In the Pancha Pakshi bird zodiac your spiritual messenger is the lively and adventurous hawk. This high flying hunter soars over the landscape for an expansive view of all. Hawk's cry was once thought to warn travelers of treachery on the road ahead as well as providing a reminder not to be caught unaware.

FINANCE

Patience will help you to advance toward meeting financial goals this year. The Full Moon on June 29 highlights your financial sector. Study options and pursue financial opportunities near that date. January and February also promise positive financial trends.

CAPRICORN

December 21–January 19

Spring 2026–Spring 2027 for those born under the sign of the Goat

Getting results. That's what it's all about for this Saturn ruled cardinal sign of Earth. You are a hard worker. Like your symbol, the Goat, you focus on climbing high and on survival. You are serious and conscientious. Recognition and achievement motivate you. Yet you will often surprise others when you reveal your wry sense of humor and subtle wit.

At the Vernal Equinox the Sun joins Neptune and Saturn in your sector of home and heritage. Nuances and hunches are present as you seek insight into hereditary and environmental factors. There is an unsettled energy impacting your home life and family dynamics during late March and early April. Do a house blessing near the New Moon on April 17 to clear any stressful energy and restore tranquility. April 18–May 2 communication with loved ones improves. On May Day assemble May baskets to deliver to friends, family and neighbors. During the first half of May a strong Mars aspect generates a competitive mood. Focus on constructive efforts dedicated to home improvements. May 19–June 28 the pace will become more relaxed. Health and vitality improve by the Summer Solstice. Express gratitude for a goal which you have reached at the Full Moon in Capricorn on June 29.

On July 1, Jupiter begins a long transit in your 8th house which will last through the end of the year. This promises a gradual but steady return on an investment. A long term financial commitment or debt can be resolved, too. Throughout July a Mercury opposition inspires others to be more talkative. Listen. Consider suggestions which are offered. After July 24 differences are resolved. At Lammas, as August begins, a favor is returned and a relationship is strengthened. August 1–6 vacation travel and visits to places of cultural or spiritual significance can be enjoyed. Mid August through September 27 a Mars influence inspires a take charge kind of attitude from others. Allow a partner to pursue a dream near the Autumn Equinox. Celebrate the start of the fall season on September 22 by sharing a toast with someone who is dear to you.

During October a retrograde Venus highlights associations which were a part of your past. There can be an opportunity to bring closure to a situation linked to a troubling memory or regret. At Halloween create a costume or decoration which symbolizes your view of the future. On November 14 both Mercury and Venus will turn direct. You will experience elation as you reflect upon how much you have grown and how far you have come. The last half of November brings positive situations regarding work. A productive balance between business and pleasure emerges, allowing you to make headway in achieving your goals. By December 11 Saturn, your ruler, completes a retrograde cycle. This allows issues related to family matters to be resolved. At the Winter Solstice on December 21 a supportive Mars aspect brings a burst of energy and overall zest for life. You can enjoy Winter sports as well as travel. Maintain a spirit of adventure near your birthday.

December 26–January 13 a Mercury aspect blesses you with quick mental perceptions and heightened awareness. You will be able to evaluate situations quickly and make wise choices. Gather information through study and research. Be receptive to learning something new. A charitable endeavor speaks to your heart during late January. It is satisfying to help a person or animal in need at Candlemas on February 2. Venus brightens your life during most of February. A close relationship brings comfort and support. February also favors artistic and cultural activities. Attend a concert or theatrical production. Stroll through an art gallery to inspire your own creativity. During March, transits in your 2nd house emphasize values and cash flow. You're able to purchase a long desired item. March 5–18 is favorable for reviewing details related to financial management. During Winter's final days you will experience a vague sense of longing. Dreams center upon a cherished ambition.

HEALTH

Uranus touches your health sector all year. Be aware of changes regarding wellness. It's important to understand what signals your body is sending now.. Stress and extreme weather can affect your health. After Uranus completes its retrograde on February 9, 2027 you will bc ablc to address health concerns easily and reach fitness goals.

LOVE

February and April promise happiness from Venus, the celestial Love Goddess. Discussing ideas about reaching career and financial goals can strengthen love. Also visiting beautiful gardens or sharing time outdoors, perhaps camping or picnicking, can set the stage for a memorable love tryst. The Full Moon on October 26 holds potential for experiencing true love. Plan a romantic stroll at moonrise that evening.

SPIRITUALITY

Neptune, an indicator of spirituality, impacts your sector of study, communication and short journeys this year. Discussion groups and publications which explore spiritual topics can open new spiritual horizons for you. India's Pancha Pakshi bird zodiac features the mild mannered wren as your spiritual messenger. The wren copes with bleak and treacherous surroundings and yet survives and thrives.

FINANCE

Two of the eclipses this year, the total solar Leo eclipse on August 12 and the February 6, 2027, partial solar eclipse in Aquarius affect your 8th and 2nd houses, respectively. This indicates unexpected developments regarding money matters. Consider approaching finance in new ways and adapting to current financial trends. From July 1 through the end of Winter, Jupiter creates a protective influence impacting investments and inherited money. This is helpful for maintaining financial security.

AQUARIUS

January 20–February 18

Spring 2026–Spring 2027 for those born under the sign of the Water Bearer

Ruled by the ingenious and unpredictable planet Uranus, this fixed sign of Air is all about expressing uniqueness. You enjoy broadening connections and making new friends. The Water Bearer's jug pours the liquid energy of the life forces to connect the greater family of humanity. Technology, philanthropy and developing a broad perspective are all incorporated into your life focus. Aquarius is a futurist and visionary.

Effort, energy and attention are focused on your finances as the Spring Equinox arrives. March 20–April 9 you will be able to address financial needs and goals. April 10–23 Venus brightens your home and family life. A decorating project or entertaining visitors can add enjoyment to living circumstances. As May Day approaches a charitable project appeals to you. You can find satisfaction in extending a helping hand to those in need. May 2–18 favors social events. A friendship is strengthened. Explore creative expression, too. An art or writing project can be very productive and successful. Late May–June 30 your health sector is favorable. You can reach a fitness goal. Brew healthy herbal blends of citrus and mint teas to sip while you honor the Summer Solstice.

July marks the start of a long Jupiter transit which will impact your closest relationships and partnerships through the end of the year. Those closest to you will experience growth and success. You will bask in the glow of the successes of a loved one at Lammas on August 1. Serve fresh salads of seasonal fruits and vegetables as you discuss all the good that has happened in recent weeks. Early August–September 10 finds Venus impacting your 9th house. This is an excellent time for vacation travel, perhaps visiting sacred and spiritual sites. On September 11, Uranus begins a retrograde cycle. This influence creates a backdrop of déjà vu and coincidences which will offer insights about your life direction through February 9. This entire time favors drawing upon memories and experiences for guidance. September 11–30 a favorable Mercury influence stimulates your curiosity and sharpens your intellect. Near the Autumn Equinox draw upon the music and spiritual traditions of faraway lands to celebrate the fall season. During the first week of October Venus turns retrograde. Social connections and business responsibilities can clash, causing complications. Keep intimate relationships, personal feelings and romantic urges in perspective. Patience and detachment restore peace. On October 16, Pluto turns direct. Secrets surface. A sense of renewal and refreshment prevails as Halloween arrives. For your costume this year consider a marine theme. A boat captain, sailor or a mermaid are some workable ideas. Embellish your costume with seashells or navy insignia.

November 25–December 18 friendly spirits send subtle messages. A ghostly encounter is likely, especially when holiday decorations are being assembled. From the Winter Solstice through January 7 intuitive perceptions come during meditation sessions or when you recall dreams. January 14–31 Mercury moves through your birth sign. This heightens mental clarity and the ability to make wise choices. February begins with a Mercury–Mars opposition. Be careful about acting upon the advice of others, however well meant it might be. Go within to judge what feels right intuitively to you. At Candlemas, on February 2nd, dedicate green and gold candles and include frankincense incense on your altar to stimulate prosperity.

On February 6 the solar eclipse in Aquarius favors setting intentions for your birthday the year to come. Write a wish list. Changes are in the air. Adapt. Be flexible. Release all that seems to be outdated or irrelevant. By late February Mars joins Jupiter in your sector of partnership. Both planets will oppose your Sun. This promises some differences of opinion to over come. A competitive and challenging mood is brewing. Listen to what others have to say before engaging in an argument. By March 2, Venus enters Aquarius. On March 4, Mercury completes its retrograde. Mercury and Venus form a stellium with Pluto in your 1st house. This promises a turn for the better regarding a controversial situation. Differences can be amicably resolved as Winter draws to a close.

HEALTH

Beginning at the Spring Equinox and continuing through June 30, Jupiter, the celestial healer, will transit your health sector. This is a promising time for overcoming health challenges. Select the best diet and develop good health habits then. You are sensitive to temperature extremes, so wearing layered clothing is a helpful way to stay comfortable when conditions vary.

LOVE

On April 26, Uranus will begin a transit through your sector of pleasure and romance. Sudden meetings and partings can occur. Love connections are entering a phase of sparkle and excitement. Late April through May 18, August 7–September 10 and March 2–19 promise happiness in love.

SPIRITUALITY

Neptune, an indicator of spirituality, influences your 3rd house all year. This encourages exploring spiritually oriented studies and attending spiritual discussion groups. In the Pancha Pakshi bird zodiac the adaptable and sociable seagull is your spiritual messenger. Tales about the seagull shared by Welsh sailors refer to this bird's kindness to the souls of those who are lost at sea. The seagull is a true odd bird, a nonconformist who uplifts humanity yet remains true to itself.

FINANCE

This year two eclipses, one on August 28 and another on February 20, will impact your finances in unexpected ways. Be receptive to adapting to new economic trends. Consider trying new financial strategies. A promising income opportunity can arise between February 7 and the end of March, 2027.

PISCES

February 19–March 20

Spring 2026–Spring 2027 for those born under the sign of the Fish

The two Fish, attached yet swimming apart in different directions symbolize Pisces. Ruled by Neptune, this mutable sign of water is about completion as well as preparation. Forgiveness, sacrifice, sensitivity to color and sound, dreams, intuition and the ability to adapt are your special gifts. Compassionate as well as loyal, you are subtle and devoted in your quest for seeking beauty.

The Spring Equinox brings enthusiasm for planning. Mercury and Mars transit your birth sign March 20–April 9. Pursue travel then. April 10–23 bring friendly influences from Venus and Uranus. New acquaintances make suggestions or offer invitations. Late April and early May accent shopping for important purchases. May Day a bargain or treasure appears, perhaps disguised as a gift. May 2–14 you'll feel an urge to decorate your home or work space. Consider adding new curtains or intriguing conversation pieces. Mid May through June 30 a Jupiter influence inspires more involvement with neighbors and community concerns. Sing a cheerful song at the Summer Solstice on June 21. Follow up with a visualization dedicated to healing and good will.

As July begins, Mercury is retrograde—plan a reunion with beloved family members, classmates or friends who have been out of touch. Choose a vacation destination which is a familiar favorite place close to the waterfront. Late July through August 6 a partner's success is a source of joy. At Lammas celebrate and honor the achievements and dreams cherished by a loved one with a feast of seasonal fruits and breads.

Mid to late August animal companions bring joy. Near the New Moon on August 12 a new pet could enter your life. Intuitive connections with wild as well as domestic animals can be very strong at the lunar eclipse near the Pisces Full Moon on August 28. Throughout September a favorable Mars aspect to your Sun inspires an adventurous mood.

On October 1, Mercury begins a long transit through your 9th house. Throughout October and November you'll enjoy spiritual as well as academic studies. At this time it's easy to assimilate new ideas. Grandparent–grandchild interactions uplift and enlighten those on both sides of the generation gap. At Halloween a good costume choice would be to portray a favorite historic or fairy tale character. What about Queen Elizabeth, a sea captain, Little Red Riding Hood or the Big Bad Wolf?

December brings strong mutable sign transits. Others are assertive, even competitive. Lighten up if another's ideas are at odds with your own preferences. Neptune completes its retrograde on December 13, allowing you to release worn out habit patterns. At the Winter Solstice, on December 21, include bayberry candles on an altar decorated with pine cones to brighten the longest of nights. On January 8, Venus enters your career sector. Friendship and camaraderie is present. Appreciation comes your way. By Candlemas on February 2 a new alliance is formed. A promising opportunity is presented. The solar eclipse on February 6 sparks a need for some peace and quiet. Answers come from within regarding choices. Mid February awakens concerns for those who are in need. A charitable project attracts you, this might involve contributing to a food pantry. The lunar eclipse on February 20 brings a surprise decision involving a business associate or partner. Old contacts are being replaced. New faces appear as March begins. Write a wish list at the New Moon on March 8. Set intentions for the year to come as you celebrate your birthday. From mid March through the end of the Winter season on March 19 the influences of Saturn and Neptune in your financial sector will set the pace. A hunch or dream can be influential regarding money management. However, balance intuition with some practical research and analysis.

HEALTH

Jupiter enters your health sector on July 1 where it remains for the remainder of the year. This favors resolving any health issues and setting new health goals. Remember. Jupiter tends to expand everything. Control calorie consumption and limit portion sizes to avoid gaining weight. Pisceans are prone to foot maladies. Always wear comfortable shoes and care for your feet with foot massages and pedicures.

LOVE

It's a Springtime of love for you. From late March throughout April, May and June, your love and romance sector is positive. Dates that are especially good for love are May 18—June 13, September 10–October 3 and December 15–January 7. Avoid rekindling an old flame which wasn't good before while Venus is retrograde October 4– November 14.

SPIRITUALITY

Neptune, the spirituality indicator, hovers mysteriously in your 2nd house all year. Juggle financial choices with emotional values. The Pancha Pakshi bird zodiac places the nocturnal Owl harmoniously with your birth sign. Many Pisceans do tend to be night owls. The darkness suggest profound access to hidden knowledge gleaned during the night along with insightful dream interpretation. Athena, the Greek Goddess of wisdom, is one of the many deities associated with the Owl.

FINANCE

Illusion is at work. Good or not, it will be challenging to clarify what is happening with finances. Cope by collecting information about current financial trends and avoiding risk. Favorable times regarding money are April through May and December.

Sites of Awe

Pompeii

I REMEMBER my mother talking about wanting to visit Pompeii. She only mentioned it a couple of times, but it sank in and planted a seed. So, as I'm planning my trip to Naples, I saw a side tour to the ancient city. I'm buying my ticket!

As we arrive, I'm already excited—even before getting off the bus.

Now I walk the ancient streets of Pompeii with a sense of awe and reverence. My feet are covering the worn cobblestones that have witnessed centuries of community, mystery, magic and Pagan rites. The air seems heavy with energy, a strong mixture of history and myth, thick with the scent (imagined or not) of distant sulfur and ash. I am here not just as a traveler, but as a Witch, a seeker of the unseen, eager to touch the remnants of a world steeped in magic and divine reverence for the Gods and nature.

The Sun strikes hard today and the stone streets are getting hot. I've just stepped through the Porta Marina gate, where I imagine the sea breeze used to come through, cooling the city during the hot nights. The entrance is at the end of the inclined road, leading to a stone archway, this being what was once the main gate to the city.

The Temple of Apollo

The first place I visit is the Temple of Apollo, where the Sun God once held prominence. The remaining columns stand tall as guardians of a sacred space

Pompeii in the shadow of Vesuvius

The wild joy of the Dancing Faun endures.

where oracles would speak in tongues, delivering messages of prophecy. As I light a small imaginary candle, placing it carefully on a fallen stone. Offering a silent prayer to Apollo for clarity and wisdom, I am imagining the temple in its full glory, some 2000 years ago, with statues gleaming with gold leaf, priests clad in flowing robes and the scent of burning laurel drifting through the air. Perhaps the Gods have not truly abandoned this place. Perhaps they simply sleep beneath the ash and ruin, waiting for someone to remember. I'm looking at the blue sky, the green grass, and between them, the stone steps as if reaching out for someone to know, remember and ascend the steps once more.

Outside, our tour group moves slowly forward, but I keep to the edges. Past the temple of Apollo, the earth smells more mineral, almost coppery. It is easy to fantasize about priests performing rituals, great clouds of incense rising, chanting echoing through the sacred space. Apollo, the God of prophecy, healing and the Sun, would have been deeply established here. I pause, taking a moment to honor him, feeling the Sun's warmth on my face as a sign of his presence and acceptance of my offering—of today's time.

The House of the Faun

A pigeon startled me from the eaves above, trying to "grace" me with a pigeon gift, long known in Italy as a sign of good luck. Fortunately (unfortunately?) he missed me. I watch the pigeon disappear into the remnants of a home—the House of the Faun. Taking it as a sign, I choose to follow this bird. The mosaic at the threshold still pulses with color: "HAVE"—

”welcome,” it says. I cross over, and for a moment, I feel something move beneath my feet, in the shallow of the ground below. Not physically, but energetically. Like stepping onto a current. The faun, frozen in dance, seems to acknowledge my presence, his eyes meeting mine with an ancient gaze.

Inside, the air is different. Cooler, and again a metallic undertone of some kind. The statue of the dancing faun holds his posture forever—arm raised, hip cocked, locked in time. I decide to place my hand on the pedestal and close my eyes. In the darkness, with my inner eye, I see fire. Not the destructive fire of Mount Vesuvius, but a sacred flame, both dancing and alive. I removed my hand, opened my eyes, and now feel a sense of reverence for the spirit that still dwells here. This faun lives!

The Forum and Public Spaces

I move on, feeling the weight of history with each step. The Forum, the heart of Pompeii, was once a busy hub of activity. Politicians, merchants and citizens of the city would have gathered here, their voices filling the air with debate, news and gossip. At least, this is how I imagine it, or would like to imagine Pompeii in the dreamworld that I carry inside. I can almost hear the echoes of their footsteps, the clatter of chariots and the cries of vendors selling their wares. I understand that the Gods were everywhere in this city, in every aspect of life. And their presence can still be felt, a residual energy that pulses beneath the surface. It takes many years to wipe away the energy of a bustling city like Pompeii.

I have stopped at the edge of the Forum Baths to see the mosaic floors and the barrel vaults. As I inhale deeply, there seems to be the scent of crushed laurel leaves, perhaps even a hint of frankincense. Were these the ghosts of offerings from two thousand years ago? I can almost hear whispered prayers under the vaulted ceilings. These are not Christian prayers—no—these are older. Invocations to the Lares—the household spirits. Whispers of women touching the marble edges of the Caldarium, praying for safe childbirth or victory for their sons. The energy here is palpable, a mixture of hope and devotion, with a slight sense of fear that their prayers may not be answered!

The Villa of the Mysteries

As I expected, the energy shifts again as I find myself entering the Villa of the Mysteries. The doorway is before me, and beyond it, that room—the one painted in deep shades of red. On the walls, is a ritual frieze, a procession of figures. They say it is Dionysian. It could be, or maybe it is something more complicated. I'm thinking something older. I sit cross-legged on the cool stone floor, as I put my back against a carved bench for support—I'm not getting any younger!

As I breathe, the air seems musty but sacred at the same time. Am I imaging this or is chalky dust rising from the floor with each breath I take? I close my eyes and feel a pulse from the silence. It is faint but it is also very rhythmic. Like a drumbeat through time. I am very happy to have visited the Villa.

The Necropolis and Mount Vesuvius

Back outside, the sky looks as if it is a stretched out piece of golden fabric. The wind is picking up. Somehow, I can smell, or sense, salt, olive and charred wood. Are these really here, or a sense from the distant past? I walk toward the Necropolis. The dead, and there are many, have tombs that are covered in moss, the inscriptions worn by time but mostly still legible. I trace one with my finger, and there it is—that earie feeling that I knew would come. Silly me. I've tapped on the shoulder of the dead.

Suddenly, I am finding myself remember the charcoal bodies that I saw earlier—one on what appeared to be a shelf and one on the ground in front of it. Perfectly preserved in ash. Now I feel watched as I sit beside the tomb, place my palms on the Earth and close my eyes. I won't speak—I'll just attempt to feel what I cannot see. The ground beneath me is warm and dry but still filled with energy. When I finally open my eyes, there is a raven watching me from the wall opposite me. It doesn't make a sound. It just waits, and stares at me. Our line of site locked between us, I sense it knows that I acknowledge its presence, and it flutters once before taking flight off to the Northeast.

I am now in the Forum, where commerce and community once thrived. I'll pause to take in the energy of those who walked here before me. I can imagine the bustling marketplace with the exchange of goods and gossip, the long discussions about politics and daily life's activities. As I stand in the center, I can imagine the weaving of energies that create the spells, that work the magic of the marketplace. Mercury is happy here! Oops! Time to catch up to the group before I am left behind. I've been taking more time at each stop than the rest of the group that has chosen to only "observe" the material.

Further along, I find myself standing in the shadow of Mount Vesuvius, the great destroyer and creator. The looming

The Amphitheater of Pompeii framed by time and trees

presence of the volcano fills me with a mixture of fear and respect, a reminder of nature's power, which is capable of destruction and renewal. Once again, I close my eyes and feel the pulse of the Earth beneath my feet. Vesuvius is no mere mountain—it is a sleeping God. I gather a handful of volcanic soil, knowing it holds potent energy, perfect for spells of transformation and resilience. It will be added to my magical apothecary at home. And, of course, some will be given as gifts to friends of like mind, that is if it doesn't get taken at customs. Fingers crossed!

The Amphitheater

Leaving the Necropolis, I make my way by the Temple of Isis. I know that Isis was worshiped here, as in most Mediterranean cities, but I am still a wee bit surprised to find this temple in Pompeii. I will now make my way to the Amphitheater. This is truly a grand structure that would have hosted gladiatorial contests and other public and religious events. The seats are carved from stone and provide a panoramic view of the arena. What it must have been like to hear the roar of the crowd, the clash of steel, the cheers that once were heard here! The energy here is raw and primal.

As I stand in the amphitheater, I realize that this is the place where many people came together. It is the part of this complex where large numbers of people, filling these seats, their hearts pounding with excitement once gathered, and it feels different—almost ghostly crowded. I can almost see the processions, the parades, the rituals that would have taken place here. The air is electric, charged with the residue of so many lives.

The Lupanar

Although there is more to see, my final stop is the Lupanar, the brothel, a place of pleasure and desire. The small rooms, decorated with erotic frescoes, look back to a time when the Gods of love and lust were honored in the most primal of ways. Here the Gods were invoked in the act of love.

The Gods of love, Venus and Cupid, would have been recognized here, their images adorning the walls, silently listening to the whispers of desire.

Departure

Exiting the Lupanar, our group is gathering and it is time to leave Pompeii. I take one last look at the city. Pompeii lives again—not in ruin, but in my memory. I can almost see the city as it once was, vibrant and alive, its streets filled with the laughter and the chatter of its people. The Gods are here, their presence a living, breathing entity that pulses through the very heart of Pompeii.

I came as a tourist, a seeker of history and knowledge. I leave as something else—a keeper of memories, for the spirits of the past.

As I walk away, I carry with me the memories of the city with its rich tapestry of history, mythology and magic. It has become a part of me—a sacred journey that has forever changed the way I see the world.

And, I will not forget the birds—white and black—and the ghosts, with a presence in both worlds.

…just enough time to buy a Faun at the gift shop!

—ARMAND TABER

owe there
was one thin
ge of which
D. Darell
spoke noe
words to any
other and
but litel to
mee and e
that was
she had but
small faith
in Blacke
Witchcrafte
or that we
men solde
themselves
to ye Devill
for she had
known ful
many who was sayd to serve the
Devill and devill a one was there
who could conjer up half a crown
or shewe any thing new.
But in White Witchcrafte the
Dame had great beleefe, saying
that Faithe in Spels and Charmes
and great hope would come or
holpen folke when the Devill
and all his folk were afraid. Twas
with their praying tales like Rob o
the Dale who when a man was
scart att some Frogges, said
'Bee good cheare I trow it
is nothing but a Noyse."

Excerpt from

The Witchcraft of Dame Darrel of York

Protection Spells: 36 Cards for Magical Self-Defense
Weiser Books
Judika Illes
ISBN 978-1578638918
$18.99

ENGAGING with magical protection doesn't have to be overwhelming and *Protection Spells: 36 Cards for Magical Self-Defense* by Judika Illes proves just that. With vivid, full-color cards that each highlight a traditional spell, charm or magical aid, the deck offers a quick and inviting way to explore the essentials of protection magic. From herbs and crystals to colors and numbers, each card acts as a touchstone for both daily reinforcement and ritual focus. It's the kind of tool you can toss in a bag, pull out when needed and still feel like you've tapped into something meaningful..

Judika Illes brings her characteristic clarity to the writing, presenting the material in a refreshingly direct and grounded voice. Rather than layering the content in dense esoterica, she keeps the language clean and confident—making it easy for beginners to jump in and for seasoned practitioners to find something of value. Her ability to distill complex magical principles into approachable language is one of her greatest strengths.

While it's not meant to replace deeper study, *Protection Spells* serves as a charming and portable resource. It's well-suited to moments when a quick dose of inspiration or magical reinforcement is needed and makes a thoughtful gift for anyone stepping onto the path—or for those simply in need of a little extra fortification.

Song of the Dark Man: Father of Witches, Lord of the Crossroads
Darragh Mason
Inner Traditions
ISBN 9978-1644119099
$195

A SHADOWED figure appears again and again at the edges of folklore and personal transformation—neither entirely demon nor mere symbol, but something older, more enigmatic and profoundly initiatory. This is the presence at the heart of *Song of the Dark Man* by Darragh Mason, a work that traces the Dark Man through Celtic manuscripts, witch trial records and firsthand accounts. Rather than casting him as a villain, Mason repositions this being as a force that challenges, provokes and ultimately awakens those who encounter him.

What distinguishes this book is its balance of historical depth and experiential insight. Mason doesn't rely solely on archival sources; he weaves in his own experiences and thoughtful interviews with contemporary practitioners, creating a tapestry that is as intimate as it is scholarly. The Dark Man emerges here not just as a mythic figure but as a living presence—one that disrupts, questions and, for those willing, initiates. Contributions from voices like Shullie H. Porter and Peter Grey anchor this presence within modern magical practice.

Judiciously written and rich with poetic moments, *Sing of the Dark Man* invites readers to reexamine their assumptions about fear, power and the shadowed gateways to personal purpose. It is a bold and reverent work—unafraid to dwell in mystery and unflinching in its call to deeper transformation. For those willing to look directly into the dark, this book may well light the way.

Liber Nephilim: A Grimoire of Fallen Angels
Frater Barrabas
Crossed Crow Books
ISBN 978-1-959883-55-5
$25.95

ENOCHIAN MAGIC, ceremonial magic, grimoire magic—these systems can be as confusing as they are empowering and there comes a moment in reading every grimoire when you think to yourself that this would all make so much more sense if you could just see the magician doing it one time. Well, this is your chance. In *Liber Nephilim*, Frater Barrabas invites the reader to join in on a magical operation he began decades ago. He describes his original workings in detail, what he learned from them, how he has altered them and why.

Barrabas explores the Nephilim, fallen angels mentioned in the Book of Enoch who fathered a race of giants with human women and taught humankind angelic magic before being imprisoned by Michael, Gabriel, Raphael and Uriel. Finding it curious that these spirits have largely been left out of the grimoire tradition. In *Liber Nephilim*, he reframes the corporealization of the Nephilim as manifestation rather than fall and their imprisonment less as punishment and more as protection. He lays out a system of 200 spirits and describes their four chiefs—Shemihazah, Azazel, Ramat'el and Turiel—as they appear when evoked, outlines their functions and elemental associations and offers the reader two paths to contacting them, the lawful path in which the operant invokes the archangels and the unlawful path in which the operant contacts Samael. Barrabas includes seals and sigils he received from the archangels in his workings along with diagrams and detailed instructions for the reader to invoke the angels and contact the Nephilim.

He also suggests several avenues of exploration along this path that he hopes the reader might engage in that he has not—for example, he believes that the four demon queens who are the wives of the Nephilim and the daughters of Lilith hold keys to further mysteries. Frater Barrabas invites the reader in to explore this magical system that is just being discovered because he enthusiastically believes that the spirits of the Nephilim still have a great deal of magic to teach. If you feel the beckoning of these powers, he gives you the tools and techniques you need to contact them. However, even readers who are not particularly interested in working with these spirits will find it worthwhile to learn from Barrabas, a ritual magician with decades of experience, by following along with the workings of a living magician in as close to real time as a practice based on centuries-old tomes allows. Until we have a time machine that allows us to peer through the keyhole during Dee and Kelley's operations or listen through a wall in Worms to the devotions of Abraham, Barrabas' *Liber Nephilim* is your best chance to ride along on the shoulder of a magician while he works out his magic.

Starlore Arcana: Constellations for Tarot, Astrology and Cartomancy
Nitasia Roland
Weiser Books
ISBN 978-1578638482
$29.95

TO GAZE at the stars is to wonder at what meaning they might be whispering for you. Offering divinatory meanings for the constellations visible in the night sky, the new *Starlore Arcana* deck from Weiser is based on John Lenthall's 1717 deck Astronomical Playing Cards. It features 56 full color cards redrawn for the modern reader and expanded to include all court cards and better align with tarot systems. Each card depicts a constellation with an image of the constellation's imagined form overlaid on the arrangement of the actual stars of the constellation, helpful for anyone who wants to connect stargazing with divination more directly. For example, the five of hearts bears both a drawing of the stars of the constellation Canis Major as well as an image of a dog. Each card also includes a translation of the constellation's name or a description if it is a proper name, e.g., Cygnus is labelled the swan while Orion is labelled the hunter.

As a pip deck (there are no trump cards,) *Starlore Arcana* uses the playing card suits of hearts, diamonds, clubs and spades. For those who have struggled in the past with correlating systems, the cards are helpfully labelled with both the playing card suit and the associated tarot suit. There is additional support for understanding the meaning of each card in both playing card cartomancy and tarot in the included guidebook.

The full color, 119 page book is where the brilliance of the deck shines most clearly. It offers the reader detailed information about the physical location of each constellation, its folklore and several different ways to read the card depending on the reader's system. It would be worth the price of the deck by itself. Each entry opens with a retelling of the constellation's mythology, followed by distinct meanings for cartomancy, tarot and divination. This allows a reader to simultaneously gain deeper insight into the constellations and the messages the stars can share while also connecting the mythology to traditional meanings in playing card reading as well as meanings typical in Rider-Waite derived decks.

The edges of the cards are gilded and the back of each card shows a night sky scattered with constellations. The deck and book are packaged in a sturdy, matching cardboard box for ease of storage. The quality of the cards, beautiful full color illustrations and thoughtful and thorough guidebook make this one of a kind system worthy of a place on every diviner's card table.

Sacred Texts Arhive
Internet Resource
www.sacred-texts.com/

LAUNCHED on March 9, 1999, *Sacred-Texts.com* has become an indispensable digital archive for anyone interested in the world's spiritual, mythological and esoteric traditions. Founded by John Bruno Hare, the site was created to promote religious tolerance and scholarship by preserving public domain texts that might otherwise be lost or inaccessible. Over the years, it has grown into one of the most visited religion-focused websites globally, often exceeding a million hits per day and consistently ranking among the top 10,000 sites in countries like the U.S., Australia and India.

Sacred-Texts.com offers an extensive collection of texts spanning a wide array of traditions, including major world religions like Wicca, Paganism, Christianity, Islam, Hinduism, Buddhism and Judaism, as well as lesser-known paths such as Zoroastrianism, Shinto and various indigenous belief systems. The archive also encompasses a rich assortment of materials on mythology, folklore and esoteric subjects, providing resources on topics like alchemy, tarot, ceremonial magic and mysticism. Many of these texts are presented in both English translation and original languages, making the site a valuable tool for comparative studies, academic reference and deep spiritual inquiry. The inclusion of commentaries, scholarly introductions and source notes adds context and credibility, enhancing its usefulness for more serious study.

For researchers, educators and spiritual seekers, *Sacred-Texts.com* serves as a comprehensive and reliable resource. Its user-friendly interface and thoughtfully organized categories facilitate intuitive navigation through a vast and diverse body of knowledge. The site's commitment to preserving works that are often overlooked or marginalized ensures that a wide range of voices and perspectives remain available to a global audience. Whether you're conducting scholarly research, preparing educational curricula, enriching your personal practice or simply exploring the wisdom traditions of the world, this archive offers unmatched depth and accessibility. It's also a treasure trove for writers, artists and creators seeking authentic inspiration from original source material.

In an era when libraries face limits and rare books are out of reach, *Sacred-Texts.com* remains a beacon of open-access learning. It preserves sacred and esoteric texts and fosters cultural literacy and understanding. A testament to the power of digital preservation, it stands as a quiet cornerstone of the spiritual internet.

When Nature Nudges

How can I tell if I'm experiencing a sign from nature or just projecting meaning onto random events? –Submitted by Lila Marquez

Interpreting signs from nature is a subtle art, blending intuition with grounded observation. Begin by cultivating mindfulness outdoors. Pay close attention to animals, weather patterns and unusual plant occurrences or natural disruptions. A genuine sign often evokes a distinct emotional response—a sudden clarity, a chill, or a deep sense of knowing that lingers. Keep a journal of your experiences and note if certain signs recur or coincide with major life events. This helps distinguish meaningful patterns from mere coincidence.

Study the traditional meanings of animals and natural elements in folklore, mythology and spiritual systems, but always temper this with your own experience and intuition. For instance, seeing a hawk might universally symbolize clarity and vision, but if your grandmother adored hawks, it might carry a personal ancestral message instead.

Avoid forcing meaning onto everything; not every falling leaf carries a message. Instead, stay open, patient and receptive. True signs often arrive when you're not searching for them—when you're aligned, present and willing to listen to the world's quiet whisper. Ultimately, discernment deepens through experience. The more you listen without needing answers, the clearer the language of nature becomes.

Second Sight on Schedule

Is there a time of day or phase of the Moon that's best for psychic work? –Submitted by Eliot R.

Yes—and no. While psychic work can be done anytime, certain times do amplify results. The liminal hours of twilight (dawn and dusk) are traditionally potent for spirit and psychic work, as they're natural thresholds between worlds and moments of atmospheric stillness. Similarly, late night—between midnight and 3 in the morning—is often considered the "psychic hour," when the mundane world quiets and intuition reigns undisturbed.

Moon phases also matter. The waxing moon is great for building psychic ability and calling visions forward. Full moons illuminate—ideal for divination, dreamwork, or mediumship. Waning moons assist with banishing confusion or releasing psychic blocks. The dark moon is perfect for deep introspection, ancestral contact and shadow work.

That said, personal rhythm matters most. Some practitioners are most clairvoyant in the morning, others when the house is still, lights are low and everyone's asleep. Track your energy, emotional state and clarity throughout the day and month. You may discover your own "psychic tide" rising and falling with surprising regularity. Create a supportive atmosphere—low light, minimal noise, perhaps a cup of mugwort or blue lotus tea—and your inner sight will respond more readily, no matter the clock or calendar.

Elemental, My Dear

What if I don't feel connected to the Elements?–Submitted by Rayna Hardy

Not everyone feels an immediate bond with Earth, Air, Fire or Water—and that's okay. Connection grows through experience. Start by observing how each Element shows up in your life: a breeze on your skin, the warmth of sunlight, the steadiness of stone, the flow of emotion. Try working with one element at a time. Light a candle and meditate on Fire. Walk barefoot to feel Earth. These small acts create sensory and energetic bonds. Over time, the Elements become more than symbols—they become companions. If one still feels distant, focus on the ones that do resonate. The others may reveal themselves in their own time. Trust that connection will come—not through force, but through presence.

Broom Closet Blues

How do I stay spiritually active even though I am not out of the broom closet? –Submitted by Anonymous

Practicing in secret can be frustrating, but it's far from powerless. Many traditions were preserved this way and privacy can deepen focus and connection. Redefine spiritual practice—invocations, mindfulness, ancestral reverence and spellwork can all be adapted discreetly.

Create a hidden altar in a drawer, box, or even in your phone's notes or images. Use coded symbols—a seashell for the Goddess, a rock for grounding, a candle-shaped lamp. Journal through poetry or gratitude lists. Kitchen Witchery works well too: brewing teas, seasoning with intent and cooking as ritual all nourish the soul invisibly. Your mind is your temple. Visualization, meditation and breathwork are potent and portable. Even mentally reciting affirmations or syncing thoughts with the Moon keeps you connected. Secrecy doesn't dilute power—it refines it. You're walking the path with care and intent. That's a kind of magic all its own.

Let us hear from you, too

We love to hear from our readers. Letters should be sent with the writer's name (or just first name or initials), address, daytime phone number and e-mail address, if available. Published material may be edited for clarity or length. All letters and e-mails will become the property of The Witches' Almanac Ltd. *and will not be returned. We regret that due to the volume of correspondence we cannot reply to all communications.*

The Witches' Almanac, Ltd.
P.O. Box 25239
Providence, RI 02905-7700
info@TheWitchesAlmanac.com
www.TheWitchesAlmanac.com

Visit Our Mythical Mystical Realm For:
*Full Service Metaphysical Supply
* Wide Selection of Occult Titles
* Rare Crystals & Minerals
* Stunning Gemstone Jewelry

All Things Rare & Magickal

Psychic Readings - Personal Magical Candles -
Mojo Bags, Baths, Charms

-Over 30 Years of Magickal Service-

AVALONBEYOND.COM

1211 Hillcrest St. Orlando. Florida 32803 (407) 895 7439

The products and services offered above are paid advertisements.

THE BUCKLAND MUSEUM OF WITCHCRAFT AND MAGICK

THE FIRST OF ITS KIND IN THE UNITED STATES

Genuine Artifacts of the Occult!

Please visit BucklandMuseum.org
for hours, ticketing, and programming.
2155 Broadview Rd., Cleveland, OH 44109
bucklandmuseum@gmail.com
(718) 709-6643

UNLOCK YOUR MAGICKAL POTENTIAL!

INFO@OLDCRAFT.ORG

Providence Coven

Providence Coven
an Alexandrian Coven
emphasizing coven work,
traditional lore and
ceremonial magick

ProvidenceCoven.org

NECTW

New England Covens of
Traditionalist Witches

Info@NECTW.org

Since 1994 Herbs & Arts has served Denver and the region, striving to be a place of healing & sanctuary for the Pagan & Wiccan communities, and all seekers of spiritual living.

We live with a simple intention, to put forth compassion, love & gratitude into the universe with the belief that if we can inspire & empower healing and spiritual connection in ourselves and others, the world will change for the better.

We make 100s of ritual oils, incenses, & bath salts for all your magickal needs. All of our ritual products are made in sacred space and at specific lunar & astrological times. Our webstore also has over 400 herbs, essential oils and other items to support your connection to spirit. Blessed be.

Herbs & Arts

Denver, CO
303.388.2544
www.herbsandarts.com

The products and services offered above are paid advertisements.

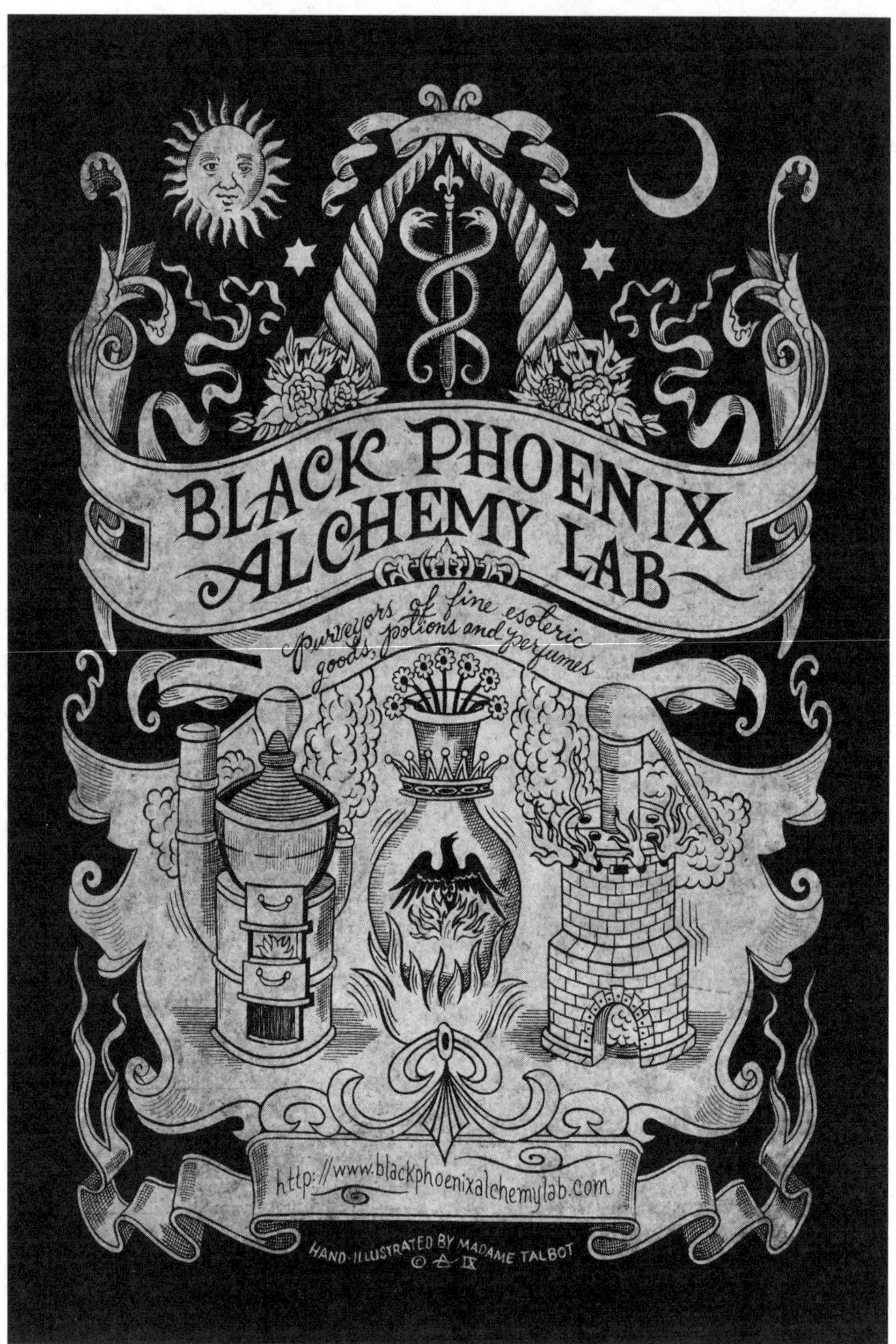

The products and services offered above are paid advertisements.

Receive 25% off your first order when you subscribe to our newsletter.

Support Independent Publishing

SHOP *REDWHEELWEISER.COM*

The Minoan Brotherhood

celebrating the mysteries unique to men who love men

seeker@minoan-brotherhood.org

The World's largest collection of objects, books and manuscripts relating to Witchcraft and the Occult

The Harbour, Boscastle, Cornwall, PL35 0HD
Tel: 01850 250111
www.museumofwitchcraftandmagic.co.uk

The products and services offered above are paid advertisements.

836 836

The

Coven

Of All Altars

www.allaltars.org

The products and services offered above are paid advertisements.

RITUALLY HANDMADE IN SMALL BATCHES

MATERIALS OF MAGIC

Oils • Incense

Seeds • Resins • Botanicals

CRAFT YOUR PRACTICE AT

ALCHEMY-WORKS.COM

Psychic / Tarot Readings

Telephone, Zoom Readings & In Person

Licensed Psychic Readers for over 35 Years In Same Location

Money Back Guarantee

New Age Products

Largest Selection of Gemstones & Tarot Cards in New England

Wiccan Jewelry, Statues, Herbs, Divination Tools & Santeria Supplies

395 Washington St., Braintree, MA, USA
OpenDoors7.com 781-843-8224

Open By Appointment And Donations Welcome

The New Alexandrian Library

www.newalexandrianlibrary.com

Near Georgetown, DE At Seelie Court

The NAL is a research and lending library dedicated to the preservation of books, periodicals, newsletters, music, media, art works, artifacts, photographs, and digital media focused on the metaphysical and esoteric aspects of all religions and traditions.

The Witches' Almanac Colophon Pendant

The late Elizabeth Pepper designed The Witches' Almanac's logo after a very special sigil that she kept close to her heart. She had a small number of sterling silver pendants made in the 1980s. Never made available to the public. Reproduced today, the sigil-pendant can also be used as a charm—for a special bracelet, or as a source of inspiration when doing private meditations or magical work.

The full pendant measures 7/8"x1/2". Bail accepts a 3mm diameter chain.
In sterling silver for $35.00, available at www.TheWitchesAlmanac.com/pendant/

The products and services offered above are paid advertisements.

MARKETPLACE

www.AzureGreen.net Jewelry, Amulets, Incense, Oils, Herbs, Candles, Statuary, Gemstones, Ritual Items. Wholesale inquiries welcome.

The Crystal Fox 311 Main Street, Laurel, MD 20707 USA. The largest new age/ metaphysical gift shop in the mid-Atlantic region. Monday-Saturday 10am-9pm Sunday 11am-7pm. **(301) 317-1980**, cryfox@verizon.net, www.TheCrystalFox.biz

Wendy Wildcraft Herbal Apothecary. Wild gifts and botanical wisdom to inspire the body, mind and spirit. **(978) 219-9453**, info@wendywildcraft.com, www.wendywildcraft.com

Coven Work Embark on a transformative journey of traditional lore and ceremonial magick. Experience expert guidance and enriching coven work in Providence, fostering growth and deep spiritual connection. **ProvidenceCoven.org**

The products and services offered above are paid advertisements.

TO: The Witches' Almanac
P.O. Box 1292, Newport, RI 02840-9998
www.TheWitchesAlmanac.com

Email (required) ______________________________

Name ______________________________

Address ______________________________

City ______________ State ________ Zip ____________

WITCHCRAFT being by nature one of the secretive arts, it may not be as easy to find us next year. If you'd like to make sure we know where you are, why don't you send us your name, email address and street address? You will certainly hear from us.

Dikki-Jo Mullen

The Witches' Almanac Astrologer
dikkijomullen@gmail.com
Sky Maiden Musings dikkijomullen.wordpress.com
Star Dates Astrology Forecasts facebook.com/dikkijo.mullen
Dikki Jo Mullen on **YouTube**

Seminars, Presentations, Convention Programs

Complete Astrology & Parapsychology Services

Paranormal Investigations

(see the website for astrology articles and information about upcoming events)

The products and services offered above are paid advertisements.

The Witches' Almanac 2026 Wall Calendar

The ever popular Moon Calendar in each issue of The Witches' Almanac is a wall calendar as well. Providing the standard Moon phases, channeled actions and an expanded version of the topic featured in the Moon Calendar are now available in a full-size wall calendar.

Harry M. Hyatt's Works on Hoodoo and Folklore: A Full Reprint in 13 Volumes

Hoodoo—Conjuration—Witchcraft—Rootwork

THE WITCHES' ALMANAC is pleased to present Harry M. Hyatt's seminal work *Hoodoo—Conjuration—Witchcraft—Rootwork.* This masterwork of Hyatt's first published in five thick volumes during the years of 1970-1978 has long been near impossible to obtain. Working closely with Michael Edward Bell, Harry Hyatt's protégé, the collected field notes of Hyatt have been supplemented with his other major work on folklore, Folklore from Adams County Illinois. Additionally, to these very important volumes has been added Michael Edward Bell's comprehensive doctoral dissertation, Pattern, Structure, and Logic in Afro-American Hoodoo Performance (1980), which uses Hyatt's *Hoodoo—Conjuration—Witchcraft—Rootwork* as its main source. Bell's dissertation may also be used as a subject-index to Hyatt's five volumes. Hyatt had also prepared an album of 4 phonograph records (8 sides in all) containing most of an interview he had recorded with one of his informants, which we are also making it available as an mp3 file to purchasers of this reprint. The audio download is available at the time of purchase. Lastly, the purchaser will have online access to searchable files of *Hoodoo—Conjuration—Witchcraft—Rootwork.*

Information:

- Page counts: "Each volume is approximately 500 pages in length."
- Number of Volumes - 13
- Book size: 8.5 x 11
- Audio files
- Ordering:
  email—sales@TheWitchesAlmanac.com
  voice—(401)847-3388
  visit—TheWitchesAlmanac.com/hyatt/
- Full Set (including audio download) $1,400

Aradia
Gospel of the Witches
Charles Godfrey Leland

ARADIA IS THE FIRST work in English in which witchcraft is portrayed as an underground old religion, surviving in secret from ancient Pagan times.

- Used as a core text by many modern Neo-Pagans.
- Foundation material containing traditional witchcraft practices
- This special edition features appreciations by such authors as Paul Huson, Raven Grimassi, Judika Illes, Michael Howard, Christopher Penczak, Myth Woodling, Christina Oakley Harrington, Patricia Della-Piana, Jimahl di Fiosa and Donald Weiser. A beautiful and compelling work, this edition is an up to date format, while keeping the text unchanged. 172 pages $16.95

The ABC of Magic Charms
Elizabeth Pepper

Mankind has sought protection from mysterious forces beyond mortal control. Humans have sought the help of animal, mineral, vegetable. The enlarged edition of *Magic Charms from A to Z*, guides us in calling on these forces. $12.95

The Little Book of Magical Creatures
Elizabeth Pepper and Barbara Stacy

AN UPDATE of the classic *Magical Creatures*, featuring Animals Tame, Animals Wild, Animals Fabulous—plus an added section of enchanting animal myths from other times, other places. *A must for all animal lovers.* $12.95

The Witchcraft of Dame Darrel of York
Charles Godfrey Leland, Introduction by Robert Mathiesen

A beautifully reproduced facsimile of the illuminated manuscript shedding light on the basis for a modern practice. A treasured by those practicing Pagans, as well as scholars. Standard Hardcover $65.00 or Exclusive full leather bound, numbered and slipcased edition $145.00

DAME FORTUNE'S WHEEL TAROT: A PICTORIAL KEY

Paul Huson

Based upon Paul Huson's research in *Mystical Origins of the Tarot, Dame Fortune's Wheel Tarot* illustrates for the first time the earliest, traditional Tarot card interpretations as collected in the 1700s by Jean-Baptiste Alliette. In addition to detailed descriptions, full color reproductions of Huson's original designs for all 79 cards.

WITCHES ALL

A Treasury from past editions, is a collection from *The Witches' Almanac* publications of the past. Arranged by topics, the book, like the popular almanacs, is thought provoking and often spurs the reader on to a tangent leading to even greater discovery. It's perfect for study or casual reading,

GREEK GODS IN LOVE

Barbara Stacy casts a marvelously original eye on the beloved stories of Greek deities, replete with amorous oddities and escapades. We relish these tales in all their splendor and antic humor, and offer an inspired storyteller's fresh version of the old, old mythical magic.

MAGIC CHARMS FROM A TO Z

A treasury of amulets, talismans, fetishes and other lucky objects compiled by the staff of *The Witches' Almanac*. An invaluable guide for all who respond to the call of mystery and enchantment.

LOVE CHARMS

Love has many forms, many aspects. Ceremonies performed in witchcraft celebrate the joy and the blessings of love. Here is a collection of love charms to use now and ever after.

MAGICAL CREATURES

Mystic tradition grants pride of place to many members of the animal kingdom. Some share our life. Others live wild and free. Still others never lived at all, springing instead from the remarkable power of human imagination.

ANCIENT ROMAN HOLIDAYS

The glory that was Rome awaits you in Barbara Stacy's classic presentation of a festive year in Pagan times. Here are the gods and goddesses as the Romans conceived them, accompanied by the annual rites performed in their worship. Scholarly, lighthearted – a rare combination.

CELTIC TREE MAGIC

Robert Graves in *The White Goddess* writes of the significance of trees in the old Celtic lore. *Celtic Tree Magic* is an investigation of the sacred trees in the remarkable Beth-Luis-Nion alphabet and their role in folklore, poetry and mysticism.

MOON LORE

As both the largest and the brightest object in the night sky, and the only one to appear in phases, the Moon has been a rich source of myth for as long as there have been mythmakers.

MAGIC SPELLS AND INCANTATIONS

Words have magic power. Their sound, spoken or sung, has ever been a part of mystic ritual. From ancient Egypt to the present, those who practice the art of enchantment have drawn inspiration from a treasury of thoughts and themes passed down through the ages.

LOVE FEASTS

Creating meals to share with the one you love can be a sacred ceremony in itself. With the Witch in mind, culinary adept Christine Fox offers magical menus and recipes for every month in the year.

RANDOM RECOLLECTIONS III, IV

Pages culled from the original (no longer available) issues of *The Witches' Almanac,* published annually throughout the 1970s, are now available in a series of tasteful booklets. A treasure for those who missed us the first time around, keepsakes for those who remember.

Liber Spirituum

BEING A TRUE AND FAITHFUL REPRODUCTION OF THE GRIMOIRE OF PAUL HUSON

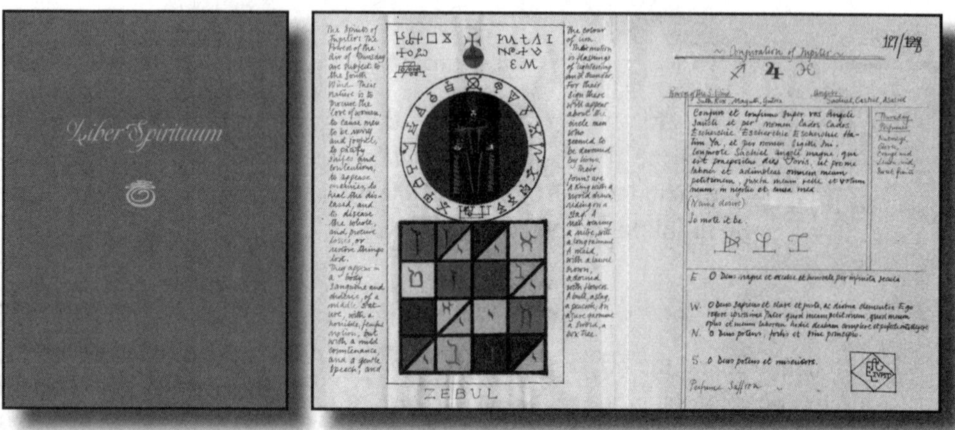

In 1966, as an apprentice mage, Paul Huson began the work of constructing his personal *Liber Spirituum* or *Book of Spirits*. The origins of his work in fact have their genesis a number of years before he took up the pen to illuminate the pages of his *Book of Spirits*. It was in his tender youth that Paul's interest in matters magical began. It was his insatiable curiosity and thirst for knowledge that would eventually lead him to knock on the doors of Dion Fortune's Society of the Inner Light in 1964, as well as studying the practices of the Hermetic Order of the Golden Dawn and the Stella Matutina under the aegis of Israel Regardie. Drawing on this wellspring of knowledge and such venerable works as the *Key of Solomon*, *The Magus*, *Heptameron*, *Three Books of Occult Philosophy* as well as others set down a unique and informed set of rituals, in addition to employing his own artistry in the creation of distinctive imagery.

Using the highest quality photographic reproduction and printing methods, Paul's personal grimoire has here been faithfully and accurately reproduced for the first time. In addition to preserving the ink quality and use of gold and silver paint, this facsimile reproduction has maintained all of Huson's corrections, including torn, pasted, missing pages and his hand drawn and renumbered folios. Preserved as well are the unique characteristics of the original grimoire paper as it has aged through the decades. In this way, the publisher has stayed true to Paul Huson's *Book of Spirits* as it was originally drawn and painted.

223 Pages
Paperback — $59.95
Hardbound in slipcase — $149.95

For further information visit: TheWitchesAlmanac.com

MAGIC

An Occult Primer

50 YEAR ANNIVERSARY EDITION

David Conway

The Witches' Almanac presents:

- *A clear, articulate presentation of magic in a workable format*
- *Updated text, graphics and appendices*
- *Foreword by Colin Wilson*

David Conway's *Magic: An Occult Primer* is a seminal work that brought magical training to the every-magician in the early 70s. David is an articulate writer presenting the mysteries in a very workable manner for the serious student. Along with the updated texts on philosophy and practical magic is a plethora of graphics that have all been redrawn, promising to be another collector's edition published by The Witches' Almanac.

384 pages — $24.95

For further information visit TheWitchesAlmanac.com

Ancient Holidays Series

INTRODUCING ANCIENT HOLIDAYS, an exhilarating new book series that immerses readers into the captivating world of ancient civilizations' spiritual calendars. Authored by the exceptionally talented Mab Borden, these books offer profound and enlightening journeys through the sacred calendars of the ancient Egyptians, Greeks, and Romans. With great excitement, we present this series, confident that it will not only provide invaluable knowledge but also kindle inspiration for our own spiritual observations.

Within each captivating title of the series, readers will delve into comprehensive explanations of the months and seasons, gaining profound insights into the significance of sacred days. Every sacred day is meticulously detailed, encompassing the deity being honored and the social and ritual activities associated with it. Additionally, each publication is enriched with information-packed appendices, which provide a wealth of knowledge, including the mapping of deity holidays to the corresponding seasons.

For further details and to order visit us at:
TheWitchesAlmanac.com/pages/the-ancient-holiday-series

Order Form

Each timeless edition of *The Witches' Almanac* is unique.
Limited numbers of previous years' editions are available.

Item	Price	Qty.	Total
2026-2027 The Witches' Almanac – Water: The Mirror of Souls	$14.95		
2026-2027 El Almanaque de las Brujas – Agua: Espejo de las almas	$15.95		
2025-2026 The Witches' Almanac – Air: Breath of the Cosmos	$13.95		
2024-2025 The Witches' Almanac – Fire: Forging Freedom	$13.95		
2023-2024 The Witches' Almanac – Earth: Origin of Chthonic Powers	$13.95		
2022-2023 The Witches' Almanac – The Moon: Transforming the Inner Spirit	$12.95		
2021-2022 The Witches' Almanac – The Sun: Rays of Hope	$12.95		
2020-2021 The Witches' Almanac – Stones: The Foundation of Earth	$12.95		
2019-2020 The Witches' Almanac – Animals: Friends & Familiars	$12.95		
2018-2019 The Witches' Almanac – The Magic of Plants	$12.95		
2017-2018 The Witches' Almanac – Water: Our Primal Source	$12.95		
2016-2017 The Witches' Almanac – Air: the Breath of Life	$12.95		
2014-2015 The Witches' Almanac – Mystic Earth	$12.95		
2013-2014 The Witches' Almanac – Wisdom of the Moon	$11.95		
2012-2013 The Witches' Almanac – Radiance of the Sun	$11.95		
2011-2012 The Witches' Almanac – Stones, Powers of Earth	$11.95		
2010-2011 The Witches' Almanac – Animals Great & Small	$11.95		
2009-2010 The Witches' Almanac – Plants & Healing Herbs	$11.95		
2008-2009 The Witches' Almanac – Divination & Prophecy	$10.95		
2007-2008 The Witches' Almanac – The Element of Water	$9.95		
1993-2006 issues of The Witches' Almanac	$10.00		
The Witches' Almanac 50 Year Anniversary Edition, paperback	$15.95		
The Witches' Almanac 50 Year Anniversary Edition, hardbound	$24.95		
2023-2024 The Witches' Almanac Wall Calendar	$14.95		
SALE: Bundle I—8 Almanac back issues (1991, 1993–1999)	$50.00		
Bundle II—10 Almanac back issues (2000–2009)	$65.00		
Bundle III—10 Almanac back issues (2010–2019)	$100.00		
Bundle IV—30 Almanac back issues (1993–2022)	$199.00		
Ancient Egyptian Holidays	$16.95		
Ancient Greek Holidays	$18.95		
Ancient Roman Holidays	$19.95		
Liber Spirituum—The Grimoire of Paul Huson, paperback	$59.95		
Liber Spirituum—The Grimoire of Paul Huson, hardbound in slipcase	$149.95		
Dame Fortune's Wheel Tarot: A Pictorial Key	$19.95		
Magic: An Occult Primer—50 Year Anniversary Edition, paperback	$24.95		
Magic: An Occult Primer—50 Year Anniversary Edition, hardbound	$29.95		
The Witches' Almanac Coloring Book	$12.00		
The Witchcraft of Dame Darrel of York, clothbound, signed and numbered, in slip case	$85.00		

Item	Price	Qty.	Total
The Witchcraft of Dame Darrel of York, leatherbound, signed and numbered, in slip case	$145.00		
Aradia or The Gospel of the Witches	$16.95		
The Horned Shepherd	$16.95		
The ABC of Magic Charms	$12.95		
The Little Book of Magical Creatures	$12.95		
Greek Gods in Love	$15.95		
Witches All	$13.95		
Ancient Roman Holidays (original first printing)	$9.95		
Celtic Tree Magic	$9.95		
Love Charms	$9.95		
Love Feasts	$9.95		
Magic Charms from A to Z	$12.95		
Magical Creatures	$12.95		
Magic Spells and Incantations	$12.95		
Moon Lore	$9.95		
Random Recollections Volumes III and IV	$9.95		
The Rede of the Wiccae – Hardcover	$49.95		
The Rede of the Wiccae – Softcover	$22.95		
Keepers of the Flame	$20.95		
Sounds of Infinity	$24.95		
The Magic of Herbs	$24.95		
Harry M. Hyatt's Works on Hoodoo and Folklore: A Full Reprint in 13 Volumes (including audio download) *Hoodoo—Conjuration—Witchcraft—Rootwork* Single volumes are also available starting at	$1,400.00 $120.00		
Sterling Silver Colophon	$35.00		
Skull Scarf	$20.00		
Pouch	$3.95		
Subtotal			
Tax *(7% sales tax for RI customers)*			
Shipping & Handling *(See shipping rates section)*			
TOTAL			

Payment available by check or money order payable in U.S. funds or credit card or PayPal

The Witches' Almanac, Ltd., PO Box 25239, Providence, RI 02905-7700

(401) 847-3388 (phone) • (888) 897-3388 (fax)

Email: info@TheWitchesAlmanac.com • www.TheWitchesAlmanac.com